SHAPE YOUR PERSONALITY—
SHAPE UP YOUR MARRIAGE

Shape Your Personality— Shape up Your Marriage

Uncover Your Personality Pattern
Strengthen Your Relationship
Achieve Mutual Understanding

Dr. Betsey Bittlingmaier

Writer's Showcase
San Jose New York Lincoln Shanghai

Shape Your Personality—Shape up Your Marriage

Writer's Showcase
an imprint of iUniverse.com, Inc.

For information address:
iUniverse.com, Inc.
5220 S 16th, Ste. 200
Lincoln, NE 68512
www.iuniverse.com

ISBN: 0-595-13167-0

Printed in the United States of America

To my husband, Lou, with love

Contents

I. Getting to Know Yourself 1

II. Winnowing Out A Pattern 6

III. Temperaments and Traits 18

    THE EMERSON 19

    THE NIGHTINGALE 24

    THE BEAU 29

    THE SHELLEY 32

    THE EINSTEIN 35

    THE AUSTEN 38

    THE MOZART 43

    THE CAESAR 46

    THE GAUGUIN 49

IV. The Emerson in Relationships 54

    EMERSON-EMERSON RELATIONSHIPS 54

    EMERSON-NIGHTINGALE RELATIONSHIPS 58

THE EMERSON-BEAU RELATIONSHIP 67
THE EMERSON-SHELLEY RELATIONSHIP 74
THE EMERSON-EINSTEIN RELATIONSHIP 81
THE EMERSON-AUSTEN RELATIONSHIP 86
THE EMERSON-MOZART RELATIONSHIP 92
THE EMERSON-CAESAR RELATIONSHIP 97
THE EMERSON-GAUGUIN RELATIONSHIP 101

V. The Nightingale in Relationships 108
THE NIGHTINGALE-NIGHTINGALE RELATIONSHIP 108
THE NIGHTINGALE-BEAU RELATIONSHIP 113
THE NIGHTINGALE-SHELLY RELATIONSHIP 120
THE NIGHTINGALE-EINSTEIN RELATIONSHIP 127
THE NIGHTINGALE-AUSTEN RELATIONSHIP 132
NIGHTINGALE-MOZART RELATIONSHIPS 138
THE NIGHTINGALE-CAESAR RELATIONSHIP 142
THE NIGHTINGALE-GAUGUIN RELATIONSHIP 148

VI. The Beau in Relationships 155
THE BEAU-BEAU RELATIONSHIP 155
THE BEAU-SHELLEY RELATIONSHIP 160
THE BEAU-EINSTEIN RELATIONSHIP 164
THE BEAU-AUSTEN RELATIONSHIP 171
THE BEAU-MOZART RELATIONSHIP 177
THE BEAU-CAESAR RELATIONSHIP 184
THE BEAU-GAUGUIN RELATIONSHIP 189

VII. The Shelley in Relationships 194
THE SHELLEY-SHELLEY RELATIONSHIP 194
THE SHELLEY-EINSTEIN RELATIONSHIP 198
THE SHELLEY-AUSTEN RELATIONSHIP 203
THE SHELLEY-MOZART RELATIONSHIP 209

THE SHELLEY-CAESAR RELATIONSHIP 214
THE SHELLEY-GAUGUIN RELATIONSHIP 220

VIII. The Einstein in Relationships 225
THE EINSTEIN-EINSTEIN RELATIONSHIP 225
THE EINSTEIN-AUSTEN RELATIONSHIP 230
THE EINSTEIN-MOZART RELATIONSHIP 237
THE EINSTEIN-CAESAR RELATIONSHIP 241
THE EINSTEIN-GAUGUIN RELATIONSHIP 248

IX. The Austen in Relationships 252
THE AUSTEN-AUSTEN RELATIONSHIP 252
THE AUSTEN-MOZART RELATIONSHIP 257
THE AUSTEN-CAESAR RELATIONSHIP 263
THE AUSTEN-GAUGUIN RELATIONSHIP 272

X. The Mozart in Relationships 277
THE MOZART-MOZART RELATIONSHIP 277
THE MOZART-CAESAR RELATIONSHIP 283
THE MOZART-GAUGUIN RELATIONSHIP 290

XI. The Caesar in Relationships 299
THE CAESAR-CAESAR RELATIONSHIP 299
THE CAESAR-GAUGUIN RELATIONSHIP 304

XII. The Gauguin in Relationships 312
THE GAUGUIN-GAUGUIN RELATIONSHIP 312

XIII. Finding the Right One 318

XIV. A Final Note 324

I

Getting to Know Yourself

"Matt just drives me wild. He is so uncooperative. He can't bother to lift a finger. He's just not a participant in the household." Barbara is speaking. She and Frances are having lunch together, and having run through the current status of their work life, have turned to a discussion of their husbands.

"What has he done?" Frances asks, trying to sound reasonably sympathetic to a complaint she's heard a dozen times.

"Well, you know I got that new furniture last week, and I'm having trouble deciding where to put a couple of pieces. Obviously I can't shift everything by myself, but can I get him to help me? He absolutely refuses."

Frances is genuinely surprised. "That doesn't sound like Matt. Are you sure he's not going to help you?"

"Oh, he will eventually, but I wanted it done last night."

Frances looks at her friend skeptically, "So what did he say exactly?"

"That he wasn't going to do it until the week-end."

"That sounds perfectly reasonable to me."

"But I needed it in place before then, and it wouldn't have taken long. It's just his usual demeaning way of making me wait and beg."

Frances protests, " It doesn't sound terrible to me, honestly. In fact, Bill would probably have said the same thing."

"So then you'd know how I feel."

"I don't think I would," Frances counters. "It sounds reasonable to me. I wouldn't want to get into heavy furniture moving after work either. Actually I think Matt and Bill are pretty much alike in their responses."

Frances is right, Bill and Matt have very similar personalities, and it's Barbara and Frances, who have quite disparate characteristics, who respond very differently in the same situation.

Tom, who is married to Maureen, is seriously irritated by her tendency to be clinging and dependent. When she calls him at the office for the third time in a day, he has been known to hang up on her. This does not really solve his problem, however, as he then comes home to a crying, panic-stricken wife.

His colleague, Larry, is puzzled by his anger. "Cindy calls me a lot too, but I think it's sort of nice. I like to know she's thinking about me, and maybe missing me a little."

"I don't feel that way at all. I just feel that she interrupts my train of thought and throws me off stride, and then she always has an excuse. I can't believe the excuses. Half of her sentences begin with "Yes, but…"

"I think Cindy does that too, but it really doesn't bother me," Larry muses.

And there we have it. The fault is not in the stars, but in the dynamics. The same personality can fit smoothly or clash with a different one. The trick, for the uncommitted is to find the right fit, and for those already in a relationship, to learn smoother ways of understanding and relating to the other person if the couple are not a natural fit.

It is a strange and seemingly irrational fact that two very likable people can have a terrible marriage while a far less pleasant couple stick it out and even seem to get along well together. This paradox can be explained by examining the interactions occurring between the two. In the case of the unpleasant, but relatively happy couple, they have probably learned ways to understand and accommodate each other's needs and foibles, undoubtedly the underlying key to a good relationship. The more clearly people understand themselves and their partners, the more likely that the relationship will be a satisfying and mutually fulfilling one.

Sometimes the most eccentric behavior can become explicable, and thereby cease to annoy, or at least irritate less intensely, when the motivations behind it are understood. Different personalities interact very differently with each other. You may thoroughly enjoy the company of a man who one of your friends can't tolerate. Neither of you are mistaken in your opinions, you simply differ in the traits you value highly and those that irritate or offend you.

It follows that if you understand your partner's personality and your own and learn to grasp how your character traits are likely to mesh with or abrade on each other, your marriage will be stronger and happier.

The secret to achieving this goal is to discover your basic personality style and that of your partner, and then to learn the specific strengths and weaknesses common to a relationship between people with these personalities. You will probably not want to limit your understanding of these dynamics to marriage, as you will probably find that you can make an accurate guess about the personality type of several people whom you know well and to profit from learning more positive ways of interacting with them.

The idea that people can be divided into patterns may sound implausible given the complexity of our personalities, but it has long been recognized that clusters of traits appear together repeatedly in people and various classifications of temperament have been devised based on this fact. Within each of the personality patterns is an intricate elaboration of specific characteristics, which makes each of us unique.

The next chapter contains a series of questions to allow you to winnow or eliminate traits that you do not possess, and through this process discover your personality.

After you have a personality designation, you can read about two people who have your pattern of functioning. Many specific details have been included here in order to flesh these patterns out. The profiles are to give you a general "feel" for each of the personalities, but it is not expected that you will conform to every aspect of the outlines. While all of the traits exemplified are typical of the personality type described, every aspect of each of the personalities is not true of everyone of that type. For example, one profile portrays a fiscally irresponsible person, although certainly, many people of this temperament are completely financially responsible. Still, it is a possibility that occurs frequently enough to make it worth mentioning as a personality marker. Not all people in another group cheat on their partners, but it can happen given their personality dynamics. If you identify with over half of the specifics given in any one portrait, then consider whether the overall description following the portrait seems to fit. If you are still uncomfortable with the designation read over the other patterns, to see if you find one that seems more accurate.

In responding to these questions, it is important to remember that your basic personality type is not going to change, but it can appear very dissimilar within a healthy or less healthy context. Emotionally healthy people will generally have overcome many of the overt behaviors or ways of responding that help to identify a personality type. For this reason, these questions should be answered within the context of your total life experience, not just your current behavior patterns. If you remember a response or action as something you used to do, but have overcome or outgrown, you should answer as if you still reacted in this way since that earlier response is likely to have been a basic personality marker.

If you are having difficulty, in answering the winnowing questions, it might be helpful to ask someone who knows you well for some input. Sometimes it is easier for a close friend to see us accurately than for us to see ourselves. For example, a person might ask someone, *"Would you think of me as indecisive?"* only to see the friend burst into laughter in response to the question, because the answer, whether yes or no, would seem so very obvious.

In an attempt to make the styles more easily identifiable and memorable, each personality type has been labeled with the name of a well-known person from the past who possessed that temperament. This may further help you to identify your type. For example, a person who is particularly focused on learning and theoretical knowledge and who sometimes seems less aware of day to day concerns is sometimes categorized as "an absent-minded professor". Here, people with these traits will be called Einsteins.

II

Winnowing Out A Pattern

Now you are ready to determine who you are through the winnowing process. By sorting out those traits and ways of behaving that are not natural to you, you will be able to tease out your particular personality style.

There is a feeling of finality and limitation inherent in some systems of personality typology, the sense that you are being told *this is who you are for better or worse,* no way out: *"We've got you pegged."* When you identify your pattern here, do not think of yourself as boxed in! Far from limiting people, this system provides a tool for change and growth. The expectation is that you will create positive changes in your life as a result of discovering more about yourself as you are now. Helping you to determine who you are will enable you to create a richer life and more satisfying relationships. In order to change, you have to know yourself first. This test gives you a starting point.

The basic personality style is an outgrowth of a cluster of traits that are generally viewed as part of our genetic endowment and are not very susceptible to change, ask any pediatric nurse if newborns are all alike.

Our individual style is open to a great deal of modification, and we grow within it. For this reason, it is important to think in terms of life-time responses. Inevitably, as people grow emotionally more healthy, they learn to act in more socially appropriate ways, changing some of their less desirable behavioral responses, and while there are no right or wrong answers to these questions, growth within the context of a personality will create new reactions to situations.

Most of our behaviors are not of the standard light switch variety, either on or off, rather they resemble the more sophisticated dimmer switch, which can create any shade from bright light to dark. Our behaviors tend to run on a series of such continuums—introvert to extrovert, aloof to warm, and playful to sternly serious, to name a few. Changes in these behaviors are usually subtle and take place over time as a result of a conscious intention to create change. When a person becomes more emotionally healthy, it means they've grown. At one time the person was acting in a way that put him or her toward one end of a continuum of behavior, in terms of a specific trait. Now they have mod-ified their behavior and moved closer to the center of the continuum, which is where the majority of emotionally healthy people are found. Because such continuum end points are quite definitive, they are often very helpful in characterizing a personality style. For this reason, it is important to respond to the questions from the perspective of your behavior over your entire life, even if you've made some conscious changes and modifications. People are different and the point of this process is to discover your unique qualities, both past and present, not to judge them right or wrong.

An analogous situation would be that of a smoker going into a restaurant, and answering non-smoking when the hostess asked about seating preference. It would be simply foolish to do that and feel uncomfortable through the meal. By the same token, if you respond on the basis of how you would like to be instead of on how you were and are, you'll find yourself in the wrong section, getting advice tailored for someone else. Since no personality style is innately better than any other, it would be doubly foolish. The differences which we might perceive between the types in terms of judging one better or worse than another are actually dependent not upon the basic type, but on the degree of the person's emotional health. People are healthier or less healthy within the context of their own personalities. No one is looking over your shoulder and there are no right answers. This is a time to be brutally honest. Once you find your personality designation, check back to the Table of Contents to locate that pattern in Chapter Three.

THE FIRST WINNOWING:

1. Do you jump into new situations quickly and easily?

Think of various new experiences that are common to most of us: starting a new job, moving to a new city, even going to a party where you don't know many of the people. Do you generally worry ahead of time or feel very apprehensive about such occasions or do you approach each new experience with pleasurable anticipation? If you can answer yes to some of these examples and no to others, your answer should be *no*.

2. Would you characterize yourself as having a high stamina level, being a very energetic person?

This question relates to your basic endurance level, how long you can keep going. If you drive yourself very hard, but run on nerves, the answer may still be *no*. With that in mind, do you find yourself very tired at the end of most days? Do you often prefer to stay home and relax on work nights or would you rather go out and do something even if you must get up early the next morning? Compare your level of energy to that of your friends, do you seem to have more stamina than most of them, or would you say you are at average or low level in terms of this trait? Unless you feel that you have high stamina, your answer should be *no*.

3. Do you view yourself as a competitive person?

Are you someone who strives very hard to be the best in whatever you are doing: the top of the class, the best salesman in the company, the best cook in your social circle? Or can you be content doing things reasonably well, even knowing that others may be even more capable. This question deals with serious competition. Some people are quite competitive when playing a game, but find that other considerations such as less stress and free time are more important to them than coming in first in real life situations. Unless you are seriously competitive in real life situations, your answer should be no.

THE SECOND WINNOWING:

Questions in this second round are dependent on the pattern of your first three answers:

Three yeses: Go to Question 1.
Yes, yes, no: Go to Question 1.
Yes, no, yes: Go to Question 2.
Yes, no, no: Go to Question 3.
No, yes, yes: Go to Question 1.
No, yes, no: Go to Question 2.
No, no, yes: Go to Question 3.
No, no, no: Go to Question 3.

1. Do you think of yourself as warmer or more reserved in style?

Do you find it easy to start a conversation with people you meet casually? Can you share thoughts and feelings with a group, even if you don't know the people well? Or do you tend to stand back and let others talk first? Does it often take time for you to get to know someone new?

If you think of yourself as warm, go to Section A.

If you think of yourself as reserved, answer Question 1a:

1a. Do you believe that when you are angry, your anger is generally what is often called "righteous anger", i.e. that it is focused on creating constructive change through criticism or making a justifiable demand?

Or is your anger primarily a gut-level response directed toward gaining the compliance of whoever has aroused it?

This is a difficult question and it is important to consider it carefully if you are to find your personality type. On first reading, it may sound as if the question has a good guy/bad guy dimension. It doesn't. It merely deals with what is going on in your gut at that moment. Do you feel a glow of righteous indignation or do you merely want things as you want them? One answer is emphatically not better than the other, but it is an important distinction to make.

If your anger centers on compliance, go to Section B.

If you feel righteous anger, go to Section C.

2. Do you believe you are more emotionally vulnerable than most people are?

Vulnerability is not the same thing as weakness. Weakness and strength are a totally different continuum. This question deals with how easily you can feel emotional pain. Very strong people are sometimes very vulnerable. Other people who are much less emotionally strong can sometimes be less sensitive to emotional pain.

Emotionally vulnerable, go to Section D.

Average to less vulnerable, go to Section E.

3. Do you have difficulty dealing with authority figures in your life whether personal or institutional?

Do the requirements and rules of organizations and institutions irritate and bother you to the point where you may have difficulty conforming to them? The question is not whether you ultimately adapt; you may have no choice but to do so. The question is concerned with whether you function best as a team player or whether your style is better suited to working on your own.

If you have difficulty adapting to people or institutions, go to Section F.

If you can adapt relatively easily, go to Section G.

THE THIRD WINNOWING:

SECTION A

1. Do you have difficulty making decisions, often wavering back and forth before coming to a conclusion?

Most people sometimes change their minds. This question concerns genuine difficulty in decision making, second-guessing yourself and even after deciding, wondering if you made the right choice.

If you have difficulty, your personality designation will be *Austen*.

If you usually have little difficulty coming to a decision, go to Question 2.

2. Do you often get over-involved in helping others?

If someone close to you is having a problem, do you take it on without being asked? Do you have difficulty saying no if someone asks you for help? Do you feel pressured by too many commitments most of the time?

No: Go to question 3.

Yes. Go to question 4.

3. Do you hold relatively fixed opinions on most political issues or do you often find yourself expressing changed or modified beliefs if the people around you disagree with you?

Everyone experiences some change in their thinking on some issues over time, this question is directed at whether your opinions are generally fluid, so that you might find yourself appearing more conservative at a conservative gathering and more liberal at a liberal gathering.

Fixed opinions: Your personality designation is *Caesar.*

Fluid opinions: Your personality designation is *Beau.*

4. Do you believe you are more emotionally vulnerable than most people are?

Vulnerability is emphatically not weakness. Weakness and strength are a totally different continuum. This question deals with how easily you can feel emotional pain. Very strong people are sometimes very vulnerable. Other people who are much less emotionally strong can sometimes be less sensitive to emotional pain.

Emotionally vulnerable: Your personality designation is *Nightingale*

Average or less vulnerable: Your personality designation is *Caesar*.

SECTION B

1. Do you provide for recreation in your life, setting aside time for it as a priority or does it take the back burner if more important issues are involved, something to be done if nothing more important is on the agenda? When you play do you do it just because it makes you happy or is it sometimes done only because of an underlying motivation such as a business or a social contact?

If recreation is a very high priority for you, your personality designation is *Mozart*.

If work comes first, your personality designation is *Caesar*.

SECTION C

1. Do you have difficulty making decisions, often wavering back and forth before coming to a conclusion?

Most people sometimes change their minds. This question concerns genuine difficulty in decision making, second-guessing yourself and even after deciding, wondering if you made the right choice.

If you have difficulty, your personality designation is *Austen*.

If you usually have little difficulty coming to a decision, go to Question 2.

2. Do you provide for recreation in your life, setting aside time for it as a priority or does it take the back burner if more important issues are involved, something to be done if nothing more important is on the agenda? When you play do you do it just because it makes you happy or is it sometimes done only because of an underlying motivation such as a business or a social contact?

If recreation is a very high priority for you, your personality designation is *Mozart.*

If work comes first, go to Question 3.

3. Do you hold relatively fixed opinions on most political issues or do you often find yourself expressing changed or modified beliefs if the people around you disagree with you?

Everyone experiences some change over time in their thinking on some issues, but this question is directed at whether your opinions are generally more fluid, so that you might find yourself appearing more conservative at a conservative gathering and more liberal at a liberal gathering.

Fixed opinions: Your personality designation is *Emerson.*

Fluid opinions: Your personality designation is *Beau.*

SECTION D

1. Do you often get over-involved in helping others?

If someone close to you is having a problem, do you take it on without being asked? Do you have difficulty saying no if someone asks you for help? Do you feel pressured by too many commitments most of the time?

Yes. Go to Question 2.

No. Go to Question 3.

2. Do you have difficulty making decisions, often wavering back and forth before coming to a conclusion?

Most people sometimes change their minds. This question concerns genuine difficulty in decision making, second-guessing yourself and even after deciding, wondering if you made the right choice.

If you have difficulty: Your personality designation is *Austen.*

If you usually have little difficulty coming to a decision: Your personality designation is *Nightingale.*

3. Do you have a lot of different projects and plans in your life that seem to keep you busy every minute or do you prefer a more focused

approach to your life and work concentrating on a few areas that are important to you.

If you're not sure on this question, the answer is probably that you are focused, the people with a finger in many different pies, are generally well aware of who they are.

Keep busy: Your personality designation is *Mozart*.

More low-keyed: Your personality designation is *Einstein*.

SECTION E

1. Do you provide for recreation in your life, setting aside time for it as a priority or does it take the back burner if more important issues are involved? When you play do you do it because it makes you happy or are there sometimes underlying motivations such as a business or a social contact?

If recreation is a very high priority for you: Your personality designation is *Mozart*.

If work comes first, go to Question 2.

2. Do you hold relatively fixed opinions on most political issues or do you often find yourself expressing changed or modified beliefs if the people around you disagree with you?

Everyone experiences some change over time in their thinking on some issues, but this question is directed at whether your opinions are generally more fluid, so that you might find yourself appearing more conservative at a conservative gathering and more liberal at a liberal gathering.

Fixed opinions: Your personality designation is *Emerson*.

Fluid opinions: Your personality designation is *Beau*.

SECTION F

1. Do you believe you are more emotionally vulnerable than most people are?

Vulnerability is emphatically not weakness. Weakness and strength are on a totally different continuum. This question deals with how easily you tend to feel emotional pain. Very strong people are sometimes very vulnerable. Other people who are much less emotionally strong can sometimes be less sensitive to emotional pain.

Emotionally vulnerable, go to Question 2.

Average or less vulnerable, go to Question 3.

2. Do you think of yourself as warmer or more reserved in style?

Have you always found it easy to start a conversation with people you met casually? Can you share thoughts and feelings with a group, even if you don't know the people well? Or do you tend to stand back and let others talk first? Does it often take time for you to get to know someone new?

Warm: Your personality designation is *Nightingale.*

Reserved: Go to Question 3.

3. Can you function efficiently within an organization or do you have difficulty fitting comfortably into institutional settings?

This question is not asking where you work, but about your ability as a team player. If you're in a corporate setting, but having difficulty conforming to their policies and structure, your answer could be no. In the same way, if you can work alone, but are aware that you could be capable of functioning in the corporate world, your answer should be yes.

I function well in corporate settings: Go to Question 4.

I don't function well in such settings: Go to Question 5.

4. In making decisions, if you turn to others for advice, do you often change your mind based on their opinions or do you usually end up following your own instincts?

All of us sometimes want the input of others on important issues, but some people are likely to make that input a dominant factor in their decision-making. Others seem to ask more out of a desire for vindication of their own opinions, rather than because they are unsure what they should do.

If the advice of others is a major influence in your decision making, your personality designation is *Austen.*

If you generally follow your own instincts: Your personality designation is *Emerson.*

5. If their is a conflict between what you feel about something and what you think about it, do you generally follow your instincts or do you generally think it through and go with what your head tells you to do?

Most of us can both feel and think deeply. Yet there is a difference between those who tend to disregard or minimize their feelings when they conflict with more rational methods of choice, and others who believe that their instincts are wiser than their thought processes, and who follow instincts if there is a conflict. This has nothing to do with how intelligent you are, or with how intensely you feel, the question is which faculty do you trust more implicitly when they conflict.

If you trust feelings more, your personality designation is *Shelley.*

If you trust thought processes more: Your personality designation is *Einstein.*

SECTION G

1. Do you often get over-involved in helping others?

If someone close to you is having a problem, do you take it on without being asked? Do you have difficulty saying no if someone asks you for help? Do you feel pressured by too many commitments most of the time?

Yes. Go to Question 2.

No. Go to Question 3.

2. Do you have difficulty making decisions, often wavering back and forth before coming to a conclusion?

Most people change their minds. This question concerns genuine difficulty in decision making, second-guessing yourself and even after deciding, wondering if you made the right choice.

Decisions are not a problem: Your personality designation is *Nightingale.*

I have difficulty deciding: Your personality designation is *Austen*

3. Do you believe you are more emotionally vulnerable than most people are?

Vulnerability is emphatically not weakness. Weakness and strength are a totally different continuum. This question deals with how easily you can feel emotional pain. Very strong people are sometimes very vulnerable. Other people who are much less emotionally strong can sometimes be less sensitive to emotional pain.

Yes. Go to Question 4.

No. Go to Question 5.

4. Do you have a high anxiety level?

Do you sometimes stay awake at night worrying about what will happen the next day? Do you hang on to unpleasant memories and rehearse what you should have done repeatedly in your head? Do you sometimes have physical symptoms such as dry mouth, stomach or intestinal upsets or muscle aches when something is bothering you?

Anxious: Your personality designation is *Austen.*

Not very anxious: Your personality designation is *Gauguin.*

5. Do you hold relatively fixed opinions on most political issues or do you often find yourself expressing changed or modified beliefs if the people around you disagree with you?

Everyone experiences some change over time in their thinking on some issues, but this question is directed at whether your opinions are generally more fluid, so that you might find yourself appearing more conservative at a conservative gathering and more liberal at a liberal gathering.

If your opinions are relatively fixed: Your personality designation is *Einstein.*

If your opinions are more fluid: Your personality designation is *Gauguin.*

III

Temperaments and Traits

You now have a name to designate your personality profile. You can go to that name to find a description of a couple of people who share this pattern with you. If you are very emotionally healthy, you may feel that many of the traits do not apply or no longer apply to you. That does not negate the basic assignment of type, but indicates that you have been working on growth and change before beginning to read this book. You will still find helpful suggestions and insights for interacting with your partner, even though you may be further along in building a good relationship than the people depicted.

Most people will arrive at the correct designation by following this process, however, there is a margin of error in all such self-report instruments and if the description does not fit you at all, read the descriptions of other personalities to see if you discover a more appropriate one. If you're still having trouble, It can be helpful to go over your answers with an objective friend. Sometimes, friends can see us more clearly and impartially than we see ourselves.

What can you do if your partner refuses to participate in the project of discovering personalities and working to improve the relationship? While working together on the relationship is certainly the optimal approach, you are not cut off from improving the relationship yourself. If you have a non-participating partner, you can answer the questions for the other person to the best of your ability to learn about the dynamics between you.

By following the recommendations for your personality type and beginning to create change based on the suggestions here, you will be creating change in the dynamics of your relationship. At some point, your partner may notice that the relationship is changing and perhaps become more receptive to cooperating with you. If not, your understanding of what happens in the relationship will continue to help you and to have a positive effect on the relationship.

Once you have identified your type and the type of the other person in your life, you can turn to the chapters dealing with relationships between your personalities. While marital relationships are the primary focus of this book, it is obvious that you will be able to understand not only the relationship you have with your partner, but also to identify the stresses occurring between you and anyone whose personality type you are able to pinpoint. This information can be just as useful in social and business contacts, and parent child interactions as in marriage.

THE EMERSON

I'm pretty sure of myself. I know who I am and I know where I stand. I take firm positions on issues and I am willing to defend them. Injustice troubles me. I'm a hard worker and always do my share. I'm something of an idealist. I think I have a pretty good sense of humor. I always try to do the best I can at whatever I'm doing.

Jim is right, he is an admirable person. He always tries to be fair. His personal honesty is beyond question. If he gives you his word on something, you have an assurance beyond most legal contracts. He relates well to most people and is highly respected at work and within the community organizations in which he participates. Everyone knows him as a hard worker. He devotes as much time to the task as is required, both at home and at work.

Jim possesses the core personality characteristics of Ralph Waldo Emerson. Honesty and justice were extremely important to this leader of the New England Transcendentalists. His primary concern was understanding and developing his moral nature. An idealist, strongly criticized by the New England establishment, he left the Unitarian ministry rather than compromise his beliefs. He had the need to do the right thing, regardless of the cost to himself or others, that is typical of this personality

Who would have problems living with such a paragon? Jim's family will tell you it's not always easy! He can be self-righteous to the point of insanity. His demand for fairness can become the height of irritating nit picking *"My portion of stew didn't have any mushrooms in it and yours had three"*. He invariably goes back to the front door from the car to double-check that it's locked and then complains that he's running late. When something goes wrong or someone makes a mistake, his anger can be frightening to behold. The more timid of his two children is really afraid of him.

Lately he's become devoted to ecology and enforces good ecological practices within his home with the thoroughness of a police state. Pity the person who unthinkingly tosses a bottle into the regular garbage!

Edith is well respected professionally. She is a hard worker, who is equally diligent at household tasks. She is well organized and there is never an item out of place in desk or kitchen. She is viewed by her friends as someone who can be depended upon in both large and small ways. She has a few quirks. There are a couple of political issues where her viewpoint seems extreme and unyielding to many. Her husband has been known to caution the unwary, *"Don't get Edith started on that!"*

Her co-workers sometimes walk on eggs around her for similar reasons. Her children were unusually well behaved through elementary school, but her teen-ager has begun to give her problems as natural adolescent rebellion conflicts with his mother's work ethic and standards of conduct and personal hygiene.

Everyone knows someone like Jim or Edith. It may be you or a member of your family, a friend or acquaintance. These *Emerson* personalities possess a unique mixture of traits common to that personality structure.

The two most consistent problems experienced by people who are interacting with Emersons is their strong need to be in control and their penchant for criticizing those around them. Their methods of discharging anger become even more of a problem in many instances, although the overt manifestations of rage will be modified as the person becomes healthier.

Average Emersons honestly believe that they know what is best for the people around them and for the world in general. This belief is rooted so deeply within their personality structure that it is relatively inaccessible to reason. They feel an impelling need to bring their own behavior into conformity with the demands and expectations of their consciences, and they judge others in terms of how well they measure up to these often unspoken expectations. In daily life these demands cause the Emerson to constantly evaluate the behavior and performance of friends and family. The closer the relationship, the more severely the person is likely to be weighed.

This is the dynamic behind both the need to control and the criticism. It is only reasonable to want to take over the steering wheel, if you suspect that anyone else in the car will run it into a ditch fairly quickly. Emersons constantly perceive themselves to be in such a situation. *"If I'm not in control something bad will happen, so I'd better take over or at least provide some strong supervision."*

It is also only reasonable to want those around us to be the best they can be. This will only happen if faults are identified and examined. As it happens, criticism also provides an excellent and relatively acceptable outlet for the discharge of anger, a powerful, but generally unacknowledged reason that the Emerson engages in it so frequently. It may be some consolation to the targets of this criticism to know that Emersons are equally rigorous with themselves.

These personalities tend to have strong political opinions and to hold them rigorously. In practice, this often means that their opponents are seen not merely as mistaken, but as utterly lacking in moral values and probity. Anyone holding markedly different religious or political views is generally going to have a great amount of on-going conflict if they are in a relationship with the average Emerson.

As Emersons become healthier, their absolutism abates and they not only become tolerant of the views of others, but adhere to tolerance as a moral imperative. The average Emerson is apt to perceive such tolerance as condoning a morally wrong belief or action. Two average Emersons on the opposite side of the same issue can destroy a family gathering or a party.

Childcare may be an area of great conflict for Emersons and their partners, since Emersons generally have strong opinions about raising children. Their standards can be diverse and amazing to the non-Emerson: Either *"All of the children must keep a journal during summer vacation,"* or *"Children must be outside playing during daylight hours—no sitting and reading a book."* Either *"Only public television channels may be watched, however good the program on another station might be"* or *"Any station may be watched, but for no longer than two hours per day with no exceptions for special circumstances."* Either *"Children must remain at the table until the adults have finished eating."* Or *"Children may leave the table when they finish eating, but only French may be spoken at the table from now until we go on our Montreal vacation."*

Emersons often view as inferior or inadequate parenting, the failure of their partner to conform to and enforce such standards.

While most of these positions have some rationale behind them, the proclamation of many such edicts is likely to create early and intense rebellion in children. A still more unfortunate outcome is that such rules tend to push the other partner into a covert alliance with the children, if not into open conflict, in an attempt to modify this absolutism.

Day-to-day issues are equally important to most Emerson personalities. It is difficult for them to comprehend that other people could genuinely disagree with their standards of housekeeping, bill paying, time management, etc., since it is simply "the right way to do it" to the average Emerson. Average Emersons may indeed regard requests to seek compromise as demands that they violate their integrity by knowingly doing the wrong thing.

Average Emerson types often display obsessive behaviors and thought patterns. They go back to check that the iron is unplugged, that the door is locked and that nothing has been left on the stove. This need to check appears reasonable and necessary to them and their demands that others follow the same routines can try the limits of tolerance for those in their families.

Anger is a perpetual problem for the Emerson. The injustices of the world and of their own personal situation are very real to them. They have a strong belief that life should be fair and the repeated experience that it is not arouses deep indignation. They do not choose to be angry, it is outside their control, and they often feel guilty about its intensity and the ease with which it is aroused. When they attempt to repress it, it comes out in other ways: complaining, criticism, fanatical adherence to causes, or excessive demands.

Emersons have unusually strong consciences, which cause them to feel guilty about a variety of concerns, though often not the issues their partners would choose them to focus on. It is possible for an Emerson to demolish a mate through criticism or rage and then to walk off without a backward glance to brood with genuine sorrow over injustice in the Third World. While this disparity in response seems utterly perverse to the onlooker, the explanation is simple. To the Emersons, the anger with the partner is perceived as justifiable rage, almost a form of constructive criticism, while the more distant suffering of those not personally known to them arouses genuine compassion, felt in conjunction with anger at those perceived to be at fault for this suffering.

THE NIGHTINGALE

I'm a loving person. People say I tend to wear my heart on my sleeve, and maybe I do, but I see nothing wrong with doing that. I am so touched by the misfortunes of others that I become really upset watching documentaries about people who are suffering. I am a good friend and I pride myself that I have wonderful friends who are there for me. I sometimes feel that I have more than my share of troubles, but that doesn't stop me, I have a heavy schedule of work and personal commitments and I try to fulfill all my obligations.

Gloria is right. She *is* a caring person and she's chosen a profession that matches that image, nursing. She has a supervisory position in a large hospital, a very responsible job. She is well respected at work and is deemed to be particularly skilled in direct patient care. She is married with two children. In addition to her work, she belongs to three diverse community organizations. She is active in all of them and can always be counted on to participate in bake sales, block parties, and potluck suppers.

Gloria's personality structure resembles that of Florence Nightingale, the nurse in the Crimean war who renounced the traditional role assigned her by Victorian society to travel to the Crimean and devote herself to the care of the sick and wounded soldiers. She endured intense physical stress and many hardships in order to fulfill her mission.

Gloria finds that her husband and children are often angry with her, complaining that she does a great deal for other people, but it is often at their expense. She is puzzled by this complaint, as she honestly feels that she does everything for them. In fact she drives herself to fulfill their needs and to see that her children have all the advantages that she feels she missed in her own childhood. Only recently, after working an eight-hour day, she stayed up until two o'clock one night finishing a costume for her daughter, Amy, to wear in the school pageant. It is true that it wouldn't have been quite as late if she hadn't first gone to a meeting of her woman's club, but it is a typical example of her willingness to sacrifice her own comfort for her children. Their other complaint is that she tends to be intrusive and often invades their privacy in ways they find both unfair and humiliating. She dismisses this charge as unfounded; feeling it is her duty as a mother to monitor their friends and activities as closely as she thinks necessary.

Her relationship with her husband is not as fulfilling as she wishes it were. She feels that the basic difficulty is that he doesn't understand and fulfill the responsibilities of a husband and father adequately, that he is simply not there for her in the way that he should be. She often tries to explain her perception of what is lacking to him, but talking about it makes her so angry that they usually end up in a fight.

She truly needs his support and understanding, yet when she tries to talk to him about what she wants and expects he often brushes her off and seems to attempt to avoid such discussions. Most of these conversations end with Gloria in tears. She often discusses this problem with her friends. They sympathize with her, but some of them also suggest that she may be making too much of an issue of this and even suggest that she has a pretty decent husband.

Martin holds two jobs. He is a social worker in a mental health clinic. After work and on weekends, he heads a literacy program run through the public library. The second job is a volunteer post and he really participates in it out of a sense of responsibility, because it's a worthwhile cause, and there's just no one else around willing to take it on.

He started with the library two years ago. He was running another volunteer operation before that, but he finally left because he wasn't getting the cooperation of the other volunteers and was experiencing a certain amount of undercutting and backbiting from the other people in the program.

He is having some of the same problems with his full-time job now. The head of the clinic seems to have no real understanding of the mental health needs of the clients and administers the program in a shabby way with more interest in profit than in meeting client needs. Martin feels that if he would only give him a free hand, he could turn it into a really well run clinic, and he is probably right. But there isn't a chance that this is going to happen.

At home, Martin views himself as an exceptionally good father. He is kind, loving, and understanding. While his work schedule prevents him from putting in as much time with his children as he would like, he believes that the hours they do spend together constitute quality time.

He wishes his wife had more empathy with the children. Of course they love her and they don't complain, but she just doesn't interact with them the same way that he does. She's not as warm and understanding, and this worries him. When he remonstrates with her, she says something to the effect that it's just as well as she doubts that the kids could handle two of him. He loves her, but has come to realize that they don't share the same goals. She just doesn't have his compassion and he's learned over the years that it's better not to count on her to join in and participate with him in his many projects in the ways he wishes she would.

As they've grown apart, it's affected their sex life, and they make love rather infrequently these days. She suggests that his weight problem may have contributed to this, a response he views as an excuse for her fear of intimacy.

Gloria and Martin both have problems with relationships and family which spring from the dynamics of the Nightingale personality. Nightingales tend to feel misunderstood. They believe that they are insufficiently loved and appreciated by those nearest to them. When this claim is examined, it often means that the Nightingale has made demands that would strain the limits of marital endurance in most relationships. *"If I start worrying at night and wake you up to talk about a problem, you will cheerfully abandon your sleep to discuss it with me."* *"Your sense of humor is acerbic and mildly malicious. This is not my style and I find it irritating. Kindly replace it with a more benign and acceptable disposition."* *"If I describe interactions with people, I expect you to agree that I was right in the way I handled the situation."*

Ironically, despite the difficulties at home, Nightingales are often well liked by their friends. This is probably a measure of the difference in the degree of attention and empathy demanded from family versus friends.

The Nightingale need for love is basic to their personality structure. The feeling of being unloved or insufficiently loved has its roots in this neediness, which often seems insatiable both to them and to those around them. *"What have you done for me lately?"* is not a joke, but often a serious and painful question when asked by this personality type.

These dynamics create a dilemma for the average Nightingale. Since they believe they are not getting sufficient appreciation within the family, it is essential to look for what they need outside and the only way to get admiration from the larger community is to earn it. Nightingales generally enjoy joining clubs and volunteer organizations and work tirelessly in them at relatively thankless tasks, often with little understanding of what drives them to such outputs of time and energy. Average Nightingales are not good team players. While they are good workers, they tend to want to set their own conditions: *"I'll help, but I'll decide what I do and how I do it and I don't want to hear any criticism."* If these prerequisites are not satisfactory to the person or organization being helped, Nightingales may withdraw their assistance feeling misunderstood and rejected.

Time spent in helping people and organizations outside the household cuts down on the hours available to the family. The partners and children of Nightingales may well feel in the role of the proverbial shoemaker's barefoot family. There simply isn't enough time to squeeze everything in, so it's necessary to cut corners and put off commitments to family members.

Average Nightingales have strong and unrealistic expectations of how their partners and children should think and act. They have a difficult time accepting those close to them as they are. The incompletely articulated desire is that their partner's change to be who they would like them to be and that entails being the person who could meet their needs most completely. The concept that the other person has a right to his or her personality and could feel violated by these demands for a systematic restructuring of him or herself is difficult for the average Nightingale to understand.

The control issue here is quite different from the need of an Emerson. Emersons will ask for outward conformity to standards, which they believe to be moral. The Nightingale's need to control is centered squarely on personality. The Emerson says, *"Do what I want you to do because it's right."* Nightingales say *"Be who I want you to be if you love me."* Both requests make for marital conflict.

Average Nightingales have a tendency to be manipulative in relationships. They wheel and deal behind the scenes to achieve the result they would like in situations. A Nightingale who wishes to cancel a social engagement can become ill in an instant. If a Nightingale wants a spouse to go somewhere or do something which he or she might not want to do, they often get someone else to ask on the theory that it will be harder to say no to a friend. If nothing else works to achieve their goals, they often turn to ultimatums and threats.

Nightingales often have problems centering on food, either being overweight, despite recurrent dieting, or becoming anorexic or bulimic. The use of food as a surrogate for love and nurturing creates this problem. When Nightingales feel unhappy, they feel empty and often turn to food as a source of momentary comfort.

Sexual intimacy is a problem in many Nightingale relationships. Feelings of being unloved or inadequately loved may make sexual arousal difficult, or anger with the partner may prohibit any display of affection.

Nightingales are natural caretakers. They can be warm and giving with those in their charge. Their willingness to take responsibility and even to be over-responsible often causes Nightingales to display co-dependent behaviors. Here the desire to restructure the personality of another person meets the personality that needs some restructuring if it is to become healthy. It's a tempting project and it is not unusual for Nightingales to form relationships with alcoholics, addicts, or the otherwise fragile or vulnerable, for the sheer pleasure of helping someone who genuinely needs help.

Should a relationship fail, it is difficult for Nightingales to let go gracefully. The need for love is too intense, and even when love no longer exists, Nightingales experience the break-up as the loss of something that was once theirs and their need solidifies into a demand. *"You must love me, you must stay with me."* Pleading gives way to manipulating tactics, which, if they are unsuccessful can be followed by rage.

THE BEAU

I possess a good sense of socially appropriate behavior. I know what to do or say on most occasions and I'm never at a loss for words. I enjoy competition and view this as a healthy trait. I have good business sense and

I'm well organized and efficient in my work. I work hard and I'm not ashamed to enjoy the results of my labors. My family and I enjoy the perks that come with a successful life. I believe I'm a likable person and people seem to like me.

George does possess great personal charm. He is admired both by his business associates and his friends. He works hard and is highly efficient and well organized. He has done well in his advertising business and has recently entered local politics.

George's personality type resembles that of George Bryan Brummel. Beau Brummel was the arbiter of fashion at the court of George IV, where his reputation was so great that the name, Beau Brummel has persisted to the present day as the prototype of poise and style. Success and appearances were both extremely important to him. He was charming and widely popular with his contemporaries and had a reputation as a wit.

George, a Beau personality, plays as hard as he works. His tennis and golf games are both well above the average level, but he remains dissatisfied and frequently seeks coaching to improve them. He enjoys parties, and when he gives one, he is an excellent host.

He is somewhat dissatisfied with his marriage, as he feels his wife doesn't put as much effort into ordering and improving her life as he does in his. She was exceptionally beautiful when he married her, but has put on about 15 pounds since the births of their children. She is certainly far from obese, still, it's not the image he would like *his* wife to project. She doesn't seem to be moving ahead with her career as quickly as he had expected either. He has never discussed his dissatisfaction with anyone, and presents the appearance of a devoted husband to the world.

Joan is a very pretty woman and she has a great sense of style. She dresses well, but her poise and bearing are such that she looks striking even in her oldest clothes. She is in a managerial position in a retail sales outlet, and hopes to be made a vice-president in her area in the next few years.

Joan believes that she comes fairly close to perfection as a wife and mother. She has excellent taste in decorating and her home reflects this. It is widely held that she gives the best parties in her social circle. She is sensitive to her husband's career needs and always willing to entertain clients or colleagues at his request. She plans a busy social schedule for them, but also makes time for them to do things together as a couple, usually a play or a visit to a museum.

Her husband sometimes complains that he needs more down time, and she responds with agreement and sympathy, but does not actually modify their busy schedule. Her children also tend to complain about a lack of free time. The schedule of tennis lessons, karate classes, dance classes and piano lessons tends to fill afternoons and Saturdays.

Beaus often give the impression, on first meeting, of being very near to the ideal personality. They are poised, pleasant, gracious, and usually physically attractive.

They are generally very good at their jobs and tend to be hard workers. They are quite competitive with a high level of drive and motivation. The negative aspect of these traits is that they often are not good team players, except when they are the team leaders. They can be quite ruthlessly competitive with colleagues and sometimes do not seek help or advice when they need it.

Appearances are exceptionally important to the Beau. They care about how they look and how anyone associated with them appears. They are conscious of status and, when they can afford it, prefer to purchase items that define them as people with both taste and purchasing power—expensive cars, designer labels, a house in an exclusive section of town.

Average Beaus seem to lack emotional depth. They know the proper things to say for various occasions, but they give the impression that there is very little genuine feeling behind their words. They also tend to lack strong views on subjects outside their personal orbit. They can appear to be in agreement with the person they are talking to, and then seem to endorse the opposite viewpoint a few minutes later when talking to someone else. This gives them an image of flexibility, a willingness to see the point of view of others, and it certainly appears to be a congenial trait initially, but it can backfire when others realize that there is no conviction behind their amiable accord. When Beaus become less healthy, they replace actual talents and accomplishments with facade, and try to bluff their way through situations that are beyond their depth. They may pretend to accomplishments that are exaggerated or even untrue, or may give events a spin to make them appear better than is really the case.

THE SHELLEY

I am someone with intense feelings. I am vulnerable and easily hurt, but that seems to me to be the price you have to pay if you want to be open to people and experience, and that is something that is very important to me. Vulnerability is not weakness. I am actually quite tough when challenged. I can be spontaneous without being impulsive. It's important to me that I represent who I am accurately and so I'm selective in the matter of friendships and possessions. I'll never be the life of the party, but my friends value my imagination and my insights.

Yes, Jean is someone whose emotional life can be quite intense. She has a deep sense of empathy for whatever is happening with her friends and family. She in deeply interested in observing the characteristics and foibles of the people around her and while she desires neither to control them or judge them, she can analyze what they are doing or where they are coming from in a dispassionate manner that can be disconcerting to many people.

Jean possesses personality characteristics similar to the romantic poet, Shelley, who was extremely sensitive in regard both to external happenings and to his own thoughts and feelings. He had more highly developed qualities of spontaneity and imagination than most people, and he had difficulty in dealing with authority in almost every form, considering most types of authority both unduly constraining and somewhat absurd.

Jean, too, is very much a free spirit, and can be contemptuous of social conventions or rules that she judges to be ill founded. She is extremely stubborn and committed on large topics that she cares about, but is generally flexible and easy-going over more mundane issues that don't matter particularly to her.

She is a therapist, and is both concerned and caring with patients. Her sensitivity is a great asset in her work, but it also makes her easily vulnerable in her personal life. She tends to be somewhat touchy in interpersonal relations, sensitive to rejection and slights. This vulnerability is partially hidden by a rather caustic dry sense of humor. She has been accused of having "a mean streak " and can be cruel when someone is too intrusive or if she feels angry or hurt.

Self-knowledge is extremely important to Jean. She feels a strong drive to understand herself and her family, both in terms of their inner needs and motivations and the interpersonal relationships between them. She sometimes wakes up at night, worrying about an interaction of the day, pulling it apart until she is satisfied that she grasps what happened.

Greg is a novelist and has published several moderately successful books. He also has a job in an ad agency, which actually provides the bulk of his income. He is good at this work, writing witty amusing copy, but he hates the agency and often mocks it and the people in it.

Greg tends to be as observer of life around him, holding himself aloof in most social situations. He is sometimes perceived as patronizing. Behind this behavior is his own uncertainty about acceptance by the people around him. He tends to be touchy and to withdraw in response to real or fancied criticism.

He is a devoted husband and father, but after an afternoon of family interaction, he is likely to pull away to read or go for a walk alone. When he is with people too long, he tends to become irascible and short-tempered.

Greg's wife believes he does much less than his fair share around the house and often complains that he is too self-centered. While he enjoys arguments about politics or literature, he tends to avoid over-heated angry discussions and to withdraw from personal confrontations.

The primary problems Shelleys bring to relationships is their need for space and time alone and their too penetrating observation of the people and interactions around them, which others often find disconcerting or even cruel.

Shelleys possess a sense of their own uniqueness, coupled with feelings of inferiority at being different from most other people. They are likely to disdain those people who engage in easy gossip or talk at length about the mundane events of their day. Yet this attitude is coupled with the desire to be able to make small talk in situations where it is socially appropriate and a painful sense of inadequacy at their difficulty in doing so. As Shelleys become healthier, of course, they learn better social skills, but it is a genuine problem for almost all Shelleys in their youth.

Shelleys have a strong need for authenticity. It is important to them to see things as they are. It is hard for a Shelley to say someone looks nice if they don't think so, or to show pleasure in a gift if they don't like it. It seems phony and dishonest to them. The child who observed that the emperor had no clothes was probably a little Shelley. This tendency to speak the whole truth can appear tactless and/or cruel depending on the situation and can be embarrassing to more tactful partners.

Shelleys need down time. They can't interact with people all day without experiencing stimulus overload. They need to spend some quiet time by themselves or at least without talking to anyone around them. When circumstances prevent them from getting the space they need, they tend to feel unfocused and usually become irritable. This can be difficult for other people to understand and may be perceived as rejection or withdrawal.

Confrontation is upsetting to Shelleys, they try to avoid it or withdraw from it. If that is impossible, or if they feel extremely strongly about something, they become vehement and stubborn opponents.

The qualities the Shelley brings to marriage include a desire for deep emotional intimacy, a good, somewhat ironic sense of humor, and high degree of sexual responsiveness.

THE EINSTEIN

I am definitely an introvert. I like people, but I really need some time and space to myself every day and I enjoy solitary occupations. I like to learn new things and I am avid in pursuing fields of particular interest. I read a lot and I like to spend time analyzing what I've read. Theories and systems fascinate me. I will approach a new theory with the glee of a child with a new toy. While I hate real confrontations and try to avoid them, I can be a bit contentious on a theoretical level and I sometimes enjoy stating a rather outrageous idea just to see how people will respond to it. My life may not seem exciting to others, but it suits me, and my quieter pleasures are fulfilling and satisfying to me.

Arthur is a computer programmer. It is both his work and his hobby. He is happiest devising new programs and stretching the limits of what can be done on the Internet. While his work is with a large computer organization and deals with more serious software, he has created several new games in his spare time.

Arthur is an Einstein. Albert Einstein lived in the realm of theories and ideas. He emphasized abstract thought and was relatively unconcerned with the mundane details of daily life. He tended to be impersonal and somewhat aloof in his interactions with others, and to give more attention to his work than to family matters.

Arthur is happily, if somewhat abstractly married. He gives relatively little attention to his relationship with his wife or children. He is quite willing to show up for parties, family gatherings or any other occasion that he is asked to attend, but is usually glad when they are over and he can get back to something more interesting. He is generally quite obliging, willing to run errands or do household tasks as needed, providing they don't take too much time away from his real preoccupation. But apart from feeding and walking his dog, he has almost no grasp of the daily details that require attention in running a household. He has several areas of special knowledge, some of them quite arcane and unexpected, and he can be a bit long-winded and something of a bore on topics that he is particularly knowledgeable about.

While he does not require a great deal of money to be happy, Arthur does tend to be somewhat close-fisted when it comes to spending. He genuinely does not understand why people want to go out to dinner if they already have food in the house or why his wife urges him to buy a new sports jacket when he already owns two.

Marion teaches at a college. She has a full professorship and has written many well-respected articles in her field. Her students find her a competent and fair teacher. She took a relatively long time to acquire her professorship because, despite her strong reputation, she is not very adept at academic politics and tends to avoid them as much as possible.

Marion does not get equally high marks at home from her husband and children. The house is, frankly, usually a mess, with piles of books, newspapers and magazines in every room. This is a household where role reversal has set in with a vengeance, and the children nag mother to pick up after herself. Her oldest daughter routinely cleans the house before inviting friends over. Marion is aware that her husband and children resent her lack of concern for the details of daily living, but she honestly has no time to do anything about it.

Marion's husband urges her to spend more time and effort on her wardrobe and personal appearance and she makes some effort to comply with his demands, but as she has little genuine interest in these things, her efforts never seem to show much in the way of results.

Her interpersonal relations with husband and children are gentle and kindly, but she brings little overt passion to the marital relationship and often chooses to retreat to her bedroom to escape the noise and confusion of family life.

Einstein personalities like Marion and Arthur are people who put more emphasis on their thoughts and theories than on observed reality. They find that they are often most comfortable alone or with just one or two close friends or family members. They are often hesitant and uncomfortable in new situations or with people they don't know well enough to be at ease with.

They approach the world from a global perspective intellectually, and are impatient with the trivia of daily life, although within the context of their own research, they are willing to be endlessly painstaking.

Often Einsteins are specialists who are genuine experts in their area, whether it is a branch of medicine, an academic specialty or a complex game like bridge or chess.

Einsteins are natural lecturers who are willing to go into endless detail with anyone who questions them about some area in which they are knowledgeable. It must be admitted that they are sometimes accused of telling people more than they want to know when they get started on a pet theory.

Einsteins tend to avoid conflict and confrontation and to agree with whatever demands the family may make for the sake of peace and quiet. When this strategy does not protect them adequately from the irritations of family life, they can eventually become angry. Whenever possible however, they withdraw rather than confronting people. Einsteins may take up solitary walks, fishing trips or frequent out-of-town seminars as methods of isolating themselves from the pressures of work or family.

Einsteins tend to be frugal, saving their money, not buying new things except when pursuing a special area of interest or expertise. An Einstein might experience no difficulty in justifying an expensive vacation to some exotic locale as a learning experience, but be quite conflicted about bringing home a few $20.00 souvenirs.

In marriage, the pervasive problem for Einsteins is remembering to focus adequately on their partners and to make adequate time for them and include them in their lives. They need to push themselves to greater assertion in stating both their needs and what bothers them.

THE AUSTEN

I think I'm a pretty nice person. I certainly try to be. I'm willing to work hard, and I try to do what's expected of me and to be nice and cooperative with everyone. I like to be a part of groups and it's been said that I'm a good team player. When I get excited or enthusiastic, I can get carried away, but generally, I feel that I'm a sensible person. Sticking with my daily routine is important to me. It keeps me focused and on track. I enjoy being with people and doing things with them.

This enjoyment is reciprocated. People tend to like Jane. She is friendly, cooperative and helpful. She would do just about anything for a friend. She is very much the traditionalist. She values the tried and true over any unknown quantity. She dislikes conflict and tries to avoid it whenever possible. It is puzzling to her for this reason that her interactions with her husband and children often become conflicted. Jane possesses the personality traits seen in the personal life of Jane Austen, the English novelist, and of many of the characters in her works.

Jane Austen was devoted to her family, and her life was centered in her home. She was sharply observant, with an eye for the small details of human interaction. Austen wrote novels of middle-class life, in which the protagonists were nice people, polite and well mannered and even the meanest characters were superficially civil in public. People speak of finding her books comforting and reassuring.

Jane is sharply observant of people and situations. She is an analytical person and tries to understand other people's motives and actions. She has a keen sense of fairness and becomes quite upset when she or her children are not fairly treated even in small matters.

One of her problems is that she tends to be quite indecisive. It's truly hard for her to make up her mind. She is considering having a third child right now. She thinks it would be a good idea and she wants to go ahead with it. After all, she enjoys children a lot and gets along well with them and she knows her parents would be thrilled to have another grandchild. But yesterday, when she was feeling quite anxious and had had a minor run-in with her son, she decided that she really ought to stop with the two she has. She thought that if she could feel as hassled and exhausted as she sometimes does with two kids, having another one would be a very foolish move. The worst of it is that she's aware that she'll probably change her mind again. She just doesn't know which is the right thing to do and she knows that she does this in many situations and that it drives her husband crazy.

Another problem for Jane is her fearfulness. She wishes it would go away, but she really can't help it. It makes her nag her children whenever they want to do anything the least bit exciting. *Don't ride your bike there. Don't dive off that diving board, it's too high. Call me when you get to your friend's house, so I'll know you got there safely.* She often cautions her husband in much the same way, worrying about when he'll get home from work, begging him not to drive unnecessarily on snowy days, fretting that his boss may be taking advantage of him. The whole family teases her about being a worrywart, but there's a bit of anger behind the teasing and she knows it.

Dan and Jane have a good deal in common with each other. He is another Austen personality, and also feels a lot of fear and anxiety, but he manages it quite differently. He's a middle management executive in a large corporation, and a lot of his worries center on his job; he feels stressed by the workload and has reached a job level where there is a reasonable amount of decision-making required of him. He is very uncomfortable with this and worries after the fact about whether he's made the right choice.

At home, a lot of the problems center on disciplining the children. Dan has very definite ideas about how kids should behave. He expects them to be obedient and respectful, to do what they're told without arguing. His wife says that his expectations are unrealistic and that his rigid demands are alienating the children from him. She thinks that he is generally too rigid, in fact and says it would be nice to have him do the unexpected thing on occasion and that she'd like to have a bit more spontaneity and excitement in her life.

Another sore spot that creates serious difficulties in the relationship shows up when Dan is in a bad mood or inwardly angry. When that happens, he may agree to take out the garbage and then forget that recyclables have to go in a separate can. Or he may say he'll put the dinner in the oven at six, so it will be ready when his wife gets home at 6:30 and then either put it in at 5:00 and burn it or not put it in until 6:25. His wife often thinks she might be more comfortable with overt anger than with this quiet sabotage.

Austens are hard workers and cooperative with the people around them and their problems in relationships often center on their fears and their needs for security. Fear can immobilize Austens on occasion and can be extremely exasperating to their more secure mates. To anyone not troubled by the same apprehensions, Austen fears often seem irrational and unbelievable. There can be a real credibility problem when one's mate refuses to do what everyone else is doing on the grounds that it's dangerous to fly, snorkel, eat octopus, go to a restaurant in another part of town, etc. The list is different for each person, and it's important to stress that we're dealing with the average degree of psychic health. As Austens become healthier, the list shortens or disappears.

Average Austens tend to be over-concerned about what neighbors and friends think. Their partners can have a great deal of difficulty understanding why the opinion of someone their spouse barely knows weighs more heavily than their own. The problem lies in Austen reliance on authority. The composite opinion of the neighborhood or group is often an authority to Austens and they find safety and stability in acceding to group mores and beliefs.

Indecisiveness is the bane of the Austen and of those in relationship with them. The problem is centered in the Austen belief that there is a right and a wrong choice to be made in whatever they do. They don't know which is the right choice, but they do know that it's important for them to find it. The truth is that there are merely options for most of our decisions and that most choices are merely picking one or another of those options, with no element of right or wrong involved. This is almost impossible for Austens to grasp. They would really prefer not to have to make many choices at all, but unless there is a clear authority to take over this responsibility, its not possible to just opt out of whatever the situation is. To allow a non-authority to make the choice would surely be a mistake, so the Austen decides, and then thinks of all the reasons to go with the opposite decision, and waivers. The husband or wife of the Austen can become enraged as the ball bounces back and forth on each issue that comes up.

The wholehearted reliance on authority is another sore point for Austen spouses. The authorities are arbitrarily chosen, but are clung to with tenacity. *"The newspaper said..., the church said..., Timmy's teacher said..., Mrs. Jones said......"* It sometimes seems to the bewildered partner that the Austen has no ability to evaluate, analyze or even just think for him or herself.

It's important to Austens that they are liked and they really want to cooperate with people both at home and in the outside world. This sounds like a good trait, but it can have a down side. The problem arises whenever a genuine disagreement occurs. They may say *yes* when they really mean *no* and then act on their real feelings despite having given lip service to the opposite course of action. The intention is to be agreeable and to avoid an argument, but it can come across as dishonesty to the person on the other end of the agreement.

When Austens become less healthy, they can become passive-aggressive in their behavior, actively thwarting the needs and desires of the people around them. The passive-aggressive person doesn't feel comfortable with open confrontation or conflict, so they engage in a kind of guerrilla warfare instead, sniping from protected locations. Passive-aggressive people may be consistently late for appointments, or "forget" them and not keep them at all, fail to follow through on commitments, sabotage other people's plans, neglect to give people messages, do things in a half-hearted slip-shod way so that they don't achieve the appropriate result, and just generally make the people around them miserable through their failure to act. The underlying dynamic in this behavior is their failure to express anger overtly.

Many Austens tend to rely heavily on conversation about daily concerns and interactions as a method of connecting with others. They expect those around them to reciprocate in this. While this sounds harmless, it can create major impasses in practice. Austens chatter about what happened at work, what was on the lunch menu, who they met on the street, or whatever else is on their minds. Then they stop and wait with the expectation that the partner will respond in the same vein. Many people are simply unable to comply. *"Nothing happened at work and I don't remember what I ate for lunch, it was nothing special."* The Austen tries again: *"How was your day?" "Fine."* Most other people are just not as interested in the minutia of daily living and find it exasperating to be asked to detail insignificant data. The Austen has difficulty in accepting this and often concludes that the partner is rejecting or insufficiently involved or committed to the relationship.

THE MOZART

I'm a very up-beat person. I like to have a good time. I enjoy being around people and they usually find me amusing and fun to be with. I have a strong impulsive streak, which can get me in trouble since I have been known to act before I think about something. My tendency to over-spend on my charge cards can be a problem. Still, I think I get more fun out of life than most people do, and I'm happy about that.

Gini certainly is a fun person and as she says, she is very upbeat practically all the time. She's the life of the party, whether or not there is one. She has a ready wit and a sparkling personality. Most people like to be around her, just to let some of her cheerfulness and sparkle rub off on them.

Gini has many of the same personality traits as Wolfgang Mozart. He was impulsive, with an enormously high energy level, he was capable of sustained hard work, but also of great overindulgence and self-indulgence. He was greatly admired for his work, but his quick wit and sharp tongue also made enemies.

While she has many friends, Gini is always eager to make more. She likes new people and new experiences, and frequently finds some new outing or adventure to relieve the tedium of the daily routine. Unfortunately, the very qualities that are so appealing to her friends, and that attracted them to her in the first place, seem to have worn a bit thin with her husband. It seems to him that while Gini presents a buoyant fun-loving *persona* to the world, she has poor tolerance for the moods and feelings of others. Any display of being tired or sad, or even slightly withdrawn, is likely to be met with annoyance, if not outright anger. *"I want to have fun and you're raining on my parade. I won't tolerate it."* is likely to be Gini's response to a desire to leave a party early, a concern about whether they can afford an expensive vacation, or just a statement that he's very tired and doesn't want to go out on Saturday afternoon this week.

It also seems that Gini's desire to have fun is specifically the desire to have the most fun possible. She accepts invitations and then if something more exciting or interesting comes along, alibis or tells outright lies to get out of the earlier engagement. She simply doesn't understand why her husband has such a problem with this. Closely allied to this difficulty is the issue of spending time together. It often seems to her husband that she would rather do just about anything than spend time alone with him. When he tries to talk to her about this, she brushes it off as untrue or foolish, but this does not deal with the issue, and he feels powerless to get her to do that.

Gini loves her children and is very good with them when she's around, but she doesn't seem to be around as much as the other mothers on the block. The baby-sitter may very well spend more time with them than she does, even outside of working hours.

Bruce is also a Mozart personality. He is a hard worker and is very well liked both at work and in the couple's social circle. He is a regional sales manager in his company and it's a job he's well suited for. He never objects to time spent in the field and his employers wish that their other employees were as open to going on business trips or taking clients out at the last minute as he is. He has taken on several assignments within the community as well. He's been an officer or member of the board of three different community organizations, and when it comes to planning a party, he's the person to turn to. He's a wonderful organizer and willing to do whatever it takes to make the affair memorable.

His wife is not always as pleased with him as his associates are. She often feels that he is just not there for her or for the children. Whether he's off at the neighborhood bar, or stopping to have dinner with some fellow workers before coming home, he is generally someplace else. She believes he has had two affairs since they were married. When she confronts him, he is contrite and promises to break things off immediately, but she's never really sure that he doesn't go back and continue the relationship later. She's never really sure where he is when he's not home and he's very rarely home. When they first started dating, she was absolutely enchanted by his vivacious personality, but at this point, she'd be willing to trade quite a bit of that vivacity for a little stability.

She is also troubled by his use of stimulants. He doesn't seem to set limits for himself. He has three cups of coffee in the morning to get going, and drinks coffee all day at work. He drinks a bit too much, and occasionally uses marijuana. He assures her that it is purely recreational use and that he would never make a regular habit of it, but at this point, she feels she can't trust him. She loves him and the children adore him, but her patience is nearing its limits.

Mozart personalities, at the average level, are people who have never really learned to postpone gratification. They want happiness and stimulation and they want it now. Naturally new and different things are considerably more stimulating than old familiar things and they are therefore always seeking something fresh and different. Since they want the maximum pleasure available at any time, they often drop commitments, people, and relationships in their search for excitement and variety.

There is an implicit demand that the people around the Mozart be upbeat, stimulating, and amusing. A Mozart can become quite irritated by depression or pessimism in those around them. Mozarts can view a failure to sparkle on the part of a partner as a personal affront. At the same time, their strong drive and high energy level will tire most other people out, until eventually, there's just no sparkle left in them for the moment.

The sense that more is always better, makes average Mozarts the life of the party, but also reluctant to leave or to have anyone else leave. Going home sounds boring, and the tendency is to party until they are ready to drop. Then when they *are* ready to quit, it's generally a total crash. *"I'm going to bed now. Don't bother me."*

Mozarts who are less healthy can be prone to having affairs. The idea of a new experience is simply too exciting to pass up. They like to dance, drink, flirt, have long intimate conversations, and thus they often find themselves tempted or even involved before they notice what's happening.

As with all personality types, the relative health of the individual will determine how serious the problems are and the personality of their partner will create major differences in the dynamics.

THE CAESAR

I'm considered a real powerhouse in my business. I don't object to the designation. I know what I want out of life and I set my sights on achieving it. I'm willing to put in long hours and work weekends if that's necessary and I can be impatient with people who are less hard working and focused than myself. If I work hard, I also know how to play hard and I like to have a good time. I consider being able to spend a fair amount of money on recreation a reasonable reward for my hard work. I know how to get along with people and I'm generally considered rather charming.

Naturally, Evelyn is able to give a fairly accurate appraisal of herself. She is used to making accurate assessments of situations and people. Evelyn is a vice-president in charge of marketing for a Fortune 500 company. She is a shrewd investor and has managed to supplement her income appreciably through her stock portfolio. She works out three times a week in a gym and plays golf and tennis regularly. She is a Caesar. Julius Caesar's most famous saying, *"I came, I saw, I conquered,"* epitomizes this personality type. Caesars are expansive people, who always seem to wish to further increase their influence and standing in everything that they do. They are natural leaders who want to take charge of any situation they find themselves in.

While Evelyn is a well-organized hard-working executive, her home life seems to run less smoothly than her career. She and her husband certainly have more conflicts than most couples. The truth is that her skills have been honed in a framework where she has been given wide decision-making initiative, and where her choices are generally respected. It is true that, as in all corporations, she must work within the confines of company policy and goals, but the experience is structured in ways that she understands and respects. Having her decisions questioned and her choices opposed by her partner for reasons that she often finds trivial or foolish tends to enrage her.

When the couple are in agreement, Evelyn is a delightful wife. She has tremendous energy and is as hard working in terms of their house and their social life as she is at her job. While she has been known to intimidate people in social settings by being somewhat outspoken and frank in her views on various subjects, she honestly considers it their problem if they can't stand up to her in discussions.

Evelyn is a no-nonsense mother. Her children know what is expected of them and also know that they had better meet those expectations. She has arranged a full program of after-school activities for them and has plenty of back up in terms of baby-sitters and housekeepers. They do some exciting things together as a family. Vacations and weekend outings are well planned and successful, but the children get relatively little of their mother's attention on a daily basis. She would love to be with them more, but there simply isn't time.

Bob is an attractive, charming guy. He gives a flattering degree of attention to the people he is with. He is genuinely interested in a wide range of people and ideas and can flatter and engage friends and associates naturally. People enjoy his company.

Bob is a true entrepreneur. He has started three different companies since he married and is currently running all three successfully. He puts in long hours, but he loves every minute of the time he spends. He is never happier than when he is successfully facing down a rival or going out on a limb with the confidence that he can bring off whatever goal he is pursuing. One result of this focus and determination is that he is a very successful businessman, the other result is that his family sees very little of him. Even when he promises to be home for a special occasion, he often shows up late because something came up at work. He loves his children and thinks he would do anything for them, but the truth is that he often disappoints them by his absence and failure to make time for them.

Bob is also something of a bully in personal relations. He certainly isn't aware of this, and would probably deny it, but his need to win in all circumstances often causes him to take an unfair advantage when he has a disagreement with his wife. He is a master at detecting weak spots and using them. *"You won't do what I want, then don't expect me home for dinner tonight,"* seems to him a natural consequence of wrong-headed behavior and he shrugs it off when his wife terms it coercion. When he considers it necessary in pursuing his own needs, he simply shouts and threatens until he gets his way.

Caesars want to be leaders, managers or directors. Healthy Caesars with their vision and energy are motivating to the people around them. They get things done and get the rest of us moving. While average Caesars also possess tremendous energy, it tends to be used less for the good of everyone around them than for their personal advantage.

It is hard for average Caesars to see the other person's point of view or to credit it as valid. They are not very sensitive to the feelings of the people around them and can be brusque and unresponsive to emotional appeals or to indications of physical or psychological weakness.

It is important to the Caesar to be in charge of anything they are involved in. Young Caesars in corporations fight their way to the top as quickly as possible, as they are uncomfortable in entry-level positions. They attempt to take control of any organizations they become involved with, and certainly make an insistent demand to be the authority in their families. This latter ploy will have mixed results depending on the personality of the spouse and the dynamics between them, but a marriage in which they do not have at least the perception of being in control is likely to be a rocky one.

Life presents some reality situations where they simply cannot exercise control. Such times are difficult for them to handle. A Caesar with a family member in the hospital is a study in frustration. They must defer to doctors and hospital policy, but they want the person healed and want it done now. Their heads tell them that they are out of their depth and often this makes them so uncomfortable that they either begin to bluster or simply stay away, not because they do not care, but because they can't handle feeling so helpless.

Caesars have anxieties like everyone else, but their approach to anxiety is to use it. While others become less focused and less capable of functioning when they are over-anxious, Caesars may even purposely increase their anxiety level in order to make themselves more focused, to give them a keener edge in whatever they have to do.

Healthy Caesars have a sense of *noblesse oblige*. They take care of those for whom they feel a sense of responsibility, spouses and children, but also their workers, extended family members and friends. Their approach may be somewhat paternalistic, but the help is genuine and generally effective. In return, they expect loyalty from those around them, and if they sense that someone has been disloyal, their enmity will be total and unforgiving.

THE GAUGUIN

I think I'm pretty easy-going. I don't like to make waves. Getting my own way has never been a big issue for me. I'm pretty adaptable. I'm willing to go along with the crowd. In fact I prefer to blend in. I enjoy simple pleasures, good food, watching television, or going out with the family. I don't have a high-powered life style and frankly, I don't want one. Most people see me as a nice guy and that's good enough for me.

Mike is considered a good guy by everyone who knows him. He's kind, considerate and easy-going. Nothing seems to bother him. He can get along with just about anybody. He is a loving husband and father, and a good friend.

While he is a more responsible person, Mike has the personality pattern of the French artist, Paul Gauguin. Gauguin started his adult life working in a bank, but soon quit in order to paint. Perpetually insolvent, he abandoned his family, first moving to Paris, and eventually, to the South Seas, where he spent the rest of his life.

While Gauguin went to extremes most people would not contemplate, an unwillingness to face problems and the desire for an easygoing life style exemplifies this temperament. This personality instinctively avoids problems and appreciates a slow paced life with adequate leisure.

Mike is well liked at work, but he doesn't seem to get promotions as quickly as some of the other people in his office, which might seem strange given his intelligence level and genial disposition. The problem is that he has very little drive. He does the job competently, but never gives it that extra push that his more dedicated colleagues supply. He is often late for work, but doesn't see this as a problem as he's willing to stay late if necessary. When confronted about lack of punctuality by his employer, he tends to brush it off and forget about it.

Problems at home also seem to center around not noticing the things that others regard as important. His wife has a growing list of tasks that need his attention. He certainly intends to deal with everything on the list, but it's growing longer as he procrastinates. Money is also an area of concern. He makes a good salary, but is reluctant to stay within a budget. Credit cards are his downfall. He seems not to understand the connection between handing the card to the clerk in the store and getting the bill at the end of the month.

Mike drinks too much. He's not an alcoholic, but there are times when his wife wonders if he's not edging in that direction. He certainly seems to have a poor sense of limits when he's at a party or even when friends come over for the evening.

Linda is also a Gauguin, kind, genial, and warm-hearted. While Mike has problems with alcohol, Linda's downfall is food. She's put on twenty pounds in the past five years, and fears she is still gaining. She starts a new diet at least once every three months, but can't seem to stick with any of them.

Linda also has job difficulties. She is a librarian, a cataloger in a college library. This was a good job choice for her as she really hates pressure and this allows her to work at her own pace. The problem is that her pace seems to have gotten slower and slower, and her colleagues and the administration are complaining of the heavy backlog and the length of time it takes for new books to appear on the shelves.

Things are a bit out of hand at home too. She only seems to get around to picking up and cleaning just before company comes. She has a problem about this with her children, who say they're ashamed to ask their friends over because the house looks like a pigpen. The strange thing is that Linda spends a lot of time on the house, it just doesn't seem to result in a finished product. She will spend a whole morning repotting her plants or rearranging a closet. This type of puttering seems soothing and pleasant to her, while the more exacting task of getting the house into some general sort of order gets put off indefinitely.

Recently Linda has developed some troubling physical symptoms. Her husband has asked her to go to the doctor to have them checked out. So far she hasn't gotten around to doing this, even though the symptoms are becoming worse. She hasn't mentioned this aggravation of the problem to her husband as she believes it will go away in time and knows that if she says anything, he'll only importune her more vehemently to go to the doctor. She has every intention of going eventually if things don't clear up, but she feels there's nothing to be so upset about, as she's sure it's nothing serious.

The essence of the relationship problems experienced by Gauguins is their unwillingness to confront people and situations. The Gauguin is truly a nice person who does not want to make waves. This means that problems are never solved or even squarely faced. This can drive those in a relationship with them berserk.

"Help me deal with this issue," the husband or wife pleads. *"No problem,"* responds the Gauguin. *"It will all work out okay, don't worry about it."* They expect leaking faucets to fix themselves, bounced checks to magically find the necessary money in the account and children with school problems to outgrow them. Their spouses feel that the entire weight of maintaining the marriage, the house, and the family is on them and that the Gauguin is off, gazing into space while they suffer. It is easy to be angry with a Gauguin, but hard to get them to focus on the fact that they have made you angry. The spouse pleads, cajoles, and screams, and the Gauguin hopes they will get over it soon and feel better.

The failure to take job requirements seriously can have a major financial impact on the Gauguin's family. While well liked by fellow employees, the Gauguin's casual approach to work can result in fewer raises and promotions at best and often in being the first to be laid off or fired in times of restructuring.

Over-indulgence is another Gauguin problem. Gauguins tend to turn to food and drink for comfort and a sense of well being. Alcoholism is not exclusive to any single personality type, but Gauguins seem especially prone to set no limits for themselves in regard to liquor. Drinking is certainly one way of achieving the enjoyment inherent for the Gauguin in tuning out from the world and its cares.

Over-eating can accompany or replace alcohol as a way to escape from the harsher aspects of daily living. The problem for the Gauguin's partner is that there appears to be no way of seriously discussing such concerns. *"You think I should go on a diet? Okay, you're absolutely right, I will."* Anyone who believes that because this conversation has taken place at five o'clock, the Gauguin will not eat two helpings of ice cream after dinner has never been in a relationship with this personality.

It sounds as though the Gauguin could never become angry. This is not true. If a situation becomes so serious or desperate that it creates anxiety, they are capable of rage. They can also respond with anger when they feel themselves being unduly pressured and are unable to deflect or defuse the person annoying them.

IV

The Emerson in Relationships

EMERSON-EMERSON RELATIONSHIPS

Edith has recently been promoted to a partnership in her law firm. She has worked hard for this promotion, but while she is pleased that it has come to her, it has brought added demands in terms of workload. She has been putting in even more overtime and coming home later than ever since the promotion.

Edith and Jim have been prominent in civic affairs and various charitable causes for many years. Now one of their favorite charities has scheduled the annual fund-raiser for a Thursday night. Jim is a member of the planning committee for the event and takes it as a matter of course that they will attend.

When Edith says she can't make it, he is incredulous at first and then quite angry. "I know all you can think about is your job, but I'm a little surprised that you could be so cavalier about something we've both worked so hard at building."

"I'm not dismissing it. I'm perfectly willing to pay for a ticket, which is the purpose behind this. They'll get the money and won't have to give me a dinner, so they'll actually come out ahead if I'm not there."

"I'd say staying away when your husband is on the planning committee doesn't show much support for him. And it's not just the money, a big turnout is important in itself. If everybody sends a check and doesn't go, they'll eventually stop holding the dinner and when they do that, most people will stop sending checks."

"You're not in my position so it's easy to say that. If you were under the same pressure I'm experiencing you wouldn't be so quick to criticize me."

"I don't buy that. If something is right, it's right and I'd try to do it regardless of any pressure and you know me well enough to know it."

"Did it ever occur to you that I might think that what I'm doing is right? My firm is paying me a good salary and they've given me tremendous responsibility. I owe them something in return and I'm not going to drop my responsibility to them to spend an evening eating and dancing. If your planning committee had thought ahead, they'd have scheduled this on the week-end when it wouldn't be as likely to conflict with work schedules."

Both partners are firmly convinced that right is on their side and as the date of the event nears, the conflict intensifies. There are nightly arguments and both Jim and Edith tend to exude an air of self-righteousness in the presence of the other. This state of mutual recrimination continues until the event takes place, without Edith's presence.

Eventually, the conflict subsides and the couple's relationship returns to its normal state. Normal relations are not exactly smooth though, since they also entail a good deal of anger and criticism. Some of the minor issues that provide continued sources of irritation are Edith's habit of straightening the house on a daily basis, causing Jim to have to look for things he left lying around, and Jim's compulsive behavior in regard to checking that doors are locked and stoves are turned off each time they leave the house. Which of them has the responsibility for walking the dog provides them with endless explorations of the concept of fairness in all its ramifications.

This marriage is often based on shared goals and ideals. They may even have met each other through a joint commitment to some political or charitable cause. Both have a strong sense of right and wrong, and are motivated to act fairly and deal with each other and the world honestly. This would seem the basis for an excellent relationship, however, the grittier details of daily life inevitably intrude, and they can rarely be resolved by reference to high ideals.

Problems in this relationship will center on conflicting definitions of what is "the right thing to do" in various situations and the propensity of both partners to be angry, critical, and demanding.

Jim and Edith will be able to minimize or avoid many of their conflicts if they acknowledge that it is their respective super-egos that are responsible for creating such intensity in their interactions.

The super-ego is formed during childhood. It is created as we absorb parental admonitions and messages and they become deeply lodged in our own consciousness. Some of these messages are quite rational and are part of the general social contract, but many of them are quite idiosyncratic, the result of the foibles and beliefs of our specific parents and other influences. Sometimes, people even have firm beliefs that have come just from misunderstanding something that they were told as children.

These beliefs, both reasonable concepts and wild cards, exist in everyone's head, but because doing the right thing is of such overriding importance to the Emerson, they cause much more trouble for this personality than they do for most others.

In this case, Jim may have had parents who put a strong emphasis on civic responsibility, while Edith's family impressed on her the importance of acting responsibly in whatever work she did.

Jim and Edith need to understand that many of the things that they see as absolutes are in actuality part of their personal belief systems, but not part of a universal standard of right conduct. This is the first step toward a happier marriage. Then, they can incorporate into their other strongly-held tenets the fact that we are all entitled to our own values and moral judgments, that no one should try to impose a moral system on another adult as long as the other person remains within the bounds of the general social contract that is the law.

The general rule of thumb for this couple could then be that it is fair to try to convince someone of your point of view, but it is not fair to denounce them if you can't convince them. If both partners understand and accept this premise, they *will* begin to put it into practice. This can be stated with reasonable assurance because one of the many good traits of Emerson personalities is that they work hard to live up to their belief systems.

If this understanding had been in place between Jim and Edith, Jim would have acknowledged Edith's feeling that her primary duty at this point was to her new career responsibilities and gone about his work for the dinner dance without rancor. Edith would have gladly paid for her ticket, as she did, but she would have also realized how important the affair was to Jim and tried to clear her schedule adequately to allow her to attend with a clear conscience.

This is a relationship in which many of the conflicts are in the areas of anger and control, especially making and meeting each other's demands. Both partners are on the same wavelength in many of the other respects that can cause acrimony in a marriage.

The other major problem is that their personalities are so very similar. The lack of stimulation that occurs from interacting with a person with different needs and motivations from the Emerson's will be missing for this couple. They tend to be earnest, serious people. They want to be good citizens and to do the right thing. This emphasis is commendable, but it can become somewhat overwhelming. They need to learn to make more room for fun in their lives and to approach the other's foibles and beliefs with tolerance and humor. Since there is no one to question the wisdom of such a righteous stance, this is less likely to happen when Emersons marry other Emersons.

GREATEST DANGER SIGNAL: Escalating anger and criticism between the partners, if uncontrolled, can create enough hostility to jeopardize the marriage.

PRIMARY FOCUS: Having fun together. Both partners tend to be serious and they can pull each other further and further in this direction until there is very little time for fun and play in the relationship. They must plan for adequate recreational time and also be aware that their daily interactions need to include lighter intervals.

EMERSON-NIGHTINGALE RELATIONSHIPS

Gloria has committed herself to helping with a plant sale for a community group from ten to one on Saturday. She announces her plans at the breakfast table Saturday morning.

"What about the kids?" Jim asks.

"What about them? You're going to be here and they pretty much take care of themselves anyway."

"How do you know I'm going to be here? Did you do me the courtesy of asking my plans?"

Gloria responds with real exasperation: "I don't have to ask your plans, you're always home on Saturday morning. I'm not asking you to do anything. They have enough to do, you won't even know they're here. Kevin has invited a couple of friends over…"

She gets no further before Jim explodes: "Oh I see, it's not enough that you've stuck me with the kids, you've invited the rest of the neighborhood in for me to watch too. Well, you can forget it; I have no intention of doing it. You're going to have to learn to consult with me before offering my services wholesale."

Gloria is outraged. "They're your children too. I watch them all week and I ask for a few hours Saturday morning and you go into a rage. I sometimes think you really hate your children."

"This has nothing to do with my children, leave the kids out of this."

"Marvelous, you refuse just to be in the house with them and it has nothing to do with them. Who do you think it has to do with."

"You, you're the one that thinks she doesn't have to ask me about my plans, that I should just fall in with whatever you've decided should be my role of the day. I have a boss five days a week, I have no intention of letting you fill in the other two days."

Gloria leaves the room in tears at this point and then goes off to the flower sale without speaking to Jim further. She knows that he won't go off and leave the children, so she assumes everything will blow over. She is infuriated when she returns home to find that Jim actually sent Kevin's friends home, and that Kevin is angry with her as well as with Jim. The remainder of their weekend is a shambles.

It is instructive to untangle the dynamics of this situation. It actually started when Gloria was asked to participate in the plant sale. This type of invitation is very difficult for the Nightingale personality to resist. They will be helping others and having fun at the same time. They genuinely enjoy the interaction with the other workers and the customers, as well as the sense of well being that comes from participating in this type of community activity. Certainly there is nothing wrong with that. All of their projects are quite commendable.

The problem is that Gloria impulsively agreed to volunteer without consulting Jim. However, this was less an impulse than a premonition that Jim might not agree if he were asked. She has been out helping others quite a bit recently, and if she were to be totally honest with herself, she would have to admit that her thoughts went along the lines: *"If I ask he might say no, but if I don't ask, he won't have any choice but to go along with my plans and with any luck, he won't be angry."* The hope of averting Jim's anger was pure wishful thinking, but this is something that

Gloria frequently does. Her timing, waiting until the last minute to announce her plans was part of her strategy, believing that since it would be too late to cancel, Jim would be forced to acquiesce.

Jim honestly had no objection to being home with the children on Saturday morning, but he consistently responds with rage to treatment he perceives as unfair. Such tactics are chalk on the blackboard to an Emerson personality. He felt furious at being manipulated, and had a righteous sense of upholding civilized conduct when he refused to agree to such a power play.

Gloria was bewildered by the strength of his anger, despite the frequency with which this interaction occurs in one form or another between them. Her explanation for Jim's response was that he is a cold aloof person who cares nothing about his children and who no longer loves her. Gloria often interprets a refusal to go along with her plans as a basic failure of love and reacts by feeling abandoned. Her reasoning, once Jim lost his temper, was that she had nothing further to lose in the relationship, so she might as well go ahead and do as she had planned. This response might be described as half anger and half misgiving over her ability to convince Jim to change his mind.

When Jim saw Gloria drive off, he felt outmaneuvered and furious. He wanted to just walk out and let her find that the kids had been left alone all morning, but his highly developed conscience and his genuine devotion to his children prevented him from taking this course. He did send Kevin's friend home with a feeling of considerable self-righteousness that left him totally unmoved by Kevin's embarrassment and misery. When Gloria returned and found what Jim had done, which he viewed as an attempt to keep some control of his life, she felt that he was truly a monster, that he had no parental feelings and that his spiteful behavior was an indication of major personality flaws.

The problems in the Emerson-Nightingale relationship revolve around the issues of love, anger and control. The Emerson is first attracted to the Nightingale because this is a warm, loving person. who possesses the caring qualities that an Emerson values highly. Because Nightingales choose with their hearts, not their heads, it is likely that they do not have complete access to the motives that create their attraction to an Emerson. In many of these relationships, the Emerson will be the initial wooer, and the experience of feeling loved and cared for in the initial courtship will be a strong component in the Nightingale's response.

Emerson personalities have a strong investment in being right, doing the right thing and seeing that the people around them conform to correct codes of conduct, codes which sometimes appear to be known only to them. When things don't "go right", the Emerson responds with criticism or anger. Emersons rarely ask for directions when traveling, because they *should* know how to get where they want to go. If they don't they are angry with themselves for this lapse from perfection, but also angry, inexplicably, with the people around them. Multiply this reaction over the many daily incidents in which things can go wrong and you realize that an average Emerson often reaches the dinner table in a state of fury.

Unfortunately, Nightingales genuinely need generous helpings of love and approval in order to function well. Whether they have a mate who is coldly critical or in a full-blown rage, they interpret the response as rejection and feel themselves unloved.

As this pattern is repeated over time, Nightingales tend to move from the posture of feeling unloved or misunderstood to demanding the reactions they would prefer. The usual request is that the partner cease to be angry and critical, a demand which is simply beyond the powers of the average Emerson. Thus, the battle is truly locked.

In defusing this situation, some of the major dynamics between the Emerson and Nightingale personalities are illustrated. Nightingales tend to see themselves in a positive light. They are often right since they are genuinely kind, helpful, caring people. But, at an average level of functioning, they have a tendency to dispense their kindness at the expense of those nearest to them. They don't take into account that the helpful gesture they wish to make includes not only some degree of self-sacrifice on their part, but also on the part of others who have not chosen to make such a commitment. In addition, Nightingales often tend to allow the end to justify the means, which causes them to behave in a manipulative manner to achieve their goals.

Emersons are deeply concerned with issues of fairness and justice. They want to be fair to others and want to be treated fairly in return. In the average Emerson, this concept may become rigid and doctrinaire, so that they are unable to coast over some of the petty injustices of daily life that other people may ignore or view as minor irritations. They often feel compelled to make a major issue of anything that smacks even slightly of unfair treatment. It is usually the Emerson who, if normal assertion of rights does not suffice, makes a major scene over someone cutting into a line or failing to wait their turn.

Control is also an important issue for the Emerson personality. They feel extremely anxious if they find themselves in a situation where they can not take charge. It is but a matter of moments for them to convert that anxiety into anger, which is a more comfortable emotion for them.

Control is an issue for Nightingales as well. With the Nightingale, the desire for control centers less on overt conduct and more on an intangible desire for the people in their lives to *be* the way they would like them to be. Thus, in this instance, Jim would like Gloria to act more fairly, and to consult him before making plans. Gloria doesn't have any such specific requirements in mind. What she wants from Jim is a basic personality change, to stop being angry, to be more demonstrative toward her and the children, and to be less critical. Jim says, "act differently", Gloria's response is, "be different".

One aspect of the Nightingale personality, in which control is often a strong component, is the couple's choice of friends. Nightingales often worry about how much they are loved by their partners, and have a strong fear of being insufficiently loved. For this reason, unhealthy

Nightingales can become very jealous of friendships their partners make outside the relationship. Old acquaintances are often puzzled, when a friend marries a Nightingale, to find their good will toward the new person in their circle met with veiled hostility or even outright enmity. In the case of the Emerson-Nightingale relationship, the Emerson will probably insist upon keeping old friends and the Nightingale will eventually either become reconciled to the fact that these people are not a threat or else continue undercutting the relationship whenever a social occasions including them occurs. In either case, the strong Emerson sense of knowing what is right and doing it, will prevent the Emerson from losing friendships to the marriage, although the issue may continue to create tension between the partners.

Obviously understanding the other person's motivation is the first step in creating change. The Nightingale personality needs to really grasp the fact that being right and doing right in even the smallest things are more important to his/her partner than they are to most other people. This is a deeply felt gut-level need. Emersons are genuinely upset and deeply troubled when they do anything they perceive as wrong or when anyone around them does. They find it difficult to grasp the concept that many of the things they consider wrong are merely options or choices and not life and death issues. Thus, on an emotional response level, an Emerson often seems to view a failure to clean the table after lunch as equivalent to larceny and a minor irresponsible impulse purchase on the part of a partner as equivalent to murder. Is their anger out of proportion? Yes, it certainly is. Is it genuine? Yes.

That's the hard part for the Nightingale to keep in mind. The immediate response to experiencing disproportionate Emerson anger is to feel unloved, a very heart-felt, gut-level response. It meets with incomprehension on the part of the Emerson: *"Of course I love you, but I'm mad at the moment"* would be the answer, if the anger could be turned off for ten seconds to let an explanation slip out. This seldom happens.

The battle rages over whatever the issue of the moment may be, but under the surface, the hidden, but very real message from the Emerson is: " *Stop trying to manipulate me. Ask for what you want and accept the fact that you won't always get it.*" And from the Nightingale, *"Can't you see I'm really hurting? It scares me when you get so angry because I think you don't love me."*

If the relationship is to improve, the Emerson must grasp that this is not a staged response, but a real need and try to meet it. This does not mean never being angry. Everyone is entitled to their feelings and trying to ignore feelings can have much worse consequences for both partners, since they will inevitably leak out in even less acceptable ways if ignored. It is possible to be truly angry, however, and to express the anger at the action rather than at the person. A statement to the effect that the behavior is enraging is very different from a statement that the person is unacceptable. In this relationship, however, that is insufficient. There needs to be some additional input, if the partner is to hear accurately what is said. They have to be reassured that they are loved even though the Emerson is truly angry at the moment. If they do not get this reassurance, the rest of the message will not be heard.

In the interaction between Jim and Gloria, Jim might have said: *"I love you Gloria, and I think you are a good person, so I want you to hang on to that, but I want you to really listen to how I'm feeling right now. I am very angry. If anyone makes plans for me without consulting me, I feel very frustrated and that my life has been taken out of my control. I'm also angry because I feel that you tend to put acquaintances and even strangers ahead of the needs of the family. I know you do it out of the best intentions, but I experience it as unfair and it really bothers me."*

This will not be easy for Gloria to hear. It would be good if Jim took her hand and held it while he spoke, to help to reassure her. It may not be as satisfying as giving way to rage, but a little pragmatism is called for here. The bottom line for the Emerson must be: *"What do I want to accomplish? Do I want to change my partner's behavior or do I merely want to ventilate anger?"* The chance to actually create change is certainly more important than the momentary gratification felt while expressing rage.

The objection that many Emerson will raise to this suggestion is that the rage is so immediate and overpowering that it cannot be controlled. This is not actually the case, if they examine their lives honestly. Do your boss and co-workers make you angrier on occasion than it is politic to express? Do you sometimes modify your response when you feel angry with friends in social situations? If you allow yourself total freedom to ventilate anger on all occasions, you are truly out of control, and need to seek professional help. Most of us know when it is "safe" to ventilate and when we have to control ourselves, and we are able to do so. We choose to ventilate anger at home because we feel that it is acceptable to do this in an intimate relationship. To a limited extent this is true, but if the anger is uncontrolled then it is damaging the relationship and failing to achieve its supposed objective of creating change in the partner.

The Nightingale personality must also work to create change. One question the Nightingale must ask before going into action is "Is what I am planning going to step on someone else's toes?" Then, "Am I being straightforward in what I want to do or am I trying to get around any obstacles through manipulative tactics?" It will be very difficult for Nightingales to forgo manipulation because they want what they want very strongly and perceive it as a real need. However, if they compare the strength of their current desire to the long-term objective of an better relationship with their partner, it is obvious that the respect and affection of a loving partner is the more important goal and is worth working toward.

Nightingales have an even more difficult realization to face. Their partners are going to be Emersons for a lifetime. Due to a combination of innate traits and environmental influences going back to childhood, their partners will continue to be both more critical and more often angry than most other people are. This is the trade-off for the many good traits Emersons possess.

In this marriage, the Nightingale must work to understand and accept the fact that this is not going to change. They long for an uncritical, easy-going partner, but that's not who they chose. Of course, no one likes people to be angry with them, but that will not lessen the reality. Emersons do become angry and critical easily. Nightingales can't change this; they can help their partners to remember to express it more acceptably. To respond with anger to an Emerson, for being angry, will merely escalate the conflict.

The wisest response to an Emerson's anger is to acknowledge it when it is appropriate, to try to respond calmly with appeals to reason when it is inappropriate, and to get away from it when it is out of control.

If Gloria had said, *"I see what you mean, Jim. It was wrong of me to neglect to consult you. I'll try not to do that after this."* Jim would still have been angry, but the acknowledgment would have kept the conflict on a more reasonable level. The appeal to reason might have come at the point of his refusal to have Kevin's friends over. *"You're right, it was a mistake to do that without checking, but Kevin will really be embarrassed and upset if he has to rescind the invitation. In effect you'll be punishing Kevin because you're mad at me."* This might or might not work on all occasions, but it is an accurate insight, and if it doesn't solve the problem immediately it is still likely to have an effect when Jim thinks it over. One of the many good traits of the Emerson is that an appeal that is not immediately effective may still influence future behavior.

Finally, if the rage is totally out of control, it is generally best to get out of the other person's way until they can get themselves together. This is the time to leave the room for both your sakes until the partner can regain self-control. No one should be placed in the position of being a verbal punching bag for a partner's rage. Leave, but remember to come back to the issue later. *"You were so furious with me, that I felt there was nothing I could say this morning, but I do want to talk about what made you angry if we can both do it calmly now.*" The Nightingale is sometimes intimidated by Emerson anger and feels reluctant to reopen the subject that aroused it. This is a mistake. Anger and love are separate issues to the Emerson. They can still love someone when they are angry and they will be ultimately much less angry if the issue can be resolved rather than left to erupt again later.

Both partners will be surprised to find that by working to create change in themselves and improve the quality of the interaction between them, that the amount of friction in the relationship can be substantially decreased with a corresponding increase in positive feelings on the part of both partners.

GREATEST DANGER SIGNAL: The greatest danger to this marriage is the intensification of anger, as each partner reacts to the other, the Nightingale interpreting Emerson anger and criticism as lack of love and responding with deep hurt and rage to the perceived coldness and cruelty of the partner.

PRIMARY FOCUS: The focus in this marriage should be on keeping open lines of communication. The Emersons wants their partners to assimilate their moral standards and behavioral codes completely, while Nightingales sustain the fantasy that their partners can become exactly the people they would like them to be. These are unrealistic and arbitrary goals, but only as they focus on discussing them and sharing their disparate viewpoints can they learn to modify their demands and have more realistic expectations of each other.

THE EMERSON-BEAU RELATIONSHIP

George is running for a city council seat in the next local election and has put out a position paper that includes several political proposals with which Edith is quite uncomfortable.

When she finally confronts him, over his stand on two issues about which she feels strongly, George is amazed at her naiveté. "You're absolutely right, my love, but in this case, the facts have nothing to do with it. These are hot political issues locally and if I were to take the stand you're suggesting I wouldn't have a hope in hell of winning."

Edith is genuinely shocked. "But that's unethical. The voters are choosing you on the basis of your beliefs and you are lying to them about what those beliefs are."

"Think of it in another way. I'm genuinely going to do more good than my opponent does, if I'm elected. I'm the better person, but being better isn't going to cut it, if I don't get the job."

Edith is decisive. "You're saying the end justifies the means and that simply is not true. You're lying to the voters."

"All right, if you say so, but it's part of the game, Edith. Don't take it so to heart. Look, you know that I'm a good person, trust me."

"But when you plan to do this, I wonder if you are a good person, George. Good people don't let the end justify the means."

Edith remains outraged, confused and angry. As the campaign progresses, her anger becomes apparent. She criticizes George's campaign at every turn, takes a marked dislike to two of his most prominent supporters and refuses to attend those affairs where a candidate's wife is usually prominent.

George is hurt and angry in turn. He makes pointed references to Miss Goody Two Shoes and spends more and more time away from home. He feels genuinely misunderstood, and when he loses the election, overtly attributes his loss to lack of support at home.

Edith, in the meantime, has generalized what she considers his duplicity in the election to their personal interactions and has started to question what he tells her about their finances, his business and even his feelings toward her.

When she says, "I wonder if you still love me, or if you're planning to leave me?" George is astonished and feels that she is undercutting the relationship in yet another way.

People with Beau personalities are physically attractive. They have an open, cheerful, wholesome look and they are exceptionally focused, goal-oriented and hard working. All of these traits make them attractive to the Emerson personality. The Emerson attracted to an average Beau probably finds that they are in substantial agreement on most issues during the early stages of the relationship. This is not surprising, as the Beau tends to be extremely congenial and willing to go along with the opinions and concepts of those around them. The Beau will appreciate the critical and analytical abilities of the partner and will find the Emerson personality interesting precisely because of the very strong views that Emersons hold. Despite these similarities, this couple exemplifies an attraction of opposites. Beaus approach life pragmatically, interested in doing what will work and in being congenial to those around them, and Emersons hold strong dogmatic positions, based on their own ethical systems. This differing approach to values will create conflict over time.

The conflict between the pragmatist and the idealist is of such a basic nature that it is generally difficult to resolve to the satisfaction of either party. These positions are deeply embedded character traits; neither George nor Edith is likely to be able to win the other to a total understanding of the partner's viewpoint.

To deal more rationally with this basic difference in outlook requires on-going discussion. In the case of George's candidacy, the couple needed to start a dialogue well before George became a candidate and to arrive at some agreement that would allow them to disagree without undue rancor on the acceptable ways to run a political campaign. This could well entail Edith's admission that this was not her field, and that she did not understand or endorse the rules of this game. Such a bargain struck ahead of time might have allowed her to look on, and perhaps disapprove, but without feeling her own sense of integrity compromised by her relationship with George.

As both George and Edith become healthier, there will be less friction between them since the more extreme aspects of their respective positions will become modified, not only in politics, but in all aspects of their lives. George will cease to place winning above personal integrity and Edith will come to recognize that moral behavior contains more complex and shaded overtones than the simple good versus bad ethic of the dogmatist.

A broader area of disagreement, which is mirrored in their differing approaches to ethical questions, is the more rigid do-it-by-the-book stance of the average Emerson in contrast to the Beau's ultra-flexible style. This can cover a range of areas in which they are likely to irritate each other.

An example would be their agreement to install a relatively moderate additional bathroom in the house: *Edith goes off to work, leaving George to deal with the contractor. She comes home to find that he has signed a contract that includes the installation of a state-of-the-art Jacuzzi. George sees no problem, they have the money to pay for it on the generous installment plan offered by the contractor, and it will enhance the value of their property if they should decide to sell.*

"But we had an agreement, you can't just make major decisions like this unilaterally," Edith says with icy fury.

George, who honestly feels that he has improved on their original plans, and that all agreements should be subject to modification if a better idea comes along, is puzzled and annoyed by her reaction. Neither has a clear understanding of the other's position.

In Emerson-Beau relationships, it is crucial for the Beau to stem a natural tendency toward making an immediate flexible response and learn to consult before implementing changes, whether in home remodeling or in less long-term decisions such as week-end plans. It is equally essential for the Emerson to work on becoming less rigid and to concede that everything is not written in granite and that modifications are sometimes rational and appropriate.

George, the Beau, needs the approval of those whom he respects in a way that Edith does not. Emersons are willing to stand against the world if their consciences tell them they are right. This may cause acute conflict in the relationship, if the Emerson partner takes on a crusade on some issue, a proclivity of many Emersons. It can be acutely embarrassing to the spouse if the cause is not one approved of by those whose opinions matter to the Beau. Even a worthy cause can create discomfort if it is pushed too stridently in social situations.

Should this issue arise and create conflict in the relationship, it is critical that the partners discuss their feelings, understand each other's point of view, and try to reach accommodation in terms of when it is and is not appropriate to discuss such matters. For example, Edith might agree not to mention her environmental concerns (on which she tends to become strident) at dinner parties for people from George's office. In return, George might agree that it is not really inappropriate for her to talk about this issue when their old friends come to dinner. She might also concede that while such a discussion is not inappropriate, refusing to eventually move on to other topics could ruin the evening.

Both personalities are very willing to confront others when angry. This is basically a good trait, since it keeps the lines of communication open. However, when both of them are very angry and are confronting each other vigorously, the results can be a free-for-all rather than a method of problem solving. They may need to designate a cooling off period prior to discussing heated issues. Both parties need to agree that raising their voices unduly or making personal attacks instead of staying with the issue are counterproductive and are to be considered out-of-bounds behavior.

Sometimes couples need to choose a method of quickly indicating to each other that the discussion in no longer proceeding productively and that they need to stop and cool off. One method of doing this is to choose a nonsense word or one that is meaningful to them that either can say to indicate that they are no longer talking productively. They then agree that when either of them says this word, they will stop and go into separate rooms for ten minutes and then try again.

This is a relationship in which both parties want to be in charge. Emersons feel upset and anxious when situations are not in their control. The Beau seeks control instinctively out of a strong competitive drive. Cooperative planning with equal participation is the only rational approach. Both partners have to be extraordinarily careful not to follow their natural inclinations to take over when an opening presents itself. The positive side of this situation is that learning to relinquish control for cooperation will enhance their interpersonal relationships at work and in social situations in addition to improving the marriage.

Emersons can be strict and sometimes quirky parents. They expect their rules to be obeyed and may sometimes have a hard time respecting a child's demand for autonomy if they conflict with Emersons needs for perfection or their sense of what is right. For example, a child who wants to turn in sloppy homework and is willing to accept a slightly lower grade as a trade off for some free time is likely to meet with very little understanding from an Emerson parent. Beaus want to be perfect parents and also expect their children to be relatively perfect. The difference in approach is that while the Beau demand could be in terms of excellence in school work, it could just as easily be that the children dress a certain way, appear poised in social situations, or acquire specific skills that might be socially useful. Obviously, both parents are in for some major disillusionment and their children may experience their home life as unusually quirky and difficult.

When both parents begin to tune in to their own and their partner's unrealistic desires, they can work together to be more down-to-earth in their demands. The major question that they will need to ask themselves is *Will what I'm saying or doing protect or help my child or is it being done to meet my own needs?* Specifically, children don't have to clean their rooms every Saturday morning, it is possible to just close the door and not see the mess, occasionally. Cookies before meals are not great, but if it happens once a month, it's not a disaster. And there are strong indications that a failed spelling test will not prevent a fourth grader from going to college.

Average Beaus can be so flexible and pragmatic at times that they appear superficial. Emersons, with their tendency to be judgmental, are particularly likely to condemn this trait. If this is a problem for the couple, it is an important area for dialogue. Beaus can use the help of the partner to make a decision about where they stand on an issue and then to stick with it. Emersons must work on understanding the difference between spineless vacillation and willingness to see the other side of an issue and be flexible in one's approach.

Money can be a major issue in this relationship. Average Beaus feel a real need for status symbols and it is important to them in terms of basic self-esteem to appear and feel successful. To the Emerson partner this is often viewed as superficial showiness and even as somewhat contemptible. If there is enough money to go around, the two can go their separate ways without too much conflict, but if money is tight, both will need to compromise. The Beau will need to decide what purchases are genuinely important and save up for them. The Emerson will have to try to understand the partner's point of view in a cooperative spirit and demonstrate some willingness to compromise, rather than merely issuing unilateral condemnations.

GREATEST DANGER SIGNAL: Sometimes one or both partners become stuck in their own value systems to such an extent that they begin to lose respect for each other. If intensive dialogue, accompanied by sincere attempts to grasp the partner's viewpoint, does not correct the situation, this is an occasion when it is important to seek professional help.

PRIMARY FOCUS: Remembering to listen to each other and work out compromises will be an ongoing task in this marriage. It is particularly difficult for this couple to really view the other's point of view with sympathy and understanding. Both partners in this marriage have strong needs to control. If the relationship is to succeed, both of them must learn to make concessions.

THE EMERSON-SHELLEY RELATIONSHIP

When Jim comes in from work and finds Jean in the living room reading, his first question is "Where are the kids?"

"Out and about, they'll be back in time for dinner."

"Isn't this a school night? Don't tell me the schools have stopped giving homework this year?"

"No, I imagine they'll get to it after dinner. It's certainly too nice out to waste the daylight hours in the house."

"But you don't know how many assignments they have or how long it's going to take them to finish. I simply cannot believe your lack of interest in our children's future. Not only are you totally irresponsible, you're actually teaching them irresponsible behavior."

"You know I really doubt that not getting a hundred in spelling will prove a major handicap in their adult life. Most of their homework seems to be dumb busy work anyway."

"Now that is truly a wonderful attitude for a mother to display to her children."

"I'm not saying it to them, I'm saying it to you and it's true. They're smart kids. If it's important, they'll learn it eventually, and if it's not, what difference does it make?"

"There is such a thing as learning good work habits and responsible behavior. Homework is about that too you know. I want those kids home and I want them home now."

"Well, you can't have them home now because I haven't any idea where they are."

If Jim was upset before, he is now enraged, "I can't believe this. If they don't come home, you don't even know where to start looking for them?"

"I'd be able to find them eventually, but they go in and out of each other's houses on the block pretty randomly most of the time. Are you aware that you're yelling at me?"

"Of course I'm yelling at you. I won't have my children raised in this way."

"Then I guess you'll have to take over raising them, won't you?"

"What does that mean?"

"It means I am not your employee. You are not my supervisor, and it means that I don't have to account to you for my actions. I'm a pretty good mother, and our kids are doing just fine at school and everywhere else, which is more than would have been the case if you had your way." Jean walks out of the room at this point, slamming the door behind her.

When the kids come home, Jim starts to yell at them, much to their bewilderment. They had their mother's permission to postpone the home-work and they often wait until after dinner to do it. Jean comes out of the bedroom yelling at Jim to leave them alone and the family settles down to yet another tension-laden dinner.

This confrontation typifies many of the differences between the Emerson and the Shelley.

A different outcome would require both Jim and Jean to acknowl-edge some ground rules. While Jim has a legitimate interest in the chil-dren's schooling, Jean is clearly right that he can not unilaterally make the rules, particularly at a moment's notice. Jim's reactions were pro-pelled far more by anger and an underlying desire to have his children follow the rules of his own childhood than by any serious anxiety over their school performance.

If he had waited until he calmed down and simply questioned Jean on how the children were doing in school, he would have learned that both of them have been doing their homework regularly and that their teachers have no complaints about them. He could then, if he felt it necessary, suggest making a few house rules regarding after school time and homework. The next step would be an attempt to reach consensus through compromise, preferably getting input from the children as well.

Jean enraged Jim by calling the homework dumb. This is the kind of situation that regularly recurs with this couple. It is important for Shelleys to elaborate on their thought processes when they make statements that their partner will misunderstand, or read further implications into. Often such comments are less controversial than they appear. Jim heard, *"I will therefore not require the children to do their homework."* This was not what Jean said, but she *did* know he would hear it that way, based on prior experience. Emersons tend to be linear and logical. Jim's thought process was: *"If the work is really dumb, then, such assignments are wrong and should be replaced by meaningful work. If this is not the case, then Jean is being flippant and irresponsible to call it dumb."*

Shelleys are more intuitive in their approach to such matters. Jean's thinking was: *"A lot of it is busy work, but it won't kill them to do it, I'm just not going to get too wrapped up in it."* This is just as valid a perception as Jim's is. Both points of view are rooted far too deeply within their personalities to be easily subject to change.

When Emersons and Shelleys are emotionally healthy, they want to see themselves honestly and to view their environment squarely, without self-deception. This basic willingness to call things as they see them, not pulling punches in order to be thought nice creates an initial bond between this couple. They admire each other for being self-disciplined. Both personalities tend to have strong sexual drives and this mutual need and its satisfaction are another point of confluence in cementing the relationship.

The freedom of the Shelley personality to go beyond the limits of the mundane and to challenge or deny conventional perceptions and beliefs will often seem liberating to the healthy Emerson, up to the point where the Shelley's lack of conventionality conflicts with personal or ethical standards. Then the Emerson will become judgmental and disapproving.

Initially, Shelleys may find the new partner's willingness to confront others and make unilateral demands exhilarating, as years of accepting bad tables at restaurants are swept away in a flash of Emersonian imperiousness. It is only fair to add that the initial fascination with this trait may pall in time due to overuse.

Control will soon become a major issue in this relationship. The Emerson has a strong need to be in control and to supervise the performance of others. Shelleys, while they have no interest in controlling anyone else, are strongly adverse to any attempt by a partner to oversee and critique their lives.

Emersons are angry people. They automatically find fault with anything that is not done the way they would do it. *"Why did you put that jacket in the hall closet? You know jackets go in the bedroom closet." "Did you actually check with the repair man that he was coming or did you just assume he would be here?"* Shelleys will not always confront their partners on such issues, because they don't care where they hang their jackets, and don't think it worth arguing about, and they assume that if the repair man doesn't show today they can always call him tomorrow. It is a mistake to believe that such conformity spells agreement. Shelleys can harbor a slow-burning irritation as these petty criticisms and demands proliferate.

Jim has a rather lengthy list of Jean's faults, which periodically send him into rages. One of them is her driving. He doesn't like it and when he is in the car with her, he can never resist making a few comments. He might on different occasions criticize which block she turns on, the route she takes or her speed, her competitive passing of another car or her failure to pass another car. From long years of conditioning, Jean is immediately anxious when she gets into the driver's seat with Jim in the car. She knows that this anxiety affects her driving performance, and she is indignant at Jim, for the criticism itself, but also because she is aware of its effect on her.

Other faults include her failure to keep the checkbook balanced, sometimes neglecting to enter checks at all, her failure to join him in his degree of indignation at the annoying habits of various neighbors, or the preparation of a particular food he doesn't like, an event occurring about once every six months, which he seems to believe must stem from personal animosity.

Jean is a lenient mother. Her children are not undisciplined, but she places great value on freedom of action and expression and sets only those limits she thinks really crucial. They are certainly allowed to do things that Jim never did as a child. It is inevitable that he considers such freedom to be license and alleges that the children are totally out of control when he is not around.

In these areas and many others, Jim does not want to take over the task, but he does want Jean to accept his supervision in doing it. Many of their confrontations center on these issues.

As Jim gets healthier, he will lose some of his rigidity, and gain more control of his temper. He will be aware of his tendency to be over critical and try to curb much of the nit-picking criticism. He will admit that many of his concerns are a desire to control rather than genuine outrage over a moral issue and understand that his need to judge is not rooted in his higher moral awareness, but in his desire to have things done his way.

As Jean becomes healthier, she may agree that on occasion she can be too laissez-faire and that Jim might be correct in suggesting that the children have slightly more supervision. She will also try to elaborate on her thought processes when she says things that upset Jim. If she takes the time to explain her underlying thinking more fully, she may find that he responds to her remarks with less alarm.

While Shelleys generally have a high level of self-control, they save it for what they consider the important stuff. They can be impulsive in other situations. Most Shelleys would not worry about having company over on the spur of the moment because the house was a mess. If Shelleys decide to go somewhere, they have no problem leaving tasks behind half-done. They postpone the trivia of daily life without guilt if they have better things to do.

These behaviors can seem alarming and undisciplined to the Emerson personality. As Jim gets healthier, he will be able to recognize these Shelley traits as liberating and positive. In the meantime, it is important that Jean curb enough of this behavior to keep him from feeling threatened or alienated.

The other side of this issue is that Shelleys can be seriously irritated by Emerson rigidity. The Emerson who can't shift plans to weed the garden when friends suggest a picnic, or who always wants to go to the same restaurant will drive the Shelley wild. Shelleys tend to bottle up and underplay the extent of their displeasure a great deal of the time, so that Emersons are sometimes unaware of just how irritating their behavior can be. When the tenth rigid response in one month occurs, and the Shelley overcomes the desire to avoid confrontation, the intensity of the rage expressed may then appear thoroughly out of proportion to the provocation. It is a good idea for the Emerson to watch for unnecessary rigidities and for both partners to be clear that this is a natural component of the Emerson personality so that they can talk about their feelings and deal with them more reasonably.

Emersons get a sense of security from being in control. It is profoundly important to their sense of well being. Shelleys don't want to control others, but harbor an intense need for freedom of both thought and action. This sets up an inevitable conflict in the relationship. When Shelleys feel that someone is trying to control them, they become deeply angry and defiant, often reacting disproportionately. Both partners should be clear about these conflicting needs and dialogue about them on an ongoing basis to avoid serious rifts in the relationship.

Both Emersons and Shelleys have a potential for anger. Emersons carry their angry feelings near the surface and are quite willing to ventilate them whenever an opportunity presents itself. Shelleys tend to hold their anger in and steam quietly. They often become depressed as a result.

Emersons, whose friends take the opposite side on an emotional local political issue, will very likely explode when they run into them, denouncing their wrong-headed views, and then forget about them. The Shelley, in the same circumstances, would be more likely to be cool to the people when they met, say nothing in reference to their politics, but drop them from the guest list permanently.

To improve the marriage, the Emerson must begin to control excessive anger and criticism while encouraging and helping the Shelley to express irritation more readily. The Shelley must remember that Emerson rage has its roots in intra-psychic functioning and is less personally directed than it appears. It is often primarily an expression of frustration with the way things are going and will blow over rather quickly if ignored. Naturally, all Emerson anger does not come under this heading, and substantive issues must be dealt with. The Shelley must consciously decide to stop avoiding confrontation. It is appropriate and necessary to speak up when angry. Assertive behavior is a tool for creating constructive solutions to disagreements.

GREATEST DANGER SIGNAL: When the Emerson is exploding more and more frequently, and/or the Shelley is withdrawn and appears depressed, it is an indication that the relationship is in trouble. Generally, this situation occurs when the Emerson's demanding behavior or anger has reached a point where the Shelley feels overwhelmed. The Shelley reacts by withdrawing, which creates frustration in the Emerson, resulting in further explosions and precipitating an emotional downward spiral between the partners. It is important to put real effort into serious discussion of what is happening and for both partners to work to correct the situation.

PRIMARY FOCUS: Inadequate communication on both sides is the biggest problem. Emersons must beware of giving free rein to their judgmental tendencies, and the automatic assumption that they are right. It is essential for them to learn to avoid denouncing their partner when they disagree. It may even help to count to ten before speaking when they know they are angry. If this does not achieve the desired level of self-control, it would be wise to go out for a walk around the block before speaking.

Shelleys must force themselves to say what is on their minds even if it seems trivial or petty. Small irritations can add up. They must learn to take the risk of talking to their partner even if they think it makes them seem petty.

THE EMERSON-EINSTEIN RELATIONSHIP

Arthur realizes that he feels disappointed with Edith. This is rooted in her inability to understand and accept the people in their lives without feeling the need to judge them: children, relatives, and even friends.

When she declares that his sister should never have had children as she has no idea of how to raise them or starts to criticize their friends taste or judgment, Arthur feels uncomfortable and angry. Usually, he says nothing, but simply leaves the room. Her moralistic stance and failure to view others charitably, along with her frequent criticisms of things that he has done, said or thought, have caused Arthur to withdraw into his work more and more. Having withdrawn, over a number of years now, Arthur goes his own way, aware of the inadequacy of their relationship and finding solace in his work, his chess club, and his computer. Edith is quite aware that their relationship is cool and has become unsatisfactory, and she has withdrawn in turn. She belongs to a woman's group and a local political club and these activities in conjunction with some good relationships with colleagues at work go a long way toward filling the void created by Arthur's coolness. Their sexual interaction has become minimal and perfunctory.

This couple's unhappiness is rooted in Arthur's unwillingness to confront and discuss what is bothering him. If he challenged Edith's criticisms, they would bite into him less deeply and might modify some of her behavior. He might have said something on the order of: *"I don't think you're at all fair to my sister. She is certainly less strict than you, but there's more than one way to raise kids, and her children seem healthy and reasonably well behaved. I think you're expecting her to follow your methods to the letter, and frankly, I often feel that you're too strict with our kids."* This would have certainly earned him an argument, but it would also have cleared the air. The problem with failure to be open about feelings and, if necessary, to confront the people around us, is that issues are never discussed, and the more opinionated critic is sometimes not even aware that he or she is being perceived as unfair and biased.

If Arthur, the Einstein, needs to learn to assert himself more, Edith, the Emerson needs to learn to exercise a degree of restraint. She is certainly entitled to voice her opinions, but she needs to work on modifying the manner in which she voices them. As she becomes healthier, she will become more aware of her penchant for believing that she always knows what is right in all situations. She will learn to appreciate that most issues are matters of style and personal choice rather than absolute right and wrong.

Emersons and Einsteins both tend to think logically, and to use linear reasoning. This similarity attracts them to each other. They believe themselves to be sensible people, responding rationally in most of their dealings. Emersons, aware that they can allow anger to overcome their better judgment on occasion, may admire the greater self-control of the Einstein personality. Many of these partners will be drawn together by common hobbies or intellectual interests.

Einsteins sometimes appear to respond to relationships totally in cognitive terms, and to lack a strong visceral component to their thinking or interactions. This is not true; they simply keep their feelings more tightly under wraps than most people do. However, the protective facade provided by this appearance of total rationality may trouble the Emerson and raise doubts about the Einstein's degree of emotional connection as the relationship develops. Einsteins will find Emerson anger irrational and upsetting to deal with. The judgmental facet of the Emerson's personality can be both irritating and upsetting to Einsteins.

Because these differences can create a slow erosion of the relationship, the importance of ongoing, honest, open dialogue between them cannot be stressed too strongly.

When Arthur is upset with Edith, he must learn to suppress all of those normal Einstein instincts, which counsel withdrawing from the situation and hiding one's feelings. Instead he needs to express the surprise, disappointment or anger that her behavior elicits. Edith in turn must go against the normal Emerson instinct, which is to maintain, " *I am right and I know what is right.*" She needs to steel herself to listen to Arthur's feelings and perceptions even if she disagrees. While listening doesn't mean agreeing, neither does it mean counter-attacking. If she views his comments as adversarial and proceeds with a vigorous counter-attack, Arthur will probably back off and the relationship will be the loser. If, on the other hand, when she disagrees, she can bring herself to say something to the effect that he has presented an interesting viewpoint and that while she disagrees, she can understand where he is coming from and respect his point of view, he will be encouraged to speak up more often.

As Arthur becomes healthier, it will be easier to express an alternate point of view on emotional or interpersonal issues without feeling threatened. The healthy Einstein knows that confrontation is never easy for introverts, but that they must learn to do it if their relationships are to grow and deepen, and that it becomes easier with practice.

Healthy Emersons accept the reality that differences in perception need not be absolutely right or wrong and that the differing viewpoint of a spouse need not be either completely accepted or totally condemned. They become more attuned to their partner's feelings and reactions, and attempt some self-restraint over their angry outbursts and critical tongues.

Both Emersons and Einsteins can be sensitive, but their sensitivities are often different enough that neither is aware of the hurt experienced by the other. It is important that both partners in the relationship stay tuned to the small cues of body language and the emotional overtones that may signal upset or hurt, and attempt to open some channels of communication over what is bothering them.

Einstein personalities generally need more personal space to themselves than the Emerson does. Einsteins absolutely *need* some time alone each day. There is a genuine urgency to their desire to limit further stimulation and withdraw into themselves in order to recharge. This compulsion is not a rejection of the partner, but is experienced viscerally as a physical requirement for solitude. It is easy for the Emerson to perceive this withdrawal as tacit criticism if it is not adequately discussed between the partners.

Emersons have no difficulty confronting people. The Einstein prefers withdrawal and will generally find the partner's anger and criticism aversive even when it is directed at other people.

When the Emerson complains about the slowness of the service to a waiter, an Einstein may want to crawl under the table. This is another area that requires on-going dialogue and mutual understanding of the other's personality and style. The Einstein must come to terms with the fact that it is reasonable to complain about bad service and to make similar complaints in other like circumstances. The Emerson must realize the importance of distinguishing between assertive and aggressive behavior and that complaints are generally more effective when they are made politely.

Both Einsteins and Emersons are quite anxious at the average level. The Einstein handles anxiety by retreating into intellectual manipulations of reality. If the anxiety stems from human interactions, these manipulations may take on paranoid overtones. *"They are out to get me at work, but I will outsmart them by..."* The clever method evolved may, however, be dependent on the other people making stereotypical responses in a lockstep manner. This behavior will be extremely upsetting to the Emerson partner: *"You're going to make enemies and possibly even get fired if you do that!"* The Emerson must present the alternative tactfully and in a non-judgmental manner if it is to be heard. However, the Einstein is well advised to listen to the Emerson who has a better gut level sense of appropriate behavior.

Emersons hate anxiety. They find it so intolerable that they rarely endure it for very long. Instead, they transform it into anger, an emotion with which they feel more comfortable. Anxiety requires the passive endurance of emotional pain; anger allows a person to attack that pain as far as the Emerson is concerned. This would be great if it occurred abstractly, but Emerson anger is never abstract; it invariably seeks a target. Thus, I am anxious about money becomes, *"You spent too much on that new stereo,"* while I am anxious about the amount of work I need to get done both at home and in the office, becomes *"You don't shoulder your share of the work around the house."*

The Einstein partner is well advised to call the Emerson on this issue. The best way to handle Emerson anxiety is to identify it and label the anger that is being expressed as the cover for underlying stress and anxiety. Emersons may well retort angrily, but they will think about it later, and if the partner is consistent in calling them on it, when it happens, the response will be modified in time.

Childcare may become an issue in Emerson-Einstein relationships. Einsteins like children, but have difficulty remaining involved in the concrete day-to-day tedium of raising them. If the choice is between playing ball with a toddler or returning to the computer, the computer is likely to win most of the time. The couple will need to discuss this frankly. The Einstein, having made the commitment to marriage and family, must now follow through, in giving time and attention to that family. If they can afford it, the couple will probably be wise to acquire some help with childcare to keep this from becoming too large an issue between them.

GREATEST DANGER SIGNAL: Work and projects can begin to drain more and more time from this couple, both of whom can easily become over committed. When they become aware that they are spending very little time together, it is important to reassess priorities. An added danger is the failure of the Einstein to do a reasonable share of household tasks. If this happens, the Emerson is liable to feel more and more imposed upon and the additional anger can result in an escalation of the syndrome of Emerson anger and Einstein withdrawal.

PRIMARY FOCUS: The quality of shared interaction should be a primary focus for this couple. Intimacy and the sharing of feelings and reactions will create the glue of this relationship. If it is lost, the marriage will come to lack that essential quality that differentiates it from a friendship. It would be helpful to create regularly scheduled times, dinner out on Friday night, or Sunday morning brunch, for example, to be alone together.

THE EMERSON-AUSTEN RELATIONSHIP

Dan and Edith have agreed to go out to dinner on Saturday night. Edith asks Dan if he has any particular place in mind.

"No, you know I don't care, wherever you like," Dan says, meaning " I am a very flexible, easy-going person and I want to make you happy."

Unfortunately Edith does not hear this hidden agenda, only the verbal commitment to accept her choice, and she makes reservations at a Mexican restaurant that a friend at work has recommended to her.

Friday night at dinner, she says that she's made the reservations at El Taco Grande for seven thirty the next evening. Dan looks vaguely uncomfortable and when she asks if something is wrong admits that he is not too enthusiastic about her choice.

She responds reasonably enough, "You said that you didn't care and this is supposed to be good. If it mattered to you, you should have said so or said that you wanted me to check back before I called."

"Well, I didn't know you'd choose Mexican."

"You didn't know what I'd choose. That's the point, you said you didn't care. I wish you could say what you mean once in a while. You do this to me all the time, and like a jerk, I fall for it. Well, you're stuck this time. The reservation's made and I'm not calling back to change it. Maybe you'll discover that you enjoy it even, and if you don't, you can just take the consequences of not saying what you mean for once."

The subject is dropped until after dinner, when Dan says, "You know the last two times we ate Mexican, it didn't agree with me, and my stomach is already a little upset today."

"Where did that come from? You just finished eating and you didn't look upset while you were taking a second helping of cake."

"Well, it's not that bad, but I'm afraid if I eat a lot of spicy food, I just won't be able to handle it."

"You're a real hypochondriac, always worried about how something will affect you. Anyway, my friends said they had some non-Mexican things on the menu, so you don't have to worry."

Dan says nothing more until they are getting ready for bed, when he asks the location of the restaurant. It is on the other side of town and in a neighborhood that he doesn't know well.

"Are you sure that's a safe neighborhood? Isn't that where there was a robbery reported last week?"

"You'll really say anything to get your way, won't you?" is Edith's retort. "There probably was a robbery there, but there was probably also a robbery

here some time in the past month. If you want to go to a totally safe environment, you'll have to find another planet."

Dan says nothing more, but he wakes up in the morning, complaining of a headache, and by mid-afternoon announces that he simply is not up to going out tonight, they'll have to cancel. Edith is furious and the remainder of the weekend is passed in grim hostility.

These interactions are classic. The Austen personality makes the ingratiating gesture that cannot be comfortably fulfilled. The Emerson feels duped when the agreement falls apart. The concept of fairness, everpresent in the Emerson approach to life, is a prominent part of the problem. The Emerson belief is that if you make a bargain, you stick to it even if it becomes uncomfortable for you. This comes head to head with the Austen anxiety over new situations and dislike of the unfamiliar as well as their proclivity for wondering if any choice that is made is the right one or if something else might not be better.

When pressed, Austens may back down, but this does not solve the problem, as they will inevitably return to the issue a little later with some new reservation, which will further inflame the rage of the Emerson. Finally, when seemingly cornered, passive-aggression is the tool of last resort for the average Austen. Emersons are perfectly aware of what the partner is up to and consider such tactics unfairly manipulative.

It is especially important for Emersons in these relationships to understand that it is simply a given that their partners are often going to be anxious in new situations, unnecessarily fearful, and ambivalent about some of their plans.

It is equally necessary for Austens to realize that things that may seem inconsequential to them are very important to their partners. Going back on a promise, not keeping an agreement, not getting places on time, failing to tell the whole truth, are things that an Emerson simply finds morally intolerable. There is nothing to be gained by arguing that a specific failure to live up to these standards is excusable and has a logical explanation, something Austens tend to do at considerable length.

The Emerson will not understand. In their book, all such behavior comes under the heading of *"Immoral actions absolutely never to be done in any circumstances".*

Grasping these basic dynamics of each other's personalities will help to create understanding and some degree of mutual acceptance. The Emerson must allow for ambivalence and ask questions about the degree of comfort the Austen will feel with certain plans, urging the partner to be absolutely honest about feelings of ambivalence or distaste for what is suggested. The Austen must realize that given this consideration, when an agreement is reached, it is necessary to face up to any subsequent anxiety or ambivalence and overcome it for the sake of a good relationship. Both partners need to credit the other with basic good will. They are not acting out of sheer malice and wrong-headed stupidity, even if it may seem that way at times.

In the previous example, Edith could have headed the whole problem off by checking with Dan about Mexican food and about the restaurant location prior to making the reservation. Knowing Dan, she realized that these aspects of the evening would be likely to arouse apprehension in him. Dan, in turn, should have known himself well enough not to offer carte blanche to Edith in terms of planning the evening. He knows that he can have problems with choices and can be somewhat rigid when he is anxious, so it is far better for him to face these facts about himself up front.

If Dan had been extremely direct in saying that he simply could not face that choice, and had at the same time taken the responsibility for creating an alternative plan, Edith would probably have been mildly irritated, but the evening could have been salvaged. *"Look this is my fault. I know it. I shouldn't have said 'any place', but I did. I'm sorry. There's a great new restaurant that just opened near my office. Would it be okay for me to call and cancel the other place and make reservations there?"*

Edith would still have been annoyed, but she would feel she was dealing with someone who was taking some measure of responsibility for his actions and was not trying to pacify her pretending to an agreement he subsequently refused to honor. It would be considerably less enraging than believing the problem to be solved repeatedly only to have it recur.

Austen personalities like to make thoughtful gestures to please their friends and families. They remember special occasions and mark them. They recall the quirks and the likes and dislikes of the people they care about. Thoughtfulness is natural and instinctive for them. They make the phone call that others intend to make but never find time for. They send "no occasion cards". This thoughtfulness is appealing to the Emerson.

Austens find Emersons attractive because they seem to have an inborn sense of what should be done in most circumstances. They are capable of making tough decisions and sticking to them. They are sure of themselves and willing to take responsibility.

When Emersons and Austens are together in a relationship there are a number of points of friction that are, initially, almost inevitable. There is a substantial theoretical opposition between the self-referenced choices of the Emerson and the dependence on outside opinion of the Austen that can become a source of ongoing annoyance to both. The Austen is often bullied by fear of the Emerson's anger, and Austen timidity, far from appeasing the partner, seems to provide a source of further irritation.

One of the main areas of difficulty is that Austens genuinely want to please their partners and often start out to do so at unreasonable cost to themselves, by saying they agree when they don't. When they find they can't follow through on a commitment they've made in an effort to be agreeable, it seems to them that the other person should understand that this was merely affability, and not hold them to it. The Emerson in this circumstance sees it quite differently and is often enraged when the Austen does an about face.

Even when Austens aren't being ingratiating, they have trouble making up their minds. Emersons, who can usually do this rather quickly, often consider an issue resolved only to find that they have to go over the same ground and discuss the same objections again the next day and again the next week. When the Austen begins to waiver, which is almost inevitable at the average level of emotional functioning, the Emerson perceives this as weakness at best, and at worst, stupidity or sabotage.

Then when Austens becomes passive-aggressive, a typical response on their part to anger and criticism, the Emerson views their partner as having stepped over some sort of moral boundary and to be operating totally without scruples.

Many Austens have a naive, innocent quality, which people find initially appealing. They melt over babies and animals. They relate easily to small children and genuinely enjoy reading to them or playing with them. Emersons are more likely to read to their children because they know it's the right thing to do and they are often less than entranced by fantasy or cuteness in their partner. They see it as a failure to grow up and take life seriously. This perceptual difference can have far-reaching consequences in the Emerson-Austen relationship.

Another issue between Emersons and Austens is the Emerson's seriousness, which is at odds with the playful, fantasy-loving nature of the Austen. Here it is a matter of respecting each other's sensibility and agreeing to disagree. The Emerson must consciously rein in the criticism that comes so easily over some piece of "child-like behavior" on the part of the Austen. The Austen must, in turn, become aware that this aspect of his/her personality is unlikely to strike a responsive chord in the Emerson, that attempting to be cute and playful too often is likely to backfire in this relationship.

It is important for the Austen to give the Emerson space. Austen dependency needs tend to make them want to be with their partners a great deal of the time. Emersons can become irritated by what they consider clinging behavior. In this situation, both sides can alleviate tensions, the Emerson by being careful to give the Austen the love and reassurance that they need to feel comfortable, and the Austen by then allowing the Emerson the time for some solitude and quiet.

GREATEST DANGER SIGNAL: The danger to this relationship lies in a mutual failure of self-restraint. The unbridled anger of the Emerson can be frightening to the Austen and lead to sexual rejection or to withdrawal, failure to communicate, and passive-aggression. If these warning signs begin to appear in the marriage, it is time for both partners to stop and evaluate what is happening between them. Professional help may be needed to put this marriage back on course.

PRIMARY FOCUS: This couple must remember to affirm each other. It is easy for them to allow mutual irritation and anger to limit the expression of positive feelings between them and to block their awareness of each other's good traits.

THE EMERSON-MOZART RELATIONSHIP

Gini and Jim are scheduled to go to his parent's for dinner on Saturday night. On Wednesday, an invitation to an impromptu barbecue at a friend's house appears in the mail. Gini has no problem making the choice of what to do. "Just give your mom a call and ask her if we can make it next week instead," she says over her shoulder, as she hands Jim the invitation before dashing off to her woman's group.

Jim only comprehends what is happening after she has left. He is immediately irritated, he puts the invitation aside until they can talk, but for the rest of the evening, a part of his attention is diverted by thoughts of Gini's irresponsibility and bad manners. By the time she returns, he is angry: "What do you mean, I should call my mother and tell her we're not coming?"

"She won't mind," says Gini. "One week is as good as another for them. It's all right, she'll understand."

"No, it's not all right. You don't just drop people if something you think is better comes along. While it may have escaped your notice, my parents do not live in a vacuum awaiting our pleasure. They make plans too."

"Not every week. It all depends on the situation. What's wrong, don't you want to go to the barbecue?"

"That is such a stupid question I can't believe you asked it. It just has nothing to do with the issue. You know I'd like to go, but if you've accepted another invitation…"

Gini cuts him off: "We go to your parent's all the time, this is a once a year party, it's different."

"Well, if they're giving a once a year party, they have an obligation to get the invitations out more than three days before the event."

"I imagine they meant to, time just gets away from you sometimes, but it's certainly not my fault that they didn't, and we don't have to penalize ourselves for their mistakes."

"I have never felt penalized by visiting my parents, I happen to love my parents," Jim huffs.

"I happen to love your parents too, but that has nothing to do with it," Gini responds, unable to comprehend his pig-headedness. "Your parents won't care. If we explain it to them, they'll say go ahead and enjoy the party."

"Of course that's what they'll say, and you're all too willing to impose on the fact that they'll say that. Well, I'm not and that's final."

"Well, I'm going and that's final."

This scene can play out one of two ways. Either the couple go their separate ways and the issue is resolved by the passage of time, but with lingering resentment on both sides, or Jim's parents prevail on him to go with Gini and he does so, but with some residual anger over her irresponsibility. Variations of this scene constantly recur in their relationship.

The difference in priorities is a given in the relationship, but the conflict resulting from this difference is not inevitable. As both partners become healthier, they may be able to understand and respect each other's viewpoints without adopting them for themselves. If Gini, the Mozart, understands that Jim, the Emerson, is not just being stubbornly obstructionist when such issues arise, but that his is a view that many people might share; and if on the other hand, Jim can realize that what he believes to be "right" is really a subjective opinion and that he does not have to be the final arbiter on ethical issues for his wife; both sides can breathe a little easier.

Part of Jim's problem actually lay in feeling that he had been deprived of the right to participate in decision-making. It is easy for the Emersons to turn anger over a control issue into an ethical criticism. Instead of assuming Jim's compliance, Gini might have told him that they had a party invitation that conflicted with the dinner at Jim's parents and asked his opinion. Jim could then have stated his viewpoint without anger. This might have allowed them to resolve the situation peacefully either by deciding to go their separate ways or checking with Jim's parents on whether they did have plans for the following week-end.

Emerson-Mozart relationships are potentially very good ones. There is a natural reciprocity between the traits of these personalities, which can make them excellent partners. The Mozart is amusing and stimulating company, and can be both focused and hard working, traits that Emersons admire. Mozarts appreciate the honesty and high standards of an Emerson partner and like the fact that they do not pull punches about what they think or want. You know where you stand with an Emerson.

Naturally, these good feelings do not mean there will be no problems. The difficulty in this pairing will rise from their contrasting philosophical outlooks. The Mozart is a natural hedonist, who views the pursuit of pleasure as a sensible and reasonable life goal. The Emerson is a moralist, who certainly enjoys a variety of pleasurable experiences, but never at the expense of moral or ethical considerations. The differences that follow from these conflicting beliefs are intense and inevitable, if both partners are operating at an average level emotionally.

Another problem that can arise between these two personalities is the demand on the part of pleasure-loving Mozarts that the people around them be upbeat and affirmative most of the time. Mozarts tend to view pessimism or even momentary glumness as a purposeful attempt to rain on their parade. The Emerson views such consistent emphasis on pleasure with suspicion, if not disapproval. Emersons benefit from the relationship with a Mozart because it encourages them to lighten up and this is good for them. However, the demand for enthusiasm on an ongoing basis may simply be more than they find reasonable or appropriate, and the natural response of the Emerson in that situation is to turn judgmental and denounce the partner as frivolous and superficial.

Mozart personalities in their constant search for new and interesting experiences do have a problem. They may jump from enthusiasm to enthusiasm never staying with anything long enough to gain depth and insight. At an average level, they can truly be "Jack of all trades, master of none". As Mozarts grow healthier they learn to be less easily distracted and to stick with projects and interests over the long term instead of moving on to something new because the novelty makes it appear more interesting to them. As they do this, the Emerson partner will perceive them as more serious and will feel able to trust them more.

There may also be economic differences between these two personality types. Money is important to Mozarts as a way to obtain the pleasures that make their lives exciting and happy. Money is also important to Emersons since they view good management skills and prudent investment as an obligation to one's family. This may cause them to be somewhat conservative spenders. Here, as both partners grow healthier, they will learn to compromise and balance their needs. The Mozart must learn to modify the desire for immediate gratification and to appreciate the partner's moderate need for financial prudence.

Finally, the Emerson will need to inhibit his/her desire to exercise control. Emersons are natural bosses. Supervising and checking up on those around them is second nature to Emersons. Mozarts simply do not accept supervision of this type. They need to be in control of their own destinies and are naturally somewhat anti-authoritarian. They have a tendency to respond to prohibitions or restrictions flippantly. They are likely to purposely do the opposite of what the other person suggests and are capable of being quite stubborn and digging in their heels when pushed. It is far better for the Mozart to confront the Emerson partner on this issue when it arises, and talk it out rather than responding to it as a dare.

In healthy relationships, the Emerson will provide grounding and stability for the Mozart, while the Mozart helps the Emerson to learn to respond more joyfully and spontaneously to situations.

GREATEST DANGER SIGNAL: A clash between Emerson obstinacy on moral issues and Mozart excess presents the greatest danger to this couple. If the Mozart pursuit of pleasure reaches a point where the partner views it as decadent or sybaritic, Emerson disapprobation can become judgmental and punitive. The marriage is in danger in such a situation and if mutual understanding and respect can not be achieved relatively quickly, it is wise to seek professional help.

PRIMARY FOCUS: Achieving and maintaining a fully adult relationship is a necessary focus in this marriage. It is easy for the fun-loving Mozart to assume a "naughty child" stance, enjoying the game of crossing the line of what is permissible to the partner in a variety of circumstances, and for the Emerson to become the scolding parent in response. This is not healthy for either party. It is necessary in a good marriage for the partners to relate to each other as equal adults.

THE EMERSON-CAESAR RELATIONSHIP

Evelyn and Jim belong to a civic club. Evelyn is president of the organization this year. They employ a part-time secretary to take care of the more tedious aspects of club business and for several years, Emma a retired secretary, has held this position. Evelyn comes home after a frustrating meeting with Emma and announces to Jim that she's going to get the permission of the board to move Emma out of the post. "She's a total incompetent. She messes up more than she takes care of. She simply has to go."

Jim is immediately censorious. "This sounds to me like a repeat of two months ago when you got someone at your job fired."

"Yes, and rightly so. My life has been a lot easier since he left and my life is going to be a lot easier without Emma."

"Have you stopped to think what it will do to her? That job is all she has left in life. It will destroy her to take it away. She probably needs the money too."

"Well, she needs to have thought about that and done a better job is all I can say. I've had it with her."

"That's not right and you know it. She does her best and nothing that we do in that club is so earth-shattering that a few mistakes are going to matter anyway."

"Look, I'm not interested in convincing you. The board will go along with me, and they're the ones I plan to talk to. I'm sorry that you have such deep feelings on the matter, but I'm frankly not very interested in them."

Jim picks up the paper and starts to read, but he can't stop thinking about poor Emma. Finally, he comes to a decision. "Evelyn, I just want you to know the consequences of what you're doing. If you are so heartless as to toss that poor woman out of her post, I'm going to resign from the club."

"That is the most disproportionate response I've heard in a long time. You can't do that. I'm the president. How will it look for you to quit?"

"That's why I'm doing it. You have no regard for anything I say. Maybe my actions will be more meaningful to you. I think what you're doing is

unkind and unfair and I will not be a party to it and I will not look the other way while you do it."

"I find it difficult to believe that, you are actually threatening me. Have you totally lost your mind?"

"No, I'm telling you that actions have consequences apart from those you plan on sometimes."

"I would suggest that you consider the possibility that your threats can also have consequences and that you are a self-righteous prig."

"Having a wife without a grain of empathy in her body is about as much consequence as I can imagine."

"Don't be too sure. There may be a few other consequences that you're not counting on and that are going to crop up where you least expect them."

This interchange is a classic case of the clash of pragmatism and idealism, and most people come down pretty sharply on one side or the other of such issues. Caesars, like Evelyn, are going to do the pragmatic thing in most situations whether Emersons like it or not. Emersons in relationship with Caesars have a choice of coming to terms with this reality and distancing themselves from their partners choices or of living in a constant state of irritation and conflict.

While it is difficult for Emersons to grasp the fact that they are not the moral arbiters of their partners, it is a necessary step in creating a healthy relationship. Caesars are adults and are not only capable, but adamant about making their own choices. Emersons, who want to stay in a marriage with a Caesar, will be forced to come to terms with this situation. It is permissible to ask pertinent questions to stimulate thought in the other person, but it is neither appropriate, nor in this case, realistic to attempt to go any further than that.

It is important for both partners to recognize that whatever the fight is about to begin with, it very often becomes a control issue, with both people more interested in the balance of power within the relationship than with the original cause of the disagreement. This is a dynamic that substantially raises the ante on all arguments.

If when Evelyn made her announcement, Jim had monitored his reaction and identified it as a feeling of moral indignation, he might have decided to slow down and think what was happening and why he was feeling so strongly about her decision. This would have allowed him to examine the possibility that his wife was not acting out of sheer malice and ill will, and even that her complaint might have some legitimate basis. This would have given him time to acknowledge that Emma was sometimes impossibly irritating, but to query if there was a way to soften the blow, such as finding her an alternate job. He could point out that this was something to consider, since other board members would ask the same question in all likelihood.

Since he was not denouncing or judging her, Evelyn would be more likely to listen to Jim's legitimate concerns. At the very least, she would not experience Jim's viewpoint as a personal attack. This approach is not going to avert all disagreement between this volatile couple, but it is likely to produce less violent arguments and to bring some conflict resolution skills into the process. Good compromise skills are absolutely essential for the success of this marriage.

A relationship between two people this strong-willed is an uncommon one. When healthy, both partners are honest and goal-oriented. They are hard workers, willing to put in long hours on projects when necessary. Problems in the relationship are likely to center around control issues, differences in value systems, and styles of coping with people and circumstances. The essential difference can be boiled down to perfectionism versus pragmatism. Since both partners have a strong need to control and both have low boiling points, this is potentially an explosive relationship. However, if both are committed to working out differences and bring an understanding and appreciation of the other person's needs and perceptions to the marriage, they can create a fulfilling relationship..

Different styles in decision making can create problems. Caesars, while not extremely impulsive, are highly decisive and want to move quickly in making choices and in meeting all perceived needs. Emersons want more time to consider the implications of any situation. Caesars say, *"Let's buy a boat today."* Emersons say, *"We'd better see how this fits the budget and find out about docking and where we can store it in the winter."* This is an area where it is important to seek a middle ground. Such conflicts can become long-term sources of conflict and mutual anger unless dealt with skillfully by both partners. In an emotionally healthy couple, the problem might be resolved, after a moderate delay while the Emersons researched the matter, by the purchase of a smaller boat.

Since both partners have a strong need to control and both have low boiling points, this will always be a relationship with explosive potential due to the inevitable conflict between perfectionism versus pragmatism. Both partners will need to be committed to working out differences and to bringing an understanding of the other's needs and perceptions to the marriage, if they are to create a fulfilling relationship.

GREATEST DANGER SIGNAL: The danger in this relationship lies in unresolved anger between the partners. They are resolute, adamant people, who expect to get their own way most of the time. It is a situation in which issues can remain unresolved over time with both partners maintaining their original positions and holding on to their anger, scorn and irritation at the other. Such unresolved issues can become cumulative over time until one or both of them reach a breaking point. Avoiding this occurrence requires that the couple agree either to talk until they arrive at a resolution to any major difference, or to seek professional help if that is necessary.

PRIMARY FOCUS: The control issue is going to be the dominant problem for this couple. It is paramount that both partners remember this. It will be an underlying issue in every argument they have. To the Caesar, control and power are closely linked and they experience being in control as the only emotionally comfortable state in a relationship. They have a gut level feeling of discomfort and intense frustration if they believe themselves to be powerless in a situation. Emersons approach control from a different perspective. It is linked to their self-image as ethical people who know and do what is right. Since, in their eyes, the rest of the world seems less capable of making correct moral judgments, they believe they need to be in control in order to secure the appropriate outcome to whatever situation presents itself. Basically, it boils down to their assumption that other people cannot be trusted to know or do the right thing.

Mutual respect for each other's choices and each other's boundaries is the only sensible compromise. Many occasions will occur when that respect seems virtually impossible to maintain, but those are the very times when keeping one's mouth shut and the issue in perspective is the most sensible course.

THE EMERSON-GAUGUIN RELATIONSHIP

Edith has been concerned for some time about the condition of the roof. She has recently painted the rooms on the second floor and worries that the old roof may begin to leak and destroy all her hard work. She has spoken to Mike about this several times and he has put her off, assuring her that he has the roofer's number at the office and will get in touch with him when he gets to work. He just seems to keep forgetting to make the call. He has also had a problem recently with persistent stomach pain and has so far refused to go to the doctor. Edith is worried about both his health and her roof. When she gets worried, she tends to clean closets and she has been on a serious closet cleaning binge for the past several weeks.

When Mike comes home and finds some of his old clothes and paperback books in a pile next to her current project, he objects. "I want those things, Edith, what are you doing in that closet?"

"Getting rid of stuff you didn't even know was there."

"Well, it's my stuff and I want it, so you're not throwing it out. What's got into you anyway? Why would anyone come home from work and clean out closets? It doesn't make sense."

Edith continues grimly with her task. "You'll have to find someplace else for all of this if you really plan to keep it. It was just piled in here one thing on top of another, you couldn't possibly have found anything if you had wanted it."

"Why didn't you just leave it and ask me to do it, if you felt it had to be done? It doesn't make sense for you to try to sort out my stuff."

"Ask you to do it? Is that some kind of joke? Are you implying I've never asked you? It takes work to clean out a closet and you haven't even been able to pick up the phone and call the roofer. People who won't make simple phone calls seldom take on projects that require physical exertion. If you don't call the roofer by the week-end, I'll find someone else."

"Don't do that. This guy's a buddy of mine and he'll do a great job. You always get all hot and bothered and want everything done yesterday. Just calm down."

"What are you going to do with this junk?"

"I'll have to figure something out. Just leave it there for now and I'll take care of it."

"I didn't clean out the closet to have a pile of junk on the floor in here."

"Well, I don't know why you started this at all without asking me about it," Mike recriminates as he walks off to turn on the television.

There is a heavy rain two days later, and Edith's worst fears are realized. The roof leaks in three places, creating large splotches on the fresh paint in two bedrooms and a hallway. She reaches for the phone to call Mike and then changes plans and reaches for the phone book to find another roofer. As long as she's calling, she makes a doctor's appointment for her husband as well.

When Mike gets home, he is torn between being upset that his buddy will be deprived of a job, and feeling genuinely sheepish about the ruined wall. However, after Edith has railed on at him for several minutes, anger *overcomes any defensiveness he feels.* "I didn't get around to doing it. This is not the end of the world, Edith. You could have made the call all along you know."

"If I had known the phone number, I would have. This is typical, your inertia causes a problem and then you get mad when anyone points it out to you."

"You've pointed it out pretty forcefully, and I've said I'm sorry. Now you're just nagging."

"I'm doing it for your own good, you have to learn to take responsibility. I did have the doctor's number, so I made an appointment for you for Saturday morning. I'm not going to let you put that off too."

Mike says nothing, but when Saturday comes, he cancels the appointment, saying he is feeling better. It will be another six months when he has to be rushed to a hospital emergency room before he discovers he has an ulcer.

This is a typical situation pitting the Emerson need to control and manage life situations with the Gauguin's refusal to face and deal with an issue.

Edith, for her own peace of mind, needs to understand that if she wants something done, she'd better do it herself. She was certainly trying to be cooperative and do the right thing by waiting for Mike to get in touch with his friend, but this is a situation in which limit setting is essential. *"I'd be happy to have your friend do the roof, but I want it done next week-end. If you get the number to me tomorrow, I'll give him a call and see if he's free."* Two days later, the time arrives to set a final limit: *"Remember I said I wanted the roof done this week-end? I'll call you at work today and get your friend's number."* If this fails, it is perfectly reasonable to go ahead and call someone else, rather than waiting for catastrophe to strike and then recriminating.

The medical problem is a genuine worry for Edith, but there is very little she can do about it. Nagging does not help Gauguins follow through even on the most serious matters. This means that the alternatives are to do it yourself if you can, and to leave it alone if it's out of your control. Gauguins can be surprisingly wily in not following through when they feel pushed into situations against their will and the natural Emerson tendency to control and criticize can backfire by creating stronger resistance to such pressure.

Mike needs to understand that becoming healthier means facing problems instead of denying and avoiding them. He needs to resolve to make a genuine effort to meet Edith halfway when something substantial is bothering her. It may help for her to emphasize, *"This is important to me, Mike."* when the issue is first raised. He must make an effort to hear her when she says this, and she must reserve the statement for things that really are important. If fixing the roof, throwing away old books and remembering to empty the dish washer without being asked, are all listed as equally important on her agenda, she is putting herself in a position where she is more likely to lose then if only the roof gets pinpointed.

This relationship should be relatively peaceful. Emersons are attracted to the kind, gentle qualities of the Gauguin. While, healthy Gauguins like the fact that an efficient Emerson can organize them and help them to become more productive and focused.

Problems in this relationship may center on the different energy levels of the partners and the philosophical differences between problem-solving Emersons, who will work to try to find a solution to even the most intractable situation, and the unwillingness of Gauguins to face their problems at all or sometimes, even to acknowledge them.

Gauguins mean to be obliging and will actually be reasonably helpful if asked in a pleasant way to do something. The problem usually comes when the Emerson gets tired of asking nicely, since no one likes to be nagged. *"Could you empty the dish washer while I start dinner?"* will almost always be willingly acquiesced to, as the request is immediate, simple and does not require undue thought or exertion. The Emerson's response, that having to ask is not fair, since the Gauguin's dishes are in the machine too, is true. The claim that they should assume half the responsibility without waiting to be told is indisputable. But, this is where fair play meets head to head with reality. It's simply unlikely to happen. It's not even attributable to laziness, they just aren't tuned into the fact that this task exists and needs to be done. So the choice generally boils down to constant recrimination and criticism versus accepting the unfair, but realistic, need to provide some structure which will allow them to do what is expected. Emersons need to accept the fact that most of the time having a pleasant relationship is a more important value than absolute equity in the area of responsibility, probably an unreachable goal in this marriage.

If Emersons want to achieve their partner's cooperation, they must try to ask for help relatively close to the time when they want something done and provide some sort of deadline that doesn't leave the task open-ended on the one hand or too tightly constrained on the other. *"The stuff in the den has to be picked up before the cleaning woman comes on Friday,"* if said on Wednesday morning, is more likely to achieve results than an open-ended: *"The stuff in the den has to be picked up."* or than the same statement made on the previous Sunday which allows too much space for putting it off and then forgetting it.

It is important to be aware of the differences in stamina, and also in energy level, between Gauguins and Emersons. Most Gauguins genuinely have less energy than the more driven Emersons do. Recognizing when Gauguins are genuinely out-of-steam for the day and accepting this reality makes more sense than being angry with them. It is equally important that Gauguins realize that sometimes their lack of steam can be a disinclination to complete the job and that they do not have to give themselves permission to quit just because there are more pleasant alternatives available than what they are doing.

Emersons can be relatively rigid and doctrinaire in their thinking, holding strong opinions and beliefs and defending them vehemently. Some Emersons place undue emphasis on cleaning and keeping things in order. In a different context, average Gauguins can also be rigid, since they can be overly dependent on convention and afraid of change. Their rigidity may show itself in the need to stick with what they know. *"We've always bought this make of car, why should we change now?" "I like to eat at the restaurant we usually go to, why do we always have to look for something new?"* Such personality traits can become a problem if they are carried to extremes. If either partner seems unduly rigid, it is time to seek professional help to learn how to modify and control these traits.

The confrontational style of the Emerson can create a problem for peace-loving Gauguins. Gauguins seeing their spouses embroiled in angry controversies or on picket lines, try to ignore what is happening as much as possible. They may not make an issue of it for fear of creating even more unpleasantness, but it makes them deeply uncomfortable and adds strain to the relationship. Emersons, who often feel deeply about causes, need to weigh the emotional cost to the Gauguins in their lives, when deciding how vociferous they want to be in supporting an issue.

Emersons are anxious people. They cross bridges before they come to them and worry about things that seem ridiculous to most Gauguins. The failure of Gauguins to worry, even when it is appropriate, drives Emersons to fury. At the same time, Gauguins are often attractive to Emersons because of their soothing personalities. It is important for both partners to understand that these differences are going to persist. They may lessen as both become emotionally healthier, but a respect for the partner's feelings and an understanding that this is a basic part of who they are, will lessen the inevitable friction that their differences in perception arouse.

Differences in their attitudes toward money can be a problem in some Emerson-Gauguin relationships. The Gauguin spends what is available and tends to give little thought to long-range goals or to the need to put money aside to replace big ticket items when they wear out.

Emersons can be driven frantic by what they perceive as feckless behavior. Emersons are genuinely better managers than Gauguins are in most cases. If this is so, it makes sense that they manage the money for the couple. However, it is also necessary that the Gauguin have some discretionary income, as Emersons can go to an opposite extreme in their goal-oriented thriftiness.

The best way to handle this situation is to sit down and plan together first, talking about all the needs of both personalities and juxtaposing them to the family budget. It is important that Emersons take the desires of the Gauguin seriously, as failure to do so will sabotage the plan before it can be implemented. When a reasonable allocation of money has been agreed upon, then Gauguins can step back, probably with a sigh of relief that dispensing it will not be their responsibility.

GREATEST DANGER SIGNAL: The danger for this couple lies in the possibility that the Gauguin may unwittingly overstep some absolute boundary in the Emerson' ethical or moral code. The Emerson is capable of viewing some behavior as unforgivable and responding with complete emotional rejection. This places a responsibility on both partners. Emersons must be clear about issues that are absolutes for them and differentiate distinctly between these "musts" and the way they react to petty irritations. It is up to the Gauguin to pay attention at such times and realize those imperatives, which impose a serious demand, since ignoring them, could seriously imperil the quality of the relationship.

PRIMARY FOCUS: It is important for this couple to do things together, to create shared commonalties in their lives. Emersons can take on any amount of responsibility, or any number of tasks, rather like the Little Red Hen in the children's story, who said I'll do it myself and did. The moral of the story, that eventually the animals who refused to help were excluded from sharing the benefits of her labors, could find a parallel in this relationship, as the Gauguin eventually becomes a more peripheral part of the household and of the partner's life.

V

The Nightingale in Relationships

For the Nightingale-Emerson Relationship—Go to the Emerson-Nightingale Relationship

THE NIGHTINGALE-NIGHTINGALE RELATIONSHIP

Gloria's widowed mother has become increasingly dependent on her in recent months and Gloria has come to the conclusion that the easiest way to handle the situation is to invite her mother to live with them. Martin is opposed to this. While, he likes Gloria's mother and often goes out of his way to help her by running errands or doing minor home repairs, he feels that Gloria is already devoting an undue amount of time to her mother's well-being, much of it at his expense. If his mother-in-law were to move in, she would become the focal point of Gloria's life, leaving him feeling deprived and deserted.

The quarrel has reached the stage where Gloria is quite weepy and very angry. "My mother has always been good to you and this is the way you repay her."

"Gloria, lots of people are good to me. It doesn't mean I want to live with them all. I know what will happen because it's already happening. We

won't have any time to ourselves. If we go out to dinner, you'll want her to come along…"

"What's wrong with that? I happen to love my mother. I never realized how selfish you were. You always talk about caring about people and wanting what's best for everybody, but now I see it was all talk and you're really a selfish, self-centered egotist."

Martin is deeply upset and hurt by this attack. "How can you say such things to me? Everyone knows that it doesn't work to have parents live with their children. It's common knowledge. I would never dream of trying to move my parents in on you. I have more consideration and more common-sense than to even consider such a thing. You're the egotist, trying to solve a problem without a moment's thought for what it will do to anyone else."

This is a no-win situation for both Martin and Gloria. They are now both going to feel miserable whether her mother moves in or doesn't. If her mother moves in, Martin will become extremely demanding of Gloria's time and attention and will feel increasing hostility toward the woman, while the mother will be in the uncomfortable position of an unwanted guest. Gloria will be in the middle, feeling constantly pulled and overburdened by conflicting loyalties.

If on the other hand, Gloria makes other arrangements for her mother, she will do so with many reservations and resentments toward Martin that will poison their relationship for some time to come.

This is a situation that should never have occurred. Nightingales more than any other personality need the undivided loyalty, attention and love of their partner if they are to be happy and productive people. When that nurturing is withdrawn, they can become emotionally dysfunctional. Nightingales in relationship must stay empathetic and aware of each other's need for this nurturing. In practical terms, this means that no plans involving commitments to the outside world should be made without consultation and mutual agreement. The line about forsaking all others in their marriage vows needs to be underlined and written in stone for them. Both want to help others and see no problem in going off to do so. At the same time, either will experience being left by the partner, embarking on a similar mission of mercy, as desertion. This is what happened to Martin. Gloria was picturing herself as the good daughter taking care of her beloved mother. Martin was experiencing himself as deserted by his wife.

Nightingales are attracted to each other because they have the same basic value system. They care about people as individuals over ideas, ideals or concepts. They consider service to others, helpfulness, and generosity to be essential elements of their personalities and to give meaning to their lives.

Nightingales at an average level of emotional health tend to have both possessive and manipulative tendencies. They have a strong need to control. Because they believe that they are doing whatever it is they may be doing from good motives, they are often out of touch with the self-serving aspect of their motivations.

Nightingales tend to be jealous of the partner's relationships outside the marriage. This can become an area of conflict. While Nightingales are comfortable with their own friends, they often have difficulty in accepting friends their partner brings to the relationship. With a Nightingale-Nightingale partnership, this could result in total isolation for the couple or in constant conflict over the relative claims and merits of opposing sets of people.

Self-observation is the starting point for dealing with this problem, followed by total honesty in discussing what's happening. If Gloria can say, *"I know how fond you are of Denise, and I think that's the problem, I really feel jealous when she's around,"* Martin will have a chance to reassure her. He can follow up by making sure that he gives Gloria plenty of attention when they invite Denise over—a quick kiss in the kitchen, a squeeze on the arm in passing—any way that the message can be conveyed, *"You're the most important person in my life".* Such a gesture will allow Gloria to relax and relate to Denise as a person instead of a rival.

If some Nightingales still find accepting friends difficult, even with strong reassurance, it is an indication of a more general problem in self-esteem, and it would be wise to seek help from a reputable therapist.

Average Nightingales have a hard time accepting criticism. They see themselves as good people with excellent motives for what they do. This may be true, but it makes it very hard for them to evaluate objectively what is said to them on occasion. This can become a double problem with two Nightingales in a relationship. For example, Martin believes he is being a kind and loving father when he buys the children candy at the supermarket. Gloria believes it is more genuinely caring to limit the children's intake of empty calories and sugar and sees herself as the *truly* loving person when she remonstrates with Martin about this. Both parties feel hurt that the other one does not understand the essential goodness inherent in their actions.

In these clashes, it is essential that both parties emphasize their awareness of the loving impulse and good will inherent in the other's position. With this obstacle in perception out of the way, compromise becomes possible. In this case, an agreement might be reached that Martin may purchase the candy, but will limit the amount, and that any excess will be saved until after the next meal.

Sexual interactions are often an area of difficulty for Nightingales. Some Nightingales do not enjoy sex or withhold themselves as a punitive gesture when angry or upset. There is a gender component to this as women in general are sexually aroused by emotional stimuli, while most men find visual stimuli more arousing. This means that men can often enjoy sex even when they are angry with the partner, while women find it difficult to do this. Women with Nightingale personalities seem to need even more tenderness, warmth, and affirmation from the partner than most other personalities in order to feel sexually responsive.

When both partners are aware of this contrast in styles, it will prevent some of the misunderstandings and conflicts that can otherwise ensue. If this becomes a recurrent problem in the relationship and cannot be dealt with through discussion and mutual attempts to work things out, professional help should be sought before the situation deteriorates. It is much harder to get back to a regular pattern of lovemaking after six months of mutual standoff, than if the problem is dealt with promptly.

Nightingales often have a potential for addictive behaviors. They are naturally expansive people and have a real enjoyment of the pleasures of good food and drink. Sometimes this leads to failures in self-control such as overeating or drinking too much. In Nightingale couples, the potential for addiction is doubled, because often neither of them is in a position to set a different example or say no. This is a possibility to be aware of, and to discuss and monitor. The various twelve-step programs are a resource that can provide help and encouragement if this becomes a problem in the relationship

GREATEST DANGER SIGNAL: This marriage will be endangered by martyrdom on the part of either or both partners. It is very easy for Nightingales to fall into self-pity, never a very attractive trait, and to complain that they contribute the lion's share to the relationship in a physical, financial, or emotional sense. Since feeling important and needed is so necessary to their wellbeing, such accusations or attitudes can cause more damage between these partners than might be the case in other marriages. When a Nightingale feels over-burdened or imposed upon, it is important to identify the precise cause of such feelings, and to initiate dialogue about it, rather than allowing the situation to continue and resentment to build.

PRIMARY FOCUS: The focus in this relationship should be on maintaining appropriate levels of contact with others. Nightingales can focus on their own interactions to the exclusion of family and friends. Eventually, this type of honeymoon closeness, with its lack of outside stimulation, can become dull and stifling. At the other extreme, they; can become so involved in outside groups and activities that there is no time left for family. As in most situations it is important to find a medium ground between these extremes.

THE NIGHTINGALE-BEAU RELATIONSHIP

Martin's 16-year-old niece, Diane, has been having a very difficult year. Her parents are in the middle of an adversarial divorce and are both trying to force her to take sides. Both Martin and Joan are angry at the parent's insensitivity to the girl, and Joan suggests that they invite her to come for a weekend visit. Martin is initially pleased, but on reflection decides that this is an inadequate response to Diane's problems and counters with the idea of inviting her to spend the summer with them.

Diane is rather plain and awkward, and her current situation has further impaired her marginal social skills. While Joan is sympathetic to the girl's plight, she feels that a summer of Diane is beyond her and simply rules this suggestion out as impossibility.

Martin moves quickly from gratitude for her original suggestion to anger at its time-limited nature. "Can't you see that her problem is that nobody gives any thought to her needs? If she's with us, she'll be different."

"Look Martin, I'm sorry for the girl, but I'm not that caring. We're going to be having a lot of company this summer and we want to go on vacation. However sorry you may feel for people, you can't just take them over and let your own life go onto hold. It won't work and I won't do it."

After further angry exchanges, Martin announces that he has reservations about how much he could enjoy going on a vacation with someone as cold-hearted and selfish as Joan. Joan responds that she can probably find someone else to go with and will be able to go to a more expensive place if she's the only one vacationing.

This impasse could have been avoided. Martin, a Nightingale, must learn to accept the fact that he cannot force his level of altruism down Joan's throat and When he tries to do this, it invariably causes trouble.

Joan is not a monster she has expressed concern for the girl, and offered to have her for a weekend.

Martin's level of commitment to the girl's situation is extreme. He has a hard time remembering and respecting Joan's needs and boundaries. His naturally expansive nature wants to reach out to whoever is hurting and make it right and this is often not realistic. In fact, he often finds out later that he has been overly optimistic about his own ability to tolerate situations he commits to. He cannot expect Joan, a Beau personality, to approach this situation from his perspective. She has stated her limits and, far from denouncing them, he must learn to respect them.

Joan is only superficially sympathetic. She really doesn't care much for Diane, and this is apparent in their argument. If she could express greater sympathy and concern, perhaps coming up with some alternate suggestions or extending the week-end offer to a week or two, it might demonstrate to Martin her sympathy and concern without inappropriately overextending their own plans and resources.

It might also be wise for Martin to examine his relationship with his sister. Such a generous offer may have a hidden motive in an old sibling rivalry agenda, showing up his sister by highlighting her maternal failings and her poor choice in husbands, through this situation.

Martin should also examine his use of an ultimatum to try and force the issue. He is employing a destructive tactic in an attempt to regain control, immediately arousing Joan's innately competitive Beau traits and causing her to respond in an inappropriately adamant manner to define her own limits. This type of interaction is a predictable dynamic between average Nightingales and Beaus and simply should not occur. They are risking harm to their own marriage in an attempt to win a battle. While Martin disguises this ploy in a charitable context, the moment he makes a threat the underlying power motive becomes apparent. Joan's response seems superficial and immature. Both of them need to return to the discussion after they have given the situation some thought and accepted the need to retreat from their original positions.

If this entire interaction were to take place between healthier personalities, both partners would be more aware of their motivations and of the specific personality components (an over-developed sense of responsibility, manipulation and unwillingness to compromise on Martin's part, and a tendency toward selfishness and lack of empathy in Joan) which create the conflict between them. They would need to dialogue about possible compromises without trying to settle the issue in one conversation, each agreeing to think about the other's point of view and talk again in a day or two.

Martin would realize that he cannot make commitments for Joan in order to further his desire to portray himself as a caring, concerned person, and would acquire a healthy skepticism of this need to assume so much responsibility for his niece. Joan has and will always have different perceptions and goals. She has to be who she is, and he should realize that this difference is actually healthy and appropriate. It may be a component of what attracted him to her in the first place. Her disparate approach is actually valuable to him in protecting him from irresponsible over-commitments.

Joan can stay aware of Martin's need to see himself as a loving, giving helper and can help him keep this orientation in proportion and to refrain from using manipulative tactics in pursuing it.

Beau personalities are out-going, poised and self-possessed. They bring energy and enthusiasm to whatever they do. It is not surprising that people find them attractive. Nightingales are extremely doting lovers; they are often eloquent in their admiration of the beloved. They care and show that they care. The Beau enjoys the admiration and flattery of the partner. This relationship can thus begin very positively.

Control issues will surface early between this couple. Beaus are goal-oriented. They are decisive, knowing exactly what they want in almost every circumstance and zeroing in to get it quickly and efficiently.

Nightingales are much more indirect. Control is extremely important to them as well. Their needs tend to be felt on an emotional plane and to be experienced at gut level, rather than being discerned cognitively. The needs of the Nightingale in conflict with the wants and desires of the Beau can create a head-on clash.

One of the ongoing tensions in the relationship is the difference in empathy between the personalities. Nightingales go out of their way to help others in a manner that can be intrusive and controlling and are beyond the comprehension of the Beau. Beaus can appear hard and insensitive to Nightingales. These personalities are at opposite poles in this regard. As usual healthy responses are never at the extremes of behavior, so they can actually help each other to grow if they are able to do it gently and not try to batter the partner into compliance. The Beau can learn compassion from the Nightingale and the Nightingale can learn that there are boundaries and that taking too much responsibility for others can destroy the acquisition of coping skills in those they are helping and make them unnecessarily dependent.

There is a marked difference in impulsivity level between these personalities. Nightingales, propelled by their greater emotional responsiveness, will often leap into things without stopping to think them through. This can be irritating to the more controlled Beau personality, particularly when commitments are made that impact on them as a couple. Nightingales can learn to consult and discuss before making commitments or approaching situations impulsively. Beaus can respond by trying to meet their partners half way, rather than digging in their heels.

It is important to Beaus to make a good impression; they feel a genuine need for the approval of the important people in their sphere. When they are together in social and business contexts, the Nightingale's appearance and behavior may fail to meet the high standards of the Beau partner. Acceptance of this difference provides the obvious solution. Nightingales need to understand that their partners really care about making a good impression and try to comply with their standards within reason. Beaus must learn to keep their demands in proportion and accept the fact that they cannot hold out for unrealistically high standards in the dress and behavior of their partners in the interest of impressing others.

Resolution of confrontations between these personalities can be difficult. Beaus have a strong drive to win in any competitive sphere and can fight quite ruthlessly if they feel frustrated in gaining their objectives. The need to control is strong with both partners and while Nightingales are less direct in their interventions, their gut level needs are very strong and can cause them to be equally adamant, although probably less pointed and more manipulative in attempting to achieve their ends.

The Beau is unlikely in the heat of battle to take Nightingale sensitivity into consideration. This adds another dimension to conflicts between them, as the Nightingale will find harsh words spoken in anger difficult to forgive. Average Nightingales tend to lose most of their objectivity in confrontations and view all disagreement as personally directed malice.

Beaus need to redefine their goals in relation to conflict when it comes to marital interactions. Average Beaus want to win and to be in control at almost any cost and this is an extremely destructive approach within a marriage. Learning to redefine the goal as conflict resolution involving mutual satisfaction will be a major step toward a healthier personality for Beaus.

Nightingales often have tremendous difficulty comprehending the difference between honest criticism and rejection. It will probably be necessary for the Beau who wants to get through to a Nightingale to surround any reproach with reassurances of love and basic worth. It is sometimes useful to hold the Nightingale's hand while explaining the problem. As Nightingales become healthier, they get tougher and learn that accepting constructive criticism provides opportunities for further growth.

Sex can become a problem in the Nightingale-Beau relationship. Women with a Nightingale personality often require more than the usual amount of emotional reassurance, nurturing and foreplay as a component of lovemaking. They need to feel deeply loved and appreciated to be responsive. If the pragmatic Beau neglects to include adequate romance in the sexual approach, the bedroom can become another arena for disagreement and reproach. Sex will be better for both partners if the Beau understands that emotional reassurance and nurturing are a genuine condition for sexual arousal in the Nightingale and provides the necessary romantic and emotional conditions to arouse the partner. In many instances, average Nightingales refuse to have sex when they are angry. Sex should never be used as a weapon by either partner. This is not a good way to gain leverage or express displeasure. It only spirals into greater anger and conflict between them.

Children of this marriage may find that their parents have differing goals and demands and that it is hard to hit upon behavior that will satisfy both parties. Beaus want to be perfect parents, but they also expect reciprocation; their standards for their children tend to be unrealistically high.

Nightingales are very loving and nurturing with young children, but they are likely to find parenting teen-agers more difficult. The teen's need to separate and establish greater autonomy is often experienced as rejection by Nightingales, who can have serious problems letting go. They can become angry, demanding, and intrusive, seriously harming their relationship with the child.

An example of the clash between Nightingale and Beau parenting styles might occur if a child complained of a minor physical discomfort. The nurturing Nightingale is likely to say, *"If you have a headache, maybe you should stay home from school today,"* while the competitive Beau is more likely to focus on the importance of being in school to review for the upcoming math test. With teenagers, the Beau may demand unrealistically high social goals, such as dating the *right* people, belonging to the right crowd, choosing the most prestigious extracurricular activities, but have no problem with the fact that they are at home less due to their increased participation in the teen social scene. The problem for the Nightingale is more likely to be feelings of rejection as the children are less available for family interactions.

The Nightingale attitude toward money is not uniform. While many Nightingales are fairly realistic in their approach, some use material things to fill the painful void that they experience in themselves, acquiring objects as a substitute for the unconditional love and nurturing that they crave. They may also use money to demonstrate their love and devotion to family members through excessive gifts.

Beaus use money as an expression of their prestige and may need quite a bit of it to create the impression of success and affluence that is important to them. If these disparate goals create financial problems, it is important to establish a budget that allows both partners an equal amount of discretionary spending money with the agreement that they will not criticize each other's choice as long as they stay within the prescribed limits.

Nightingale personalities have a very hard time letting go and will remain committed to a relationship as long as there is the least possibility that it could be viable. Beaus want the best out of life in every respect. They generally choose their partners carefully for this reason. However, unhealthy Beaus would have few qualms about leaving a relationship if someone they perceived as better came along. Both of these responses can be dysfunctional. As they become healthier, Beaus will be less quick to change partners for superficial advantage, while Nightingales will come to understand that if a relationship is genuinely beyond reasonable hope of repair, it is foolish to continue to hold onto someone out of feelings of desperation.

GREATEST DANGER SIGNAL: The greatest danger for this relationship lies in a lack of equality between the partners. If either one becomes significantly stronger than the other does, and in effect takes charge of decision-making in the relationship, the marriage will begin to deteriorate. Mutual respect and compromise are always important components in a marriage. They are essentials in this relationship.

PRIMARY FOCUS: This couple needs to focus on keeping the romance in the marriage. This provides the glue for the bonding of these two personalities. The small tokens of love and reassurances are especially necessary to Nightingales, while Beaus are always invigorated by small attentions and by the innate glamour that they experience in a setting which they deem romantic, whether it involves candlelight and soft music or a rigorous adventure in a remote setting. The partners will be united by romantic experiences, even thought their motivations come from very different needs.

THE NIGHTINGALE-SHELLY RELATIONSHIP

Gloria invites friends from out of town for the weekend without con-sulting Greg on the assumption that he will be happy to see them. Greg doesn't voice any objection when she tells him what she's done and he is the perfect host when they arrive, chatting amiably and making drinks. He helps Gloria clean up after dinner Saturday evening and gets up the next morning and puts the coffee on for breakfast before she gets to the kitchen. Then after lunch on Sunday, he disappears and Gloria finds him up in the bedroom, reading a book. When she remonstrates with him, he responds irritably that he just needs some time alone.

He reappears in time to say good-bye to their guests, but Gloria feels humiliated and upset by his behavior. "I don't understand you. What happened?"

"I can only take so much of those people, let's face it, they're pretty nerdy and after a certain amount of time, it gets to me. I'm sorry, but I can only stand the discussion of trivia for so long."

"You seemed to be enjoying yourself Saturday night."

"I was. They amuse me for a while. Their simplistic conversation is quite entertaining in moderation, but I can only take so much of them."

"They've been our friends for five years. Why have you suddenly become so patronizing?"

"Until they moved away, we only dealt with them in small doses. Two days of them is more than anyone should be asked to endure."

"You always liked them. You went out of your way to socialize with them. How can you say such things?"

"I didn't always like them, I always tolerated them because you liked them."

"That's not true, I know how you felt."

"You always know how I feel, don't you Gloria? Knowing how other people feel better than they do is one of your special gifts, isn't it? Well, how I feel now is that I never want to see them again, so if you invite them, I'll go away for the weekend." When Greg walks away, Gloria follows him.

"You're doing this to get to me, aren't you? You really enjoy hurting me."

"Yes, all of my thoughts are centered on that, it's a real preoccupation of mine. I have no life of my own, it's all devoted to you, so that whatever I do occurs only within the context of your needs."

"I hate your sarcasm. Why do you have to be like that." Gloria is crying as Greg walks out the door, gets in the car, and drives off.

As soon as he drives away, Gloria is beset by another concern. Suppose he doesn't come back? What if he's so beside himself he gets into an accident? What if he leaves her? She worries for the next two hours until he returns and goes off into the bedroom without speaking to her. She follows saying tearfully, "We have to talk."

"Stop being hysterical. If you don't leave me alone, I'll leave for the night. I don't want to talk, I've told you how I feel, now stop harassing me."

Clearly, the problems started when Gloria, the Nightingale, didn't clear her plans with Greg. Taking the responses of Shelleys for granted is a mistake. Because Shelleys are self-contained does not mean that they do not hold strong opinions. Greg actually didn't mind having company, and would have agreed to invite them if he had been consulted, but the fact that he was not, allowed him an easy way out, in his own mind, when he tired of them.

While Greg is usually willing to have visitors, he hadn't accurately predicted how much of his time and energy were to be involved in the weekend. He was amiable as long as he felt able to be and then suddenly his amiability quotient ran out. When that happened, he left. Being with people expends a certain amount of energy and when it gets used up, Shelleys tend to cut off, often in midstream.

If Greg had been more self-aware, he could have prepared Gloria for this possibility. *"It's fine with me if they come, but two solid days without respite is going to be too much for me. Can we arrange for me to opt out of a couple of the outings you've planned?"* With that arrangement, Greg could have recharged his energy level in short doses and made it through the weekend. With some awareness of the problem, Gloria could also have suggested that he take some breaks from the company if he didn't think to do so.

The next chance to retrieve a deteriorating situation occurred after the company left. Gloria felt upset at that point and began to remonstrate with him. Greg experienced himself as attacked and responded in a typical manner for an average Shelley, a mixture of irony, sarcasm, and that bluntness which goes further than is necessary, and so seems just mean. Gloria has never understood this aspect of Greg's personality and experiences herself as rejected and unloved when it surfaces.

A change in tactics at this point might have saved the situation. Shelleys dislike being remonstrated with and experience it as unwarranted intrusion. They respond poorly to sentences beginning *"How could you have..."* They are generally quite open to discussing a situation as long as it is done without the supposition that they are guilty of something. If Gloria had said, *"I was surprised when you disappeared after lunch. I wondered what had happened?"* Greg would have been willing to tell her and would probably have done so without belittling their guests.

Greg didn't want to explain himself particularly, and it seemed easier and more amusing to mock the people who had so recently jangled his nerves, than to explain that he had felt over-stimulated. To Gloria it was indicative of a malicious nature. Saying such things about friends seemed cruel and inexplicable. Then when her further remonstrations, drove Greg right out the door, she was both frightened and astonished.

Greg needs to be aware that Gloria perceives as a genuine character defect what he sees as harmless ventilation and to try to modify his sarcasm when talking to her. At the same time, Gloria needs to understand that sarcasm and irony are an inherent part of Greg's personality and take what he says with a grain of salt. This is hard for Nightingales who want their partners to be as kind and loving as they are. Greg actually is a kind person, but he is never going to be kind within the particular context that Gloria would prefer, and she will need to learn to understand and accept that.

Greg knows that he really frightens Gloria when he leaves during an argument, and he sees it as justifiable retaliation for her nagging. The problem is that it is overkill. He does not comprehend that she really fears that he will leave her because he has driven off in anger. When he understands this, he can modify his response at least to the point of saying, *"I can't handle this now, and I'm leaving, but I'm not leaving you, I'm just getting away from this particular confrontation for awhile."* It's hard to do this in moments of anger, particularly when the thought of permanent separation is not at issue, but it is an important step in improving their relationship.

Nightingales frequently perceive Shelleys as needing care and protection, which brings out their strong nurturing instincts. Average Shelleys have a tendency toward depression and may find the sympathy and concern of the Nightingale initially attractive, however, as the relationship matures, that same nurturing approach can begin to seem intrusive and oppressive.

The problems that are likely to occur in this marriage lie in the basic personality structures of the partners. Nightingales are naturally expansive. They are overtly emotional people who express their feelings easily and fully. Shelleys draw into themselves. They feel very deeply about many things, but they have a strong sense that those feelings can never be adequately put into words and they fear that expressing them directly cheapens them. Nightingales like to be with people, to spend a lot of time with those they care about; Shelleys enjoy the company of their friends, but also need a large measure of space and solitude to function well.

Shelleys are naturally irritable people, easily annoyed by the small idiosyncrasies of those around them. They may easily experience questions and comments about their activities as intrusion. Nightingales have a great deal of trouble handling the disapproval of those they love. This puts this couple on a natural collision course.

Nightingales must overcome their need for immediate conflict resolution. They are warm, open people and there is nothing more satisfying to them than to rehash and resolve disagreements. Making up is half the fun for them. We have to talk, they carol, and they generally intend it to be a long and satisfying exploration of just what happened with each moment of misery described, poked at, and experienced anew.

This is intensely distasteful to the Shelley. Shelleys are unequaled at suffering, but they generally aren't able to share it up front. It is an interior process and too much closeness is suffocating to them. A week or two, or maybe six months later, they'll have the experience in a shape that will enable them to discuss it, but immediate rehashing generally doesn't work for them. It is painfully aversive, and they cringe and feel resentful when it is forced upon them.

Both Nightingales and Shelleys are sensitive, but the sensitivities are so different that there will generally be problems in understanding one another in this area. Nightingale sensitivity is overt. They melt over babies and puppies, they cry easily; they can have hurt feelings in situations beyond the understanding of their spouses. Shelleys feel this lack of restraint to be in poor taste. Often people don't realize they've hurt the feelings of a Shelley until they find that they haven't seen them for two months and begin to wonder why.

Shelleys have a tendency to despise anyone making a scene, even though, at an unhealthy level, they often make them themselves. Nightingales are well advised to make a conscious effort to modify their behavior in this respect. They must understand that just because Shelleys give no dramatic surface indication of pain, it doesn't mean they don't hurt. Shelleys, for their part, should work to develop a greater understanding of the partner's needs and feelings so that they can respond less censoriously to their partner's stronger overt reactions. After all, it is not actually wrong to display greater emotion, simply a different response style.

Shelleys are highly disciplined and self-controlled in dealing with what is important to them. They may have messy desks or messy houses, they may drink with friends until three in the morning, but when they make a decision to do something, unless they are quite unhealthy, they demonstrate a solid inner control. It is hard for them be sympathetic when a Nightingale spouse decides to diet and is discovered eating chocolates two days later. This is an area where Nightingales will need to try harder and Shelleys must learn to be both forgiving and encouraging. They can help by providing structure, *"I know it's hard for you to diet, but let's agree not to have any junk food in the house, so you won't be tempted and let's plan enough stuff to do on the weekend, so you won't be sitting around thinking about food."*

Nightingales have a need to control in relationships. Shelleys have no interest in controlling, but they will fight being controlled with every resource at their disposal. It's important in Nightingale-Shelley relationships for both partners to be aware of these personality interactions.

They will understand what is happening in many of their conflicts if they remain aware of this dynamic. When a Nightingale says, *"We must go to the zoo this weekend,"* or *"We must devote Saturday to this task,"* or *"You really ought to call your mother,"* the Shelley naturally and spontaneously responds, *"Says who?"* The Nightingale needs to learn to suggest without implying a demand, and the Shelley must try to stop experiencing every suggestion as an unwelcome imperative.

Nightingales and Shelleys handle anger differently. Nightingales confront. *"You have done this and this and this to me, and have destroyed me utterly."* seems to the average Nightingale a temperate and rational accusation against a spouse for relatively minor offenses. Some personality types can handle this, *"How you do exaggerate,"* they reply and go about their business. The Nightingale harbors an unrealistic hope that the Shelley will admit to being hopelessly in the wrong, and is thus more completely shattered by the obvious distaste with which the Shelley views their denunciations.

Shelleys have an instinctive desire to avoid confrontation, but they do not simply back away or concede when faced with such an approach, instead they tend to react to an intemperate display of emotion with disdain, so that whatever the original disagreement, it is made considerably worse,

The Shelley desire to avoid confrontation is not a healthy way to handle disagreements either. While it is genuinely difficult for the Shelley to articulate grievances or respond to accusations immediately, there is a method of resolving the impasse. If the Nightingale indicates a need to talk, but a willingness to wait until the Shelley is ready, preferably within a day or so, the resulting dialogue will be more productive and satisfactory to both partners.

GREATEST DANGER SIGNAL: The danger for this relationship comes from the clash of values between the Shelley's need for honesty and authenticity at any cost, and the Nightingale's belief that it is sometimes necessary to tilt or manipulate circumstances or perceptions to create the desired result. The conflict between these belief systems, if unresolved, can leave the partners perceiving each other as a heartless, uncaring monster in the former case, and as a lying scheming manipulator in the latter. Awareness of the difference in value systems and ongoing dialogue about what happens between them can modify the behaviors of both parties to a mutually acceptable degree.

PRIMARY FOCUS: The focus in this marriage should be on emotional understanding and communication. The partners are both sensitive and tend to be emotionally intense but their styles of handling their feelings can cause hurt and anger between them. If both partners focus on honest communication of their feelings and remain willing to understand and accept the contrasting style of the other person, the relationship can prosper.

THE NIGHTINGALE-EINSTEIN RELATIONSHIP

It's four o'clock, Saturday afternoon, and Arthur is at his computer. He's been there since breakfast, apart from a quick sandwich break. Gloria has done some gardening, dealt with the children, gone out to run errands and has now returned to find him still at work.

"Aren't you about ready to stop for the day? It's beautiful out. I'd like to go for a walk."

"Not now. I'm really in the middle of something here," Arthur responds, eyes focused on the screen.

Gloria does not give up. "Would you at least stop long enough to talk to me for a minute?"

"I'll lose my train of thought if I do. Please, Gloria, I'm at an important point. If you just leave me alone now, I'll talk to you in a little while."

"That's all you ever want isn't it, just to be left alone? This isn't a marriage. I'm running a catering service." Gloria responds feeling rejected and imposed upon. "You never give a moment's thought to me or the children.

You should have married a computer, it's the only genuine relationship you're capable of having."

"All right. That does it. You've achieved your objective. You've managed to destroy my train of thought. What's wrong with you, Gloria? If you want to go for a walk, go. If I wanted to go for a walk, and you didn't, I wouldn't pester you."

"Do you know you are totally maddening? You just don't get it, Arthur. I don't want to go for a walk. I want to spend some time with you. I want to feel that you love me and enjoy my company."

"Of course I love you. I wouldn't have married you if didn't."

"Yes, you did do that, but I didn't realize that the day of our wedding was the last one we'd actually spend together. You haven't been there for me since."

The anger and pain in Gloria's voice is inscrutable to Arthur. He does love her and if he thought it would really resolve the situation, he would stop and go for a walk with her. However, since prior experience has taught him that the walk will only be an occasion for further remonstrance on the times he has failed to be with her, he shrugs and returns to his computer, while Gloria leaves the room in tears.

Compared to the stormy confrontations in some other relationships, this may seem low-keyed and none too serious, but the damage in this interaction is cumulative, and, eventually can become pervasive.

Gloria needs to feel loved and cared for to stay psychologically healthy. When she doesn't get enough attention and is not affirmed sufficiently, she feels empty and rejected. If these feelings are not addressed, they will eventually give place to deep-seated rage. If Arthur does not begin to focus on her needs more adequately, he is going to have to cope with more and more unpleasant scenes and with a wife who resorts to scheming and manipulation to achieve her goals.

The safest thing for couples in a Nightingale-Einstein relationship to do is to create a structure that can provide for adequate time for the Einstein to devote to work and projects and for an emotionally acceptable level of interaction and joint time to meet Nightingale needs. This will require compromise on both parts. *"We will go for a walk or find some mutually agreeable joint activity together every Sunday afternoon, but we'll go our separate ways on Saturday,"* or *"We'll devote an hour on Wednesday evening to just spending time together."* The details are irrelevant, but it is important that it be mutually acceptable and pleasant.

That time together is the Einstein contribution to compromise, the Nightingale's compromise consists of understanding that the Einstein needs time and space alone and making a commitment to honor that need.

Nightingales are initially attracted to Einsteins by a mothering impulse, a desire to help someone they perceive as needing to be taken care of. They will socialize them and help them to become more outgoing and self-confident. They may also sew on their buttons and replace their more disreputable old clothes. They will encourage them to enjoy life more. Einsteins sometimes seem in need of parenting, often neglecting to care for themselves, and appearing a bit disheveled. This aspect of their partner touches Nightingales, who want to be needed.

For their part, Einsteins have no objection to having their physical needs met, as long as not much active participation in the process is required. Thus, they are happy to have meals provided, clothes cleaned and pressed, and bills paid, but if the Nightingale moves on to wanting to straighten the papers on the desk, the honeymoon will definitely end abruptly.

Since Einsteins are generally not deeply concerned about initiating social interactions, their part in establishing connections with other couples is likely to consist of agreeing that relationships are theoretically useful and good. They will be happy to participate in them as long as they don't interfere too much with their work or projects.

Problems in this association will evolve around the Nightingale demand for greater intimacy and more time together, and the Einstein proclivity for focusing too extensively on work or other projects and hobbies that exclude a partner.

Another difficulty for the Nightingale is that many Einsteins will be unable to share their emotions as deeply and openly as the Nightingale would like. This is not a conscious choice. They don't know how to do it. They do feel deeply, but they cannot master the rich emotional vocabulary that comes naturally to their partner.

Until Nightingales become healthy, there is an insatiable quality to their personalities. They continually demand more from the relationship. Repeated recriminations on this subject are truly a mistake. Einsteins are good solid citizens, whose commitment to the marriage in practical terms is solid. Einsteins rarely take lovers or go off on drunken binges. Nightingales who can learn to accept them for who they are will find them loyal and committed, trying to change them will only cause damage to the relationship.

Self-controlled Einsteins may not understand the more impulsive aspects of their partners, but generally they do not let that impulsiveness upset them unduly. It may become a problem if Nightingales indulge in buying sprees or set up social occasions without consulting their spouses. In these instances, compromise and setting guide lines for future situations should iron out the difficulties between them. *"After this, I'll remember to check before planning a dinner party, if you will agree that we **can** have dinner parties."*

Nightingales when angry or upset tend to find a release for their feelings in angry confrontations with whoever has upset them. This does not provide much satisfaction in this case. Unhealthy Einsteins may respond with paranoia believing that their partners are purposely destroying their lives, while those who are healthy will probably label the partner as hysterical and totally disregard what is said. Nightingales would be well advised to wait until they have cooled down and can speak quietly and rationally about what is upsetting them if they want to be taken seriously.

Sexual problems in the relationship are most likely to occur when Nightingales seek reassurance of their love and worth through sex, once again the Einstein response is likely to be rated inadequately demonstrative. Einsteins need to try harder. It is acceptable to ask partners for some direction in how to meet their sexual needs more fully. Loving tactful phrasing is crucial when doing this, lest the partner hear: *"Anything for a peaceful life, just tell me what to do."*

This couple approach childcare from almost diametrically opposite points of view. Nightingales often seem to care too much for their children, doing things for them that they are capable of doing for themselves, supervising them too closely, and becoming over involved in their lives.

Einsteins love their children, but give the impression that they would be just as happy if they lived somewhere else. If both partners can accept these as unhealthy extremes, and attempt to modify their positions, stepping back from over involvement and working on connection, respectively, everyone in the family will profit. The greatest obstacle to creating balance is that often over-involved Nightingales believe they are behaving appropriately and, instead of stepping back, attempt to push Einsteins to their relatively intense level of interaction. Both partners need to be aware of their natural inclinations and work toward moving in a more moderate direction.

Average Nightingales are innately expansive and usually express this trait through wanting more of those good things they value: more food, more clothes, more jewelry, and more vacations. Average Einsteins are innately fiscally conservative, desiring to keep what they own, old sweaters, old furniture, and hard-earned money. These opposing traits can create misunderstanding and conflict.

In this area, as in childcare, it is necessary that both partners recognize that they represent extremes, and attempt to move toward reasonable compromises. One approach is to take turns in financial choices: *"We'll go camping in a National Park this year, and then next year, we'll go* to Italy." If this is a major problem, a financial counselor may be able to help chart a middle course.

GREATEST DANGER SIGNAL: When the Nightingale is increasingly vociferous about feelings of rejection and abandonment, and the Einstein has withdrawn from the family and started to regard the partner as an enemy, the relationship is in serious trouble. Professional help will probably be necessary to bring both partners back from the brink.

PRIMARY FOCUS: The focus here must be on keeping the relationship balanced. It is easy for the Nightingale partner to assume a caretaking role, which can result in the creation of a parent-child dynamic between the couple. Nightingales need to remember that both family and relationship needs are joint responsibilities, while Einsteins must guard against the inclination to totally cede responsibility for daily family life to their partners.

THE NIGHTINGALE-AUSTEN RELATIONSHIP

When Martin and Jane first married, Jane had several close friends that she went out with for the evening on a regular basis. She also belonged to a bridge club that met one evening a month. At first after their marriage, Jane tried to make regular plans with other couples, either inviting them to dinner, or planning a night out. Soon Martin began to have a problem with one couple. He didn't get along with the woman and found her abrasive. Finally he said he'd rather not see them any more, he just didn't feel comfortable with them. A few months later, he started to have difficulties with a second couple for a different reason. He then told Jane that he really hated having the bridge club meet at their house. He felt like an outcast in his own home when all those people came over.

Jane was extremely understanding about Martin's problems with her friends. She was deeply in love, and didn't want to do anything that would make her husband uncomfortable. It was only after two years of marriage, when Martin began to complain of the last friend she still saw regularly, her old college roommate, that she looked back and realized that he had systematically eliminated from her life everyone that she knew before they were married and that they spent very little time socializing with anyone outside of work hours.

When she became aware of this, Jane began to reach out and attempt to reestablish some of the relationships that she had neglected and discouraged. She didn't ask Martin to participate, but felt that she could at least meet friends for lunch or go out with them occasionally. She and Martin were spending all their free time together and it was becoming claustrophobic.

When she told Martin that she would be out one evening to meet an old friend, she was surprised at his negative reaction. "I know you don't like her, but I do and I thought that if I met her without involving you, it would be all right."

"What am I supposed to do for the evening? Sit home and twiddle my fingers? If we're married, I think it means that we should try to have a social life together, not just go off our separate ways."

"I suppose so, but you don't like any of my friends. Where does that leave me? I can't have a social life with you if you don't want to go anyplace with anyone."

Jane had zeroed in on the problem. Many average Nightingales don't like to share their partners with the rest of the world. They can be jealous of friends, family, even their own children. In a Nightingale-Austen relationship, the Nightingale is almost always the dominant partner, and tends to enforce this isolation upon the sociable Austen successfully for a time. Eventually, the Austen begins to experience the constant togetherness as oppressive. But Nightingales vociferously oppose any modification of this situation.

When Nightingales and Austens become self-observant, they can be aware of what is happening and talk about it. Martin needs to realize that the real fault he sees in Jane's friends is that they take her attention away from him. He must work to come to terms with the fact that Jane loves him, and that he comes first with her, but that, paradoxically, he will be less able to keep her love if he can not agree to share some of her affection and attention with others. The intimacy that feels so warm and comforting to him can be stifling to other people. Jane can help him with this by realizing that it is difficult for him and by giving him ample reassurance of her love and support.

Jane must learn to set limits on Martin's behavior. It is important for the relationship that she stop Martin from dominating her and making her decisions for her. Learning to say no is hard for Austen personalities, and particularly hard if the person they love is easily hurt. As Jane asserts herself more regularly, however, it will become much easier for her and Martin will begin to accept her standing up for herself with better grace.

Nightingales find that Austens try very hard to please anyone they care about and this helps the Nightingale to feel secure. Nightingales like to take care of people and this meets a willing recipient in the average Austen who can feel safe in this relationship. Both personalities like to talk at some length and use long conversations to cement relationships. Nightingales and Austens can stay up for hours engaged in deep emotional conversations.

The insatiable needs of the average Nightingale for love and reassurance, and the strong desire to comply with the loved one's desires, of the average Austen are likely to create problems in the relationship. Average Nightingales make powerful demands on their partners in terms of allegiance, exclusivity and responsiveness. *Show me that you love me* is a recurrent plea based on a recurrent need. Average Austens are unlikely to set the limits on this behavior that other personalities might. Instead, they respond to their partners demands well past the bounds of any reasonable expectation. Then when they finally find themselves in an untenable position, they feel taken advantage of and rebel. By the time this happens, however, the relationship may have been substantially damaged.

NIGHTINGALE-MOZART RELATIONSHIPS

Bruce, the Mozart, announces at the breakfast table that he will be going bowling with some friends from the office after work that evening. Gloria feels immediate pain and anger. "You were out last night, don't you ever want to stay home with me? What time will you get back?"

In an attempt at appeasement, Bruce says he'll be home early. The bowling is over by 9:00. I should be home by 9:30 at the latest." This is extremely unlikely and Gloria challenges the estimate, based on her previous experience of Bruce's nights out. In an attempt to end the confrontation, Bruce assures her that this time it will be different.

Bruce is coaxed by his friends to stop for a few beers after bowling and comes home slightly high at 11:30. Gloria is furious and the ensuing argument keeps them up for another hour. Gloria's accusation can be summarized as: "You never want to be home with me. You obviously don't love me. You're totally irresponsible." Bruce makes the usual predictable response, "I was home all day on Sunday. Of course I love you. The time just got away from me. I'm sorry."

The next morning Bruce is feeling a bit sheepish and is afraid to mention the fact that he has a civic association meeting to go to that night, so he says nothing. Gloria hopes that she has made some impact on him the night before and is willing to be pleasant at breakfast. The morning goes well for both of them.

After work, Bruce hurries home to find that Gloria has gotten there ahead of him and is preparing an elaborate meal. "Gee that looks wonderful. Only I need to eat fast. I have this meeting downtown at 7:30. Can you put this in the refrigerator for tomorrow and I'll run out and get us a pizza tonight?"

The ensuing argument is carried on at the top of Gloria's lungs, and Bruce escapes half way through it. He has a pizza on his way to the meeting and afterwards, knowing that he faces more recrimination if he goes home, purposely stops at a friend's house until he believes Gloria will be

The Austen's desire to please others is acceptable to Nightingale partners when focused on them. However, when the Austen tries too hard to please the next door neighbor, the boss, or the children's teachers, the Nightingale can become quite censorious. Nightingales simply don't see why anyone would do this and rightly perceive it as unhealthy behavior. The Nightingale response, however, is based much more on jealousy and a desire to be the sole focus of the partner's attention than on any objective appraisal of this dynamic.

Austens grow by letting go of the inordinate need to please others. It is important that they do this with their partners as well as the outside world. The result of constant striving to please at the expense of their own needs is that eventually the pleaser begins to feel that their partner is taking advantage of them and naturally begins to resent this; unconscious anger then surfaces in a variety of small irritating ways that can undermine relationships.

Average Nightingales tend to be controlling. At the beginning of the relationship, this may meet the dependency needs of Austens and be perceived as caring and loving. However, in a long-term relationship, the Nightingale will need to work on curbing this need to make all the decisions. While this tendency is pervasive in Nightingale-Austen relationships, it is particularly likely to create problems in raising children. Nightingales love their children, and tend to be highly opinionated about appropriate child care techniques and responses. Do what I do is their demand which covers food, discipline, entertainment, and even how to respond in conversations with the children. Nightingales and Austens are both loving parents and both do well in handling young children. It is important for both partners to realize that there is no single correct response in terms of parenting and that being a loving, caring parent is quite adequate, even if the details of expressing this love are different for different people.

The larger problem for Nightingales tends to occur when the children become older. Because Nightingales have such intense needs for love, they often encourage dependency in their children. This is a huge mistake and can backfire very badly, either by making the children fearful and dependent, or by causing them to rebel and withdraw from family life. It is important for Nightingales to be in touch with any tendencies they may have to do this and to control them. The Austen partner can help by reminding them of the problem in a diplomatic manner when they see it occurring.

At an average level of emotional health, both Nightingales and Austens have a tendency to be untruthful at times. The Nightingale does it to control in situations where they have a vested interest in the outcome. Austens tend to say that those things they want to be true are true. Their view of what is happening has an element of fantasy in it as if all their daydreams were the reality.

The difference in the two approaches is informative. A Nightingale might neglect to tell the partner about a friend's telephone call in an attempt to discourage the relationship, possibly even feeling justified in doing so, rationalizing that the partner does not really like that person anymore anyway and simply doesn't have the strength of mind to put an end to the relationship on their own. Austens would never do this, and would be very angry if they found out it had been done to them, but they might give a substantially inaccurate report of a quarrel and firmly maintain their perception of the occurance to the total frustration of the partner. The Austen would be unconsciously doing a rewrite of the interaction to make it go the way they wanted it to. Clearly both kinds of dishonesty are counterproductive in relationships and anyone with either of these behaviors should focus on working to overcome them.

The expression of anger can be a significant problem between Nightingales and Austens. Average Nightingales can become intensely angry and confrontational, sometimes over relatively minor issues that don't go their way. This can be extremely frightening and intimidating to the average Austen who will often try unsuccessfully to placate the

partner's rage. Both for the sake of the relationship and for their o growth and mental health, Nightingales must learn to control t anger and become more philosophical, accepting the reality that th cannot always go the way they would like them to. When their pa does express anger irrationally, average Austens must remembe this rage is very much like a child's tantrum and should be respon in the same way. The attempt to placate is doomed and only enc this behavior by rewarding it. The Austen must learn to say, "W *are ready to talk about this, I'll be happy to discuss it, but I won't at," and* then to leave the room or, if necessary, the house.

GREATEST DANGER SIGNAL: The danger in this relat that the balance of power will become uneven. Austens who d frontation can fear the anger of the Nightingale and becom tory and superficially obliging, even over issues on whic strongly. The Nightingale, in this situation, can become uneven partnership serves neither of them well. Auste emerge in passive aggressive behavior, which is much mo to live with than a contrary opinion or choice, while Nig tration with passive aggression can easily move from sim to outright rage.

PRIMARY FOCUS: Honesty should become a prima ing this relationship to grow. Nightingales can restr achieve their goals or to show themselves in the be Austens tend to use day-dreaming and denial in e They state as achievements those things which are r hopes and deny aspects of their lives which they feel to some idealistic standard. The relationship will pretenses are dropped and both partners begin thoughts, perceptions and feelings openly and even for the best of reasons.

Gloria is not in bed. The argument is heated and unproductive. The next morning, Gloria is still angry and there is silence at the breakfast table. Bruce mentions that he'll be home right after work, to which she responds that she may not be there.

Bruce takes her at her word. Since she says she's not going to be home, he agrees to go out to a movie with some friends, despite knowing on some level, that Gloria is bluffing. She sits home through the evening getting angrier every moment, but also worrying that something terrible might have happened to him as he distinctly said he was coming home.

The dynamics of this interchange are apparent. Bruce is casting himself in the role of the bad little boy, defying his mother and behaving irresponsibly, as a method of establishing some autonomy in his marriage.

There is an underlying assumption on the part of both partners that Gloria, the Nightingale, is within her rights in attempting to control Bruce's schedule, and that her analysis of the interaction is the correct one. However, while Gloria is allowed to consider herself right, she is not allowed to get what she wants, Bruce's attention and company. Bruce doesn't mind being termed "bad", and sometimes rather enjoys the role, while he continues to do as he wishes. The level of anger between them, if they do not create change, will soon destroy all their love and respect for each other.

Change can only occur in this relationship as both partners grow in insight. Bruce must come to terms with his constant need for more stimulation and fresh experiences. His upbeat personality and whole-hearted enjoyment of life are fine traits, but they must be balanced by the realization that sometimes pleasure must be postponed; and that the happiness inherent in a good marriage will produce more real joy over time than the transient good time that he must forego on occasion.

Gloria, for her part, needs to differentiate between the roles of wife and mother. Her attempts to control and make decisions, to rein Bruce in, have the opposite effect. The more she tries to limit him, the more he tries to escape her control and elude her limits.

For this couple, a contract based on mutual needs, may be a sensible way to proceed. Gloria may really need at least three nights a week when they can be home alone together or go out to dinner or a movie alone. She requires this on a gut level to be assured that Bruce loves her and that even with all his activities and friendships, he does honestly place her and the marriage first in his life.

Bruce may need the assurance that he can participate in up to three activities a week without being open to recrimination and sulking at home. It may also be important to Gloria to see Bruce's weekly schedule at the beginning of the week, so that she can make some plans for herself if she chooses to. Both partners need to agree that their plans are not engraved in stone. If occasionally things really pile up for Bruce, he needs to know that he may be able to take another night out as long as he doesn't take advantage of this flexibility, squeezing out an extra night every week. Gloria should have the assurance that if things are going really badly for her some week and she asks for some additional time together, that he can be sensitive to her need.

With this type of understanding in place, most of the scenes like the one depicted would simply never occur. Bruce would take his nights out for bowling and the community meeting without experiencing recrimination and since he could be honest and up front about what he was doing, the misunderstanding, deception, and hurt feelings would be avoided.

This will be hard for Nightingales, who will feel that such a compromise does not meet their needs sufficiently. However, it is an opportunity for genuine emotional growth. If the Nightingale can begin to accept the fact that all of one's needs will not be met by the partner in the relationship, the next step will be to begin taking responsibility for meeting those needs in other ways. Average Nightingales believe that their partners have the obligation to make them happy and fulfilled, and as they turn inward and look for that fulfillment within themselves, they become healthier, more attractive people.

The compromise, which this contract represents, is just as difficult for average Mozarts. It requires them to sometimes say no to amusement, to the impulse of the moment, to friends. But this is equally an occasion for Mozarts to experience some emotional growth. As Mozarts develop impulse control and acknowledge that they have some responsibility toward those people who they claim are important to them, they will become more solid and substantial people. They will find that the long-term pleasures inherent in a good marital relationship are deeper and more truly fulfilling than the satisfaction of each ephemeral impulse could ever be.

This specific contract is not the answer for every Nightingale-Mozart interaction and it will be necessary for couples in this relationship to sit down together and honestly discuss their needs to come up with the compromises that will work for them. However, if both people are absolutely honest in differentiating between what they would like and what is bottom line necessity, then compromise can be found in almost any situation. The couple can become locked in a mutual desire to triumph at the others expense, if the Nightingale says: *"I need to have you home every night and I also need to know that I have unlimited buying power."* and the Mozart replies, *" I need to be out six nights a week and to take a separate vacation.* Such a triumph, if either of them brings it off, will be made at the cost of the marriage.

These personalities have much in common. Both are doers, enjoying a great variety of activities. Both have relatively high energy levels. But while the Mozart seeks new experiences, more and different kinds of stimulation, the Nightingale wants togetherness, closeness, and intimacy with the partner.

The Nightingale needs the love of the Mozart partner and experiences the partner's absence or friendly interest in other people and activities as rejection and lack of love. The Mozart feels oppressed and stifled by the Nightingale demand for closeness, often specifically a desire to be alone together, and responds by staying away more; sometimes starting a new relationship in an attempt to get away from the Nightingale's tenacious grasp and multiple demands.

When Nightingale personalities at the average level feel frustrated, they become angry and manipulative. They can act in blatantly dishonest ways in an attempt to achieve their goals, believing that their needs are reasonable, and that this excuses whatever they may do in order to attain the desired result. If the manipulative behavior is seen through or uncovered by the partner, it contributes substantially to the further degeneration of the relationship.

GREATEST DANGER SIGNAL: The danger for this marriage is that it could easily become a parent-child relationship with the Nightingale scolding and remonstrating with the naughty child Mozart. This dynamic is not good for either partner. It may be necessary to seek professional help to create the necessary change in the relationship.

PRIMARY FOCUS: Spending quality time together should be the focus of this relationship. It is very easy for the Nightingale to complain, demand and remonstrate with a partner in an effort to gain greater compliance with his or her needs. It is equally easy for the Mozart to look upon time alone with the partner as "down time" before the next fun event. It is important that the couple make a strong effort to make their time together meaningful and pleasant.

THE NIGHTINGALE-CAESAR RELATIONSHIP

Bob and Gloria are planning to go on vacation to the Caribbean. When Gloria volunteers to call the travel agent and arrange for flights and the hotel, Bob astonishes her with the information that he's already booked the flights. "How could you if we just decided?" I knew you'd like my idea, so I went ahead and booked it. It's more romantic that way, isn't it? I thought you'd like it."

Slightly dubious, but won over by the appeal to romance, Gloria agrees. "And the hotel, what hotel did you book?"

"I didn't. You can never really tell from brochures, I figured we'd wait until we got there and check them out before we chose one."

Gloria is appalled. "You can't do that. All the rooms will be taken. You have to book weeks in advance. Everybody knows that."

"We've been through this before Gloria. Remember when we went to Cape Cod and you wanted to book ahead. Remember the great place I found?"

"I remember we spent the first three hours of our vacation looking for a room."

"But it was worth it. I got us a great place. Trust me."

Gloria does not trust him, and after worrying about it for several days, calls the travel agent and surreptitiously books a hotel.

The rest of the scenario is predictable whether Bob actually finds a room when they arrive or not. He is furious at her duplicity. They barely speak to each other for the entire vacation and both vow never to go on vacation with the other again.

Bob, as a Caesar, believes he has a near omnipotent ability to see that his needs are met, but if he had more insight and less of a penchant for control, he would never have devised this arrangement. Gloria had an indication that Bob's power drive was somewhat out of control when he made the plane reservations without consulting her. Bob knows he can sometimes get around her by using a romantic appeal and she allowed herself to be swayed by him. Certainly, when he said he would not make reservations, she needed to set some limit on his grandiosity.

As Bob becomes healthier, he will be aware of his desire to take total control and acknowledge that it is an unreasonable position. He will understand that while taking chances and then getting things to come out right is a great game to him, it is not perceived in that light by Gloria and really does cause her great anxiety.

Emotional health for Gloria consists in learning to fight fairly, giving up her practice of doing things behind Bob's back. If she doesn't agree with him about something, she must learn to tell him so, and to abandon manipulation as a tool for control. Both partners need to learn to compromise.

Caesars know what they want and focus on getting it. They are direct and forthright and they don't spend much time worrying about their images or other people's reactions to them. What people think of them if they go after what they want is the least of their worries. This is a refreshing stance for the Nightingale personality, perennially craving love and validation from others. When creating a relationship is at the top of the agenda, the Caesar can be extremely centered on winning the partner's affections. The Nightingale, as the focus of these attentions, will find the thoughtfulness and concern irresistible.

Caesars find the Nightingale sensitivity, warmth and caring, attractive. They sense Nightingale unhappiness and are gratified by their own ability to quiet some of that pain. They can be the alter ego for the Nightingale, stepping into the role of defender and protector. *"I won't let them hurt you anymore,"* says the Caesar, and the Nightingale responds, *"My hero."*

What could possibly cloud such a fairy tale romance? The pleasure for Caesars is partly in the conquest, and once the honeymoon is over, it's time to move on, there are new fields to conquer. Suddenly, the Nightingale is alone and hurting again, feeling abandoned and unloved. *"Why aren't you there for me like you were?"* is the increasingly despairing Nightingale plaint. The Caesar, who understands courtship as a time-limited activity with a beginning and end, is likely to be unsympathetic. *"I am there, but we're married, and I have other things to do now. Leave me alone,"* is likely to be the Caesar response.

Control is a major problem in the Nightingale-Caesar relationship. Caesars are overt controllers, wanting things their way and tolerating little disagreement in anything that matters to them. Nightingales are equally dedicated to having things their way, but do so by indirection, manipulating and behaving quite deviously, if they are emotionally unhealthy. Clashes between Caesars, who discover they have been manipulated and Nightingales, who were only trying to help, can create major marital damage.

Nightingales are very sensitive; Caesars are not. Nightingales are often deeply upset over Caesar words and actions. Caesars all too often are either oblivious or mocking when they encounter their partner's misery, seeing it as over-emotionalism and self-pity.

In a healthy relationship, both partners will realize that they are at opposite ends of a continuum and that healthy responses are somewhere in the middle. Nightingales need to be aware that they can be too sensitive and too easily hurt and make conscious efforts to toughen up a bit and not take minor upsets or slights so seriously. Caesars need to become aware of their lack of sensitivity and try to respond more sympathetically to those around them. Role-playing can be helpful for both partners in this context. If the Caesar acts the part of the Nightingale and tries to feel the pain and hurt, while the Nightingale attempts to experience the Caesar drive to do what needs doing, to focus on immediate objectives, both partners will come to a healthier understanding of the other's needs.

The Nightingale need for approval and validation can run squarely in the face of Caesar needs to get what they want or to get the job done. Nightingales can be reduced to tears when the Caesar gives the impression of being oblivious to the feelings of the people around them. *"How could you act that way? Didn't you see what he must have thought? Don't you realize that you embarrassed her?"* These Nightingale refrains fall on relatively stony ground with Caesars.

In truth, not everyone is as sensitive as the Nightingale and probably sometimes when Nightingales are humiliated by what others must think, others have thought nothing of it. However, there are also times when Caesar insensitivity is genuinely inappropriate. Again, both partners must strive to move toward a middle ground. Caesars need to monitor themselves more closely, particularly in those areas that are most upsetting to their partners, while Nightingales must try to get a sense of proportion about just how horrifying Caesar words or actions really are to those around them.

Both Nightingales and Caesars can be quite confrontational and they will probably have some quite spectacular battles. The problem is that neither average Nightingales nor Caesars feel constrained to fight fairly and both will do just about anything to win. In the heat of battle, both are likely to aim for maximum damage to the other. Healthy behavior for both entails monitoring what they say in anger and learning to involve the head as well as the gut in confrontation.

Calling time out when things begin to get out of hand is an excellent idea in this relationship. The agreement that either can call for a cooling off period when the argument begins to get out of hand will be beneficial. Another tactic that can be helpful is written communication. It is very hard for Nightingales and Caesars to hear each other in the midst of a conflict. It is sometimes useful for both parties to write out their positions in a disagreement and then sit down and read what the other has to say, this strategy can remove some of the emotional heat from the disagreement and allow more rational considerations to be entertained.

Sexual needs can be an area of disharmony due to differing perceptions of what constitutes good sex. Caesars tend to have high sex drives, but are often unwilling to devote the same amount of time and romantic interaction to the interlude as the Nightingale. In this instance, both partners needs will be better satisfied in their love making, if they can talk outside the bedroom about what they find arousing and how to satisfy each other. Caesars who can fulfill the romantic expectations of their Nightingale spouses will discover that they are improving their own sex lives as well, by gaining a more interested and responsive partner.

Both Nightingales and Caesars are loving, concerned parents. Their styles are markedly different. Caesars like to roughhouse with young children, and are likely to demand that older children face challenges and roll with the punches. Nightingales are more likely to be protective, often overprotective. Thus, when a three year old takes a tumble, the Caesar will typically say, *"Jump up, you're okay,"* while the Nightingale runs forward to comfort the child. Caesars expect schoolyard fights and rough play; Nightingales are often uncomfortable with it. Once again, if they both work toward a central position away from either extreme, the children will benefit.

Unfortunately, both parents tend to be controlling. The Caesar can be an overt authoritarian, with a *"do it because I say so"* attitude. The Nightingale can be equally arbitrary, but can also use manipulation and guilt to control. *"If you love me, you won't ever do that again."* Obviously, both of these stances are misguided. Children thrive and become independent and capable as they are given choices, and have their opinions and needs respected. Both partners want this for their children, and it is a matter of becoming more aware of those hidden motivations in their own personalities which put them at odds with their ultimate parental goals. If both partners remain aware of their needs to control, they will be able, to help themselves and each other to moderate their positions in this regard.

Average Caesars sometimes seek partners outside the marital relationship. While most people find this behavior unacceptable, it is particularly hard on the Nightingale. If this is a problem in the relationship, it is important that it be faced honestly and immediately and that professional help be sought. This is particularly important to the Nightingale, who sometimes tries to make the best of a bad situation, and wait for it to pass. Things will get worse, not better. If your partner will not come with you, seek a therapist for yourself.

GREATEST DANGER SIGNAL: The escalation of quarrels is the greatest danger to this relationship. Both partners enjoy confrontation on some level. The Caesar often takes pleasure in conflict engagement for its own sake. The competitive aspect is fun and a Caesar can unconsciously begin to utilize game-like strategies of conflict in a marriage. The Nightingale, while genuinely suffering, can, at the same time, revel in the drama implicit in such situations. Both partners should be aware of the serious consequences of this behavior and make a joint effort to move from confrontation to discussion and compromise in their approach to conflict resolution.

PRIMARY FOCUS: Spending quality time together is the primary focus for keeping this relationship on track. Both partners can be good company and like to have fun. If they do things they both enjoy together on a regular basis, it will provide the glue to keep them together through the difficult times and problems.

THE NIGHTINGALE-GAUGUIN RELATIONSHIP

Linda loves to ski and prior to her marriage tried to spend three or four weekends skiing every winter. When she and Martin started seeing each other, he overwhelmed her with his attentions, and she let her enthusiasm for the sport wane temporarily. However by the time they entered their second year of marriage, she was ready to head back to the slopes.

The first time she suggested to Martin that they go to a ski lodge for a week-end, he agreed, but he found that he did not enjoy the sport and resented being left on the beginner's slope while Linda was off on more advanced trails. He also resented her camaraderie with the other skiers and still felt left out by her at the end of the day as she talked and laughed with the others in the lounge.

When they returned home, he announced that skiing was not for him and he was never going again. Linda accepted this readily. But in a few weeks, she announced that she was planning to go on a day skiing trip with some old friends the following weekend. To her surprise, Martin exploded, "You mean you're going to leave me home alone all day Saturday?"

"Yes. What's wrong with that?"

"Well it's not my idea of a marriage, spending the week-end by yourself."

"Come on, Martin, it's not the week-end, it's a day. I'll be back in time for dinner."

"I don't think you should go. You know I hate to be left alone all day. And what's more, I don't like the people you're going with."

Linda feels bad that Martin is unhappy, but she does go. She has a good time and once she's away from the house, she doesn't think anything more about Martin and his demands. It comes as a surprise to her that when she gets home, that Martin is in a foul mood, he barely speaks to her and is still angry and miserable the following day.

The repercussions of her day out keep Linda home for almost a month, but her friends continue to urge her to come with them, and she finally agrees.

The earlier scene is intensified this time, and has an added component. Martin accuses her of being romantically involved with one of the other men in the group. Linda denies this heatedly and then puts it out of her mind as a momentary aberration. It is not. The more Martin thinks about it, the greater is his certainty that this is the case. When she gets home, he is hysterically angry and rages at her in a way that she finds frightening. At this point, she decides that her pleasure in skiing is not worth the scenes and promises Martin she won't go anymore.

On the surface, since Linda, the Gauguin feels unable to continue meeting her friends, Martin seems to have achieved his goal, but their relationship is permanently damaged by this interaction.

Martin needs help with his possessive feelings and in this instance, marital counseling would seem the obvious step toward improving the marriage. Linda tends to ignore Martin's anger until he forces her to pay attention, and then to acquiesce in order to have peace and quiet. Martin needs to confront and overcome his unfounded fears and to understand that the type of togetherness that appeals to him is unlikely to be acceptable to most partners.

As Martin grows healthier, he will learn to control his jealousy and to accept Linda's need for friends in her life. He will cultivate friendships of his own and learn to accept her friends rather than believing himself threatened by them.

Linda needs to learn to listen to Martin, even when he is saying something she doesn't want to hear. When she brushes aside his complaints without giving them adequate thought and attention, she reinforces his fear that she doesn't love him very much. It is reasonable for her to set limits on his demands for total mutual involvement, but it is necessary that she set those limits within the context of a conversation where she reassures him that she does love him and that his needs are important to her.

Nightingales are attracted to Gauguins by their kindness, gentleness and generally pleasant dispositions. Gauguins find Nightingales attractive because they care about them and the easy-going Gauguin generally likes everyone, waiting to be chosen, rather than initiating any action. Thus, Nightingales generally take the initiative in establishing this relationship. Problems occur when Nightingales begin to feel that they aren't getting sufficient payback in terms of love, caring and attention. This personality, at an average level, is often jealous and possessive, resenting the partner's friends and preferring an exclusive one-on-one relationship. This often extends beyond old friends to activities the partner enjoyed before marriage. Then if the partner fails to comply with their demands for full time togetherness, they experience themselves as rejected. Gauguins hate scenes and confrontations and when their Nightingale partners become tearful, emotional or angry, they tend to withdraw. This intensifies the Nightingales feelings of rejection and abandonment and makes matters still worse.

Nightingales are overtly sensitive people. They laugh and cry readily. They leave you in no doubt of their current emotional state. Gauguins find overt displays of emotion uncomfortable. They would rather not talk or even think about the things that bother them. In a

Nightingale-Gauguin relationship, Gauguins instinctively withdraw when they feel an emotional storm on the horizon. They must learn to curb this impulse and to stand by their partners when they are upset. Being present does not mean that they must endorse Nightingale perceptions of a situation. In fact, only by listening and staying with Nightingale partners can Gauguins present a calmer more balanced perspective on whatever has upset the Nightingale.

Nightingales need to learn to create some distance from their feelings when they become overwhelmed by their emotions. It seems natural to Nightingales to affirm and justify their feelings of anger, deprivation or rejection. The problem that occurs when they do this is that it tends to increase their emotional reactivity making things seem even worse. As they become healthier, Nightingales learn to talk to themselves in ways that lessen rather than increasing their pain and anger.

Nightingales want to be emotionally close to those they love. They would like to share their lives in every possible way. While Gauguins will generally agree to do this verbally, their ability to actually share their feelings and emotions is likely to be limited by their inherent reticence. If both partners are aware of this personality difference, it is less likely to cause friction between them. Nightingales must accept the Gauguin limit when it comes to the expression of emotions, while Gauguins can work on stretching that limit for themselves in order to reassure and please their mates.

Dealing with confrontation can be a major problem in this marriage. Most Nightingales would claim to hate showdowns and angry quarrels as a method of problem solving and they appear honestly miserable when fights develop, but they rarely shirk a confrontation with their partners when an issue occurs. Gauguins hate arguing and they will go to considerable lengths to avoid it. The relationship can suffer from this discrepancy in tolerance level, since when Gauguins are repeatedly forced into arguments, they become resentful and evasive as they attempt to appease and avoid the anger that comes so easily to their

Nightingale mates. If there is too much confrontation for them to handle, they will begin to withdraw into themselves more and more. Nightingales view the Gauguin refusal to fight as rejection and a lack of commitment to the marriage. When the partner starts to withdraw from confrontations in self-protection, the Nightingale is likely to feel abandoned.

In a good Nightingale-Gauguin relationship, both partners will work to minimize the gap. The Nightingale will attempt to become less agitated during disagreements and to keep emotions in check, while the Gauguin will be aware that the tendency to back off and avoid conflict is not constructive and will stay with the discussion. Nightingales will still be stronger and more persistent in conflicts. They need to remember that if they win every argument hands down, they are going to pay a heavy price for their transitory triumphs.

There is often a difference in energy level in this marriage. Nightingales are energetic go-getters who have ample stamina for the tasks they set themselves. Gauguins seldom set themselves tasks, so the issue arises when Nightingale projects require Gauguin involvement. The main question that Nightingales must ask in this circumstance is whether the chore is a necessary one. *"We're moving in two weeks and we won't be ready unless you help with the packing"* or an arbitrary desire that poses no real urgency *"It would be nice to clean out the garage".*

When the task is truly necessary, Nightingales should first get the Gauguin's agreement that it does have to be done and that the couple will have to do it and then get further agreement on when, what, and where. Gauguins who say yes to a general plan will not inevitably then begin to pull their weight. *"It should take about four hours to get the books and your clothes sorted and packed, could we agree that we'll both devote an hour a night after dinner to this?"* is a better ploy than *"Will you be responsible for packing the books and your clothes?"*

When the chore is an arbitrarily chosen one, Nightingales will probably be happier in the end if they acknowledge that the price of their partners involvement is too high and do what they want done themselves.

In their relationship with their children, average Nightingales tend to be overly controlling. They tend to encourage their children to depend on them and to view too much self-reliance as defiance or rejection. Average Gauguins are likely to accept the Nightingale definition of what constitutes appropriate parenting in general, but not to see what the fuss is about in terms of daily issues. This leaves the Nightingale essentially in charge.

Nightingales assume this role easily, but find that as sole disciplinarians, their children often see them as the bad guys. It is natural to resent this situation. The solution lies in involving Gauguins in broader discussions of childcare issues and listening to and discussing their beliefs and feelings. Gauguins who believe that homework is the child's responsibility may well refuse to become involved in a battle over whether homework must be finished before dinner.

As Nightingales become healthier, they become less controlling and intrusive in their children's lives. Working to modify a need to control is a big step toward greater emotional well being for Nightingales.

Gauguins become healthier as they assume a greater degree of involvement in the day to day issues of child care and participate in limit setting, which is, after all, a necessary component of parenting.

Many Nightingales and Gauguins have a potential for addictions. If this is a problem in the relationship, it is important to recognize it and get help. Optimally, both partners will seek help if there is an addiction problem, but if the addictive partner refuses to participate, it is important for the other person to seek the support of one of the self-help groups such as Al-Anon or to seek help through individual therapy.

GREATEST DANGER SIGNAL: An imbalance of power is the greatest danger to this couple. When one partner is able to dominate a relationship consistently, it is inevitable that the other person will become increasingly resentful and passive-aggressive. This is more insidious because it can occur without either party having a conscious awareness of what is happening. It is easy for the high energy, active Nightingale to take the lead in making choices and suggesting things that need to be done. It is up to both partners to be aware that whoever suggests a plan, strategy, or project; full discussion and mutual agreement must precede its implementation.

PRIMARY FOCUS: Achieving a balance in their needs for emotional intimacy is the primary goal for this couple. It is important for both of them. It is always an issue for the Nightingale, who cannot experience full emotional well being without the sense of being deeply loved. A degree of effort and focus is always necessary to create such involvement, and this does not come easily to the Gauguin, but it will be worth doing, since it will result in a mutual experience of gratification and well-being for both partners

VI

The Beau in Relationships

For the Beau-Emerson Relationship—Go to the Emerson-Beau Relationship
For the Beau-Nightingale Relationship—Go to the Nightingale-Beau Relationship.

THE BEAU-BEAU RELATIONSHIP

George and Joan both have good jobs and a reasonable amount of discretionary income. They are thinking about buying a new house and haven't done so only because they cannot agree on the location. George has his heart set on something in the country, two or three acres preferably. To find a house that they could afford with that much land would mean looking for something about 45 minutes from the city where they both work. Joan is adamant in declaring that this would impose undue hardship on her and she is simply unwilling to consider it. She would also like to move, but her choice is a house in an older section of the city that has been rediscovered by young professionals. George feels there is not much benefit in moving at all if they are going to stay in the city, He is skeptical of the

155

advantages of refurbished housing and wants something with the latest in bathrooms and kitchens that doesn't require extensive remodeling.

They have been stuck on this issue for the past six months and neither of them has been willing to compromise. Both are holding on to their anger at the intransigence of the other and this unresolved issue is brought in to any other disagreements they may have.

Now another matter has presented itself. Joan has been offered a position as a trainer with her organization. This is a promotion, but it is going to require extensive travel and may compel her to be away from home on an unspecified number of weekends. They have always done extensive entertaining, much of it in connection with George's business. George is seriously concerned about how this promotion will interfere with his need for a hostess and is opposed to her accepting the offer.

Joan is furious. "You are so selfish and self-centered, I can't believe it. You are perfectly willing to impede my career so that I can play the little wife with your business associates. It is incredible to me that you have the gall to state such a position, let alone maintain it."

"It's important to me, Joan. We have to make decisions like this based on the total picture. You never were much of a team player."

"Look who's talking. You don't know the meaning of the word. If the situation were reversed, you wouldn't even consult me."

"The situation couldn't be reversed, you don't happen to have a career that requires outside entertaining, I do. This is a minor promotion for you, but it could have a major effect on me and on our future. You're the one who's selfish and self-centered. This is just another example."

"Another example of what? It's another example of you down playing my career while you boost yours."

"It's the same as trying to find a house. You get fixated on what you want and won't even seriously look at anything I suggest."

"That could be because everything you suggest requires an hour's driving time and would isolate us from all our friends. I don't feel like making

a long trek home when I'm tired at the end of the day. Joan stalks off and both issues remain unresolved.

Whether Joan accepts the promotion or not, their relationship remains quite dysfunctional at this point and there seems little hope of improving the situation unless this couple, both Beaus, learn the art of negotiation and compromise.

It is hard for Beaus to give up the need to win in situations of this nature, but unless they both agree to do that, they are in real danger of destroying their relationship.

As both Joan and George become healthier, they will accept the fact that in functional marriages, compromise is not despicable wishy-washiness, but an essential skill. It involves actually hearing the other person's need and trying to think of ways to accommodate it while still meeting one's own essential requirements.

In the case of the house, George might settle for an acre and a half instead of three. They could then begin to explore what was available within a reasonable driving distance with this new specification. Joan might find twenty or thirty minutes from the middle of town an acceptable compromise.

In the case of the job offer, they need to get down to specifics and talk about concrete needs. How often does George entertain? How often is that entertainment a necessary part of doing business? If the answer is twice a month, then Joan needs to do some negotiating on her end. Will she have at least two weekends a month at home? In truth, she will not want a job that requires her to spend all her weekends away from home, so this is going to be important from her own perspective as well as George's.

It is also important that George hear the underlying issue in this confrontation, which is Joan's fear that he does not put the same value on her career that he does on his own and that she views this as a lack of respect for her and for her work. As George becomes healthier, he will become more sensitive to such nuances and provide his wife with the respect and reassurance that are important to her.

It would be very natural for Beaus to find each other attractive. They both value the characteristics that are strengths in this personality type: poise, efficiency, organizational skills, drive, and a good sense of style.

Problems in the relationship will occur relatively quickly, however, since both are strongly competitive and expect to get their way. This is impossible in a day-to-day relationship where both people are capable and opinionated. Unfortunately average Beaus tend to become increasingly ruthless when they experience themselves as crossed.

Beaus like to make choices that demonstrate their taste and discrimination in clothes, careers, friends, housing, home decor, food and wine. Perceptions of what constitutes the best choice can often differ and when the couple's opinions of what comprises the best option diverge, neither is likely to give in easily or gracefully.

Confrontations between Beaus can be heated and bitter. It is particularly necessary that the couple learn to confine themselves to the issue when they disagree. It is easy for Beaus to move beyond the basic disagreement into personal disparagement in the heat of an argument. If they value their marriage, the couple will agree that this is not acceptable and that when either of them steps outside the bounds of civility, they will stop arguing until they have cooled off and are able to limit their discussion to the issue at hand.

One effective way of handling this problem is to use a code word that either partner can employ to stop all discussion when the confrontation loses focus. It must be agreed between the couple that as soon as the code word is invoked, they will go into separate rooms and cool off before returning to the matter at hand.

It is natural for average Beaus to want to be in control in any situation in which they are involved. The difficulty in Beau-Beau marriages is that quite apart from any larger issues, both partners are likely to become demanding and intransigent over quibbles such as which route to take to get to the airport, which television program to watch, or which restaurant to go to. It is important for Beau-Beau couples to label this sort of thing for what it is, a control issue, and to make guidelines to allow themselves to deal with it rationally. Simple examples that will save wear and tear are: letting whoever is driving pick the route with no squabbling, and taking turns choosing restaurants on alternate weeks.

Money issues could become a problem in these marriages if the couple differ in some of their goals. The difficulty is heightened because many of the goals Beaus set for themselves are expensive ones. The couple must acknowledge that they both demand value and excellence in their consumer purchases and devise a reasonable system for achieving compromise in meeting their needs without overspending. They might decide to take turns in choosing what high-ticket item was to be the next major purchase. Another possibility would be to agree to a certain amount of discretionary income for each partner to use freely or save toward a larger purchase.

GREATEST DANGER SIGNAL: Growing mutual intransigence is the greatest danger for this couple. These are two strong competitive personalities, used to getting what they want. It is a continuing challenge to them to willingly seek compromise over conflict and to put a spouse's need on a par with their own in considering options. Because Beaus do want the best of everything, and they can only have the best of marriage through doing this, they will be able to learn this skill.

PRIMARY FOCUS: In-depth communication is a necessary focus in this relationship. Beaus are skilled conversationalists. It is easy for them to talk about plays, movies, restaurants, work, or books. They have more difficulty talking meaningfully about themselves and their feelings. This more difficult level of self-revelation is what creates genuine intimacy between two people. They will find their marriage and their lives enriched as they trust each other and share themselves more deeply.

THE BEAU-SHELLEY RELATIONSHIP

Greg has reached an impasse in his writing. He has been unable to produce more than a paragraph or two a day for the past two months. He has become more and more depressed by this drying up and is increasingly irritable and incommunicative with Joan.

When Joan tries to talk to him about his behavior, he becomes furious. "You don't know what you're talking about. You have no understanding of what I'm going through, so just shut up and leave me alone."

"I understand that you're giving in to self-pity and navel gazing. If you made yourself write something whether you said anything or not, you'd get past it. Instead you sit and look out the window all day and feel that no one understands your suffering. And you're right, I don't. I don't understand how a grown man could be so self-indulgent and foolish."

"What you know about writing could be put on the back of a matchbook cover and still leave room for all the advertising."

"You'd like to think so, but I've done pretty well with the material I have to write for my job, which has included several manuals of procedures."

"And as far as you're concerned, this is just another manual of procedures that happens to be called a novel. Just go away and leave me alone."

Variations of this conversation continue several times a week until Greg gets past his writer's block. Unfortunately, by that time, the accusations and counter-accusations have done some severe damage to their relationship. Greg, the Shelley, perceives Joan's Beau personality as insensitive, superficial and lacking in empathy. Joan repeats that she would never advise anyone to marry a man who writes for a living and that she would lose her job if she let herself depend on the inspiration of the moment to decide whether or not to work.

The problem Joan and Greg are having has its origins in what is important to each of them. Greg is concerned with his integrity as an author and as a person. To write for the sake of having produced something seems to him a violation of his own vision and a misuse of his talent. He finds Joan's suggestions unthinkable, tawdry and lacking in respect for him and his work.

It is important to Joan to succeed at work. Efficiency and organization are her watchwords in the workplace. She demands results of herself and those around her. Greg's cries of artistic integrity are simply self-indulgent to her. You produce it and if you don't like it, you work on making it better, that's all.

Both of these approaches are valid within the context of their own situations. If Joan and Greg are to salvage their relationship, they will have to agree that they are coming from very different perceptions of value, self-worth and integrity. Joan must be efficient and productive in her job, and Greg, if his work is to meet his exacting standards, can not write until he is satisfied that he is saying exactly what he means with sensitivity and polish.

In the case of Greg's writing block, Joan needed to be aware that this was outside her range of competence and to back off and leave him alone. Greg, in turn, could have been sensitive to the effect his depression and irritability were having on Joan. He could have reached out to her to the extent of saying that he appreciated her tolerance of his moods and that he knew he was being hard to live with at the moment.

The Beau personality can find the deep feelings and sensitivity displayed by Shelleys attractive. Shelleys may find the poise and self-assurance of the Beau equally intriguing. Beau-Shelley relationships truly represent the attraction of opposites and this difference in perception and basic self-awareness provides the basis for much Beau-Shelley conflict.

Beaus will wonder what Shelleys are agonizing about and become impatient with their seeming inability to stop suffering and just get on with life. Shelleys will wonder in turn if there is any real substance behind the smooth facade the average Beau presents to the world.

While there are major differences in sensitivity levels between these two personalities the capacity of Beaus to adapt to those around them will generally prevent this from creating difficulties. The problem that may occur is that the Shelley may make a demand on the Beau for greater authenticity, noting that the same qualities that allow Beaus to concur with their partner's opinions and feelings come into play with others, even strangers.

Beaus may be puzzled by being faulted for being agreeable and have difficulty comprehending the demand being made of them. If it is a serious problem in the relationship, it may be advisable for them to seek therapy to help them to develop a greater sense of self.

The tendency of Beaus to be socially agreeable may collide with the total inability of most Shelleys to say anything except exactly what they mean. Shelleys are unlikely to smooth over differences of opinion for the sake of affability. They hold strong views on anything of substance that they think about for very long and when they come up against someone espousing an opposing view, they are likely to either attack or totally withdraw depending on the situation.

Both of these approaches are likely to be unacceptable to socially adept Beaus and the fall-out after dinner parties and other social occasions, particularly those involving Beau business associates, can be intense. Beaus need to come to terms with the concept that they cannot be held responsible for the actions and opinions of their partners, and that the only reasonable thing to do is to clearly separate themselves from the unacceptable behavior and then not worry about it. When it comes to business affairs, Beaus are probably better off not including the Shelley partner, who won't want to come anyway. When Shelleys become healthy, they become more socially adept and learn to handle these occasions more smoothly.

There are other occasions where this situation may be reversed. Beaus generally have no difficulty returning merchandise to stores or sending back food in restaurants. Such situations may prove embarrassing to Shelleys, who must then realize that they are not responsible for the actions of their partners, but also that what the Beaus are doing is acceptable assertive behavior, which they would be wise to emulate rather than cringing at.

Introverted Shelleys may find Beau partners abrasive in the morning when some Beaus are known to sing, chatter, and generally make noise. This is a personality difference that is unlikely to change, so that mutual consideration is the keynote to minimizing conflict. Beaus must try to keep the noise level down. Going to another part of the house to chat with an extroverted friends by phone may be helpful. Shelleys need to be clear about the fact that their early morning grumpiness is often disproportionate. In this case, the natural tendency of the Shelley to withdraw from the situation may be appropriate.

Differences in stamina level are a related difficulty. Shelleys will usually be unable to dance through the night, although many of them can talk through the night given a stimulating conversation. If both partners remain aware that there is a genuine physical difference between them, they can be more tolerant of each other's needs in this area.

GREATEST DANGER SIGNAL: Unacknowledged anger can become a major danger to this couple. Shelleys can nurture a growing resentment of Beaus as superficial, consumer spenders, and they can feel jealous of their easy poise in social situations. While Beaus will be more willing to address Shelley shortcomings, they may do so in a manner that fails to penetrate the partner's defenses. Such a situation can gradually undermine a marriage. The couple need to put aside time for discussions of what is bothering them in the relationship and make a major effort to hear and address the issues the partner presents.

PRIMARY FOCUS: Seeking a middle ground in establishing emotional balance will be important to this relationship. The Shelley thrives on intensity, while the Beau is really more at ease when not delving too deeply into feelings, keeping things light. Finding a comfort level that both partners can sustain with each other will be a challenge. If they can establish this sort of emotional compromise, it will enhance the strength and stability of the relationship.

THE BEAU-EINSTEIN RELATIONSHIP

Joan and Arthur are attending an out-of-town seminar on aspects of computer programming in which Arthur is a member of a panel discussion. There is a certain amount of tension prior to the scheduled event as Arthur is trying to go over some last minute changes in his notes, and Joan has interrupted him in an unsuccessful effort to get him to wear a different tie. They are still mildly snippy to each other as they enter the conference room.

The seminar lasts for two hours during which Joan silently brainstorms strategy for a meeting she will be chairing at work the following week. She wonders how many people in the audience are actually interested in the panel, and checks her watch to be sure it hasn't stopped, all with a look of rapt attention directed at whoever is speaking.

After the usual conversational interlude, Joan and Arthur head for lunch. Arthur is still on a high from his morning's presentation and begins immediately to explain to Joan why he disagrees with one of his colleagues on the panel.

Joan cuts him short. "I managed to remain in the room through what was near the top of the list of life's most boring experiences, that's enough; don't tell me more about it."

Arthur is understandably hurt. "I thought you were interested in my career."

"I'm interested in the fact that people in your field seem to think you're good, but spare me the details. I can't imagine anyone with a spark of life in them finding that stuff as endlessly fascinating as you seem to."

Arthur says nothing further. Joan after a brief interlude begins to analyze the dress and hairstyles of the two women on the panel in unflattering terms.

Goaded by this, Arthur says, "They happen to be nice, intelligent women who have more on their minds than their next beauty parlor appointment."

"Nerdy, Arthur, and you know it."

"If the only thing you got out of the morning was the pleasure of putting down two very pleasant capable people, I think you'd better not come to these seminars after this."

"That would be a real hardship! However, if I don't come you may wind up doing a presentation without your tie on and with non-matching socks, so for the sake of your reputation, I think I'll have to show."

Arthur leaves the lunch to return to the conference. He has said very little, but he is very angry with Joan and feels quite depressed with his life. Joan puts the incident out of her mind and goes to a movie.

This rather typical Beau-Einstein interaction would be improved by greater understanding of each other's personalities on the part of both Joan and Arthur. Arthur, an Einstein, continues to hope for Joan's approval and affirmation. It seems to him that before they were married, she spoke in quite glowing terms of his intellectual abilities and seemed to respect them. This is an inaccurate perception. Joan actually admired the success he had achieved in his field, she knew almost nothing about what he thought or did. She has come to take his success for granted after a few years of marriage and is now left with the reality of a husband who spends a great deal of his time discussing abstract problems and concepts that do not interest her. Arthur continues to hope that she will come to understand and appreciate what he does, and that his colleague's esteem will impress her. He is repeatedly hurt and depressed when this doesn't happen.

For her part, Joan sees a trip to another city as a chance to meet interesting people, see some sights and eat in new restaurants. When she finds the people boring and they end up at the local diner so that Arthur can hurry back for the next session, she is disappointed and angry. On both counts, it would be better if Joan didn't attend seminars with him.

These problems may diminish, as both people become healthier and less extreme in their positions. Joan will be able to see that her emphasis on external appearances is excessive, and that she needs to cultivate an appreciation for Arthur's abilities, even if she does not want or need to know all the details of his work. She will be able to let him know that she values his intelligence and conceptual scope instead of disparaging it out of irritation.

Arthur will come to value Joan's area of expertise as well. Social graces are another area of intelligent functioning. Joan's intuitive knowledge of how to achieve a poised, attractive facade will be a genuine asset, when she stops presenting it as an end in itself. He will be willing to admit that he can enhance his presentation of material by looking dignified, confident, and authoritative. Mutual respect will replace the automatic debasing of the partner' abilities that is the context of many of their interactions now.

A Beau personality will find someone who is a marked success in any career field interesting and attractive. In academic and scientific settings, this person is often an Einstein. The Beau energy, organizational skills and general competence will be attractive to the Einstein. This is likely to be a marriage in which friendship is the dominant bond rather than romance.

One difficulty that may emerge rather quickly in the relationship and create more dissension than it would seem to merit is the contrast in the value the partners place on appearances. Beaus generally work toward perfection in this area. Poised, well groomed, clothes color-coordinated, well matched and well fitting, they seem to be ready at a moment's notice should the fashion industry need them. Einsteins frankly have better things to do and don't want to waste their valuable time on such nonsense. Einstein dress styles generally range from *very* casual through eccentric to definitely weird.

This difference will not matter to Einsteins, who in fact will probably not notice it that much, but it will be of great concern to Beaus, who consider the person they are walking down the street with as, among other things, a fashion accessory. Those Einsteins who are reasonably docile in this area and allow the Beaus in their lives to dress them as they wish will probably have the least irritation and upset from this value difference. Einsteins, who dig in their heels, and refuse to cooperate, will truly upset their partners, provoking ongoing bouts of rage, frustration, and despair. They will suffer ongoing damage to their own self-esteem as the Beau partner explains in detail how humiliating it is to be seen on the street with such a person.

Einsteins may well experience the average Beau as superficial and shallow. The ability of Beaus to see the other person's point of view and to change opinions easily and pragmatically will appear to the Einstein to be the most gross and unprincipled sort of selling out for petty advantage. They will despair of the short interest span of their partners when they wish to explain a beloved theory in minute detail or lecture for forty-five minutes in response to a question. Beaus will find Einstein partners long-winded and boring in these situations and implore them to lighten up.

Einsteins are inwardly sensitive and can be easily hurt. This often escapes the notice of those around them, because they tend to hide their feelings quite successfully in most situations and rarely challenge those who hurt them. They must overcome their natural instinct to retreat into themselves when hurt, and learn to tell their spouses when they are offended or angry. Beaus can be caustic and insensitive to Einstein partners and need to be aware that they are damaging their marriages and harming both the partner and themselves when they neglect to monitor what they are saying. The Beau, when thinking about it, is a master of the carefully phrased constructive criticism. They must learn to be tactful at home as they are at work or socially.

Beaus, like most of us, function best when they have the respect and recognition of others. They have a very real desire to look good and to be perceived as capable. They want to stand out from the crowd. This need conflicts with Einsteins, who often want to shield their thoughts and themselves from others. This has implications not only for those situations where the couple are together in public, but also for their mutual possessions. The choice of a car can be harrowing when one partner wants a low-budget American sedan in a neutral color and the other one is thinking of an expensive European sports car. Compromise is called for in these situations and it is important that both partners actually listen to each other and accept the other person's needs and opinions as honest and genuine. On many such choices, housing, vacations, and home decor, for example, the Beau-Einstein couple must accept the wide discrepancy between their tastes and realize that the price of a good marriage is compromise, sacrificing total satisfaction for either partner in many of these areas.

Beaus have no problem confronting people who make them angry. Most Einsteins find conflict upsetting and avoid it whenever possible. They may begin to feel persecuted by a Beau partner, who often challenges and confronts them over issues. In the interest of a more harmonious relationship, Beaus need to learn to use the same tact at home that they exercise so successfully in their careers. While Einsteins must push themselves to overcome their natural diffidence and stay with a controversy, expressing their opinions and needs as vigorously as their Beau partners. It is hard for Beaus, with their strong competitive drives to concede points gracefully, but if they can view it as another skill to be mastered, the marriage will be the winner.

Beaus are natural extroverts, while introversion is inherent to the Einstein's make-up. This difference has further ramifications, such as noise level. Beaus may like to have the radio or television playing in the background, the sound invigorates them. It interferes with the thinking processes of most Einsteins. Earphones were invented to preserve this marriage. Other issues may include how often the couple will entertain and the number of guests, and choices in recreational pursuits. Sometimes the couple can agree to go their separate ways in regard to an introvert/extrovert issue. In other instances, compromise will be an important tool. Beaus will have to remember that while it will be possible for them to demand what they want strongly enough to get it by sheer force of high energy and remorseless insistence, that done too often, this tactic will be pursued at the expense of the relationship.

Beaus perceive themselves as naturally organized, efficient and extremely capable. They are absolutely correct. However, the deduction they reach, that this gives them the automatic right to be in control, is not quite accurate. Einsteins will be grateful to Beaus when they do some of the coping with daily detail that interferes with the Einstein's more abstract interests. However, if they feel their partners are taking over and making large decisions which effect them, without adequate consultation, Einsteins are likely to become angry and emotionally withdrawn.

Einsteins must be alert to their own tendency toward passivity and push themselves to express anger when they feel it. Beaus must be equally watchful of their tendency to automatically assume the decision-making role because it is so easy for them.

Einsteins have a high level of anxiety and fear with which it is often hard for Beaus to empathize. Average Beaus tend to repress and deny their anxieties to prevent them from interfering with their functioning and they have little understanding of the Einstein's inability to do this. The natural tendency of Einsteins is to obsess over their anxieties, running them over and over in their heads and making themselves increasingly miserable.

If fear, anxiety, and obsession are serious problems, it is time to look for professional help. But even relatively healthy Einsteins will be made anxious by situations that Beaus take in their strides. Healthy Beaus will try to encourage their partners to let go of their fears by sympathizing, but also putting them into some sort of perspective. *"I know how concerned you are about the fact that we have a leak, but really all we have to do is call the roofer and he'll fix it. We know how to correct the situation and we're going to."* or *"It is upsetting that Billy got a bad grade in math. Should we get him a tutor or would you like to go over his homework with him to see if you can help him?"*

Humor can often help in lightening the worries of Einsteins. It is important that it be sympathetic humor, however, directed at the situation, not making fun of the partner for feeling concern. In the case of the bad math grade, *"I know it worries you, dear, but I really do doubt that it's going to keep him out of college."* This approach should emphasize lightness and avoid sarcasm and must be used with caution, since some Einstein personalities will find such comments, however gently made, mocking or oppressive. If the response alleviates concern, proceed; if the remark was not helpful, drop the approach.

Einsteins love their children, but in moments of preoccupation tend to forget about them or at least to want them to go away. The daily routines of childcare can be relentless and oppressive to the Einstein personality. Thus, disagreements in the area of childcare are less apt to be about what is said or done than about involvement in itself. It is important that the Einstein remember to be there on a continuing basis both for the sake of the children and for the sanity of the Beau partner who does not want to be left by default with the entire responsibility.

Disagreements about money are likely to arise in a Beau-Einstein relationship. Beaus need to spend, and feel that they do so prudently getting good value for their money. Einsteins often disagree with this assessment. The Einstein has a gut-level need to economize and save, and Einsteins are adept at making emotional needs into rational, logical imperatives. What is likely to happen is that the deep emotional need of Beaus to display their sense of self-worth through their possessions will be met by the deep emotional need of Einsteins to hold on to what they have. Realizing that both of these positions are essentially emotional rather than rational is the first step toward reaching effective compromises. Possibilities include the couple agreeing to either a new patio or a European vacation this year, but not both. A smaller scale compromise might be *"If we are going to host a neighborhood barbecue, that's going to cut into the amount of current cash available for getting a new television, we can put off buying the TV for a* few months."

GREATEST DANGER SIGNAL: Growing separation is the main danger for this relationship. An unspoken mutual agreement can evolve to go separate ways as the partners face the incompatibility stemming from Beau's outward focus on appearance and the Einstein's lack of concern for such things and need for solitude.

PRIMARY FOCUS: Beaus who notice their partners withdrawing into themselves should examine whether they are consistently making most of the decisions in the relationship or behaving competitively instead of cooperating in decision-making.

Einsteins, who notice their partners seem unhappy or angry much of the time, are probably allowing themselves to spend too much time in their own private worlds. Remembering how important it is to Beaus to be affirmed, they need to listen to their partners needs and be there for them.

THE BEAU-AUSTEN RELATIONSHIP

George's professional association has a seminar in a neighboring state that he would like to attend. Normally, this would be fine, but Jane is in her ninth month of pregnancy and the baby is due the third day of the conference. Jane doesn't want him to go and is feeling very weepy and angry.

George doesn't see the problem. "I'm a two hour drive away. If you go into labor, you'll give me a call, and I'll drop everything and get right back. Don't worry, it's going to be fine. This conference has important networking potential for me, and if I stay home, I'm going to be in a bad mood, thinking what I'm missing, so you're really better off if I go, believe me."

"A good husband wouldn't think of leaving his wife at a time like this. What will my friends think when they hear you've left me on my due date? What will my mother say?"

Nobody will think anything if they have good sense. I'm not going to Europe. You could even come with me, if you wanted to."

"And drive two hours in labor to get back to the hospital? You really are out of your mind, George."

"You're convinced that you're going to have the baby on time, but both Cindy and George Jr. were late, why should this one be different? You don't really expect the baby, you just want me to stick around and hold you hand for the next two weeks. Well, I'm not about to do it."

"Go, just go, but I'm going to remember this for a long time, I warn you."

"Nothing like a loving supportive wife when a man's trying to move ahead in his career," says George as he drives off.

When Jane goes into labor, she calls her best friend and her mother to take her to the hospital. Both of them urge her to call George, but she refuses to do so. She is hurt and angry, and all of her passive-aggressive instincts have come to the fore. She makes a point of telling everyone in the hospital that her husband is attending a conference and doesn't know that she has had the baby. When George calls home, he finds out from the baby-sitter that he is a father. He drives home in a rage, narrowly averting both an accident and a speeding ticket.

There are two ways that this scenario could have had a happier ending. First, the conference was one George wanted to attend, but it would actually not have been terrible if he had missed it. So, he could have said to himself, *"Jane will really feel terrible if I go off and leave her at this time and since I love her, I will sacrifice this particular conference to our relationship."* Or if he decided he was going to attend, he might have consulted with Jane first instead of announcing it as a *fait accompli*. If he had said, *" There's a conference that I'd like to attend, but I know it's right at the time the baby is expected. I don't want to leave you at that time. I certainly don't want to miss the baby's birth,"* Jane might actually have discussed it rationally with him. *"How far away is it? How long will it take you to get back? How important a conference is it for you?"*

Part of the problem was the way George announced his intention of leaving town. It left Jane feeling abandoned and unloved, hard feelings for a dependent Austen to handle. It also aroused Austen concerns in the areas of conventionality, *"What will I tell people?"* If he could have keyed in to her concerns and his concerns for her first, she would have felt less vulnerable and perhaps been able to accommodate his needs. Or they could have compromised by George agreeing to make a daily commute to the conference and be home at night.

In a healthier relationship, Jane would be less vulnerable and less helpless. She would understand and control some of her dependency needs, so that George would not perceive her as always demanding care and attention. If someone always needs you, it's hard to discern when you *really* are needed. She would have been able to acknowledge his professional obligations and the fact that she was not being deserted. George, for his part, would be sensitive to her needs, realizing that things that seem trivial to him are truly important to her and giving them credence on her behalf even if he didn't understand them. He would discuss the pros and cons of his attendance rationally with her. *"These are the business advantages of going, I will be able to drop everything and get back if you go into labor. You have a good support system as backup. What do you think?"* Naturally in a healthy relationship, Jane would call immediately when she went into labor and George would drop everything and head for home.

Beaus are sure of themselves, upbeat, usually physically attractive people. Austens find their optimism, efficiency and poise attractive. Beaus enjoy Austen admiration and are attracted in turn by the good qualities of the Austen, particularly their organizational skills and their sense of loyalty.

Austens are extremely attentive and thoughtful to their friends and lovers, they find the perfect little token or the funny greeting card. The Austen will remember the one-month anniversary of when the relationship began and will often commemorate the occasion in some way. These attentions can be seductive to the Beau.

As the relationship progresses, the philosophical differences between the two personalities will begin to create stress. The conventional values and loyalties of the Austen will inevitably come into conflict with Beau pragmatism. Beaus can become irritated and impatient with Austen over-blown concern with themselves and the ramifications of whatever they are thinking or doing. This is the same focus on detail that produces Austen attentiveness, but in average Austens, it can also produce whining and complaining over petty inconveniences: *"Why does it have to rain on Saturday?" "The neighbors cat has been digging in our yard again." "I should never have had that coffee, it kept me up all night, I'll never get through the day."*

The differences in level of sensitivity will be an ongoing concern in this relationship and often leave the Austen feeling misunderstood. One of the difficulties that Austens have is that they project their levels of sensitivity onto other personality styles, so that they try to protect their partners. Thus, the Austen may be loathe to express anger and pain, on the one hand, but may also interpret as an intentional slight or affront things that the Beau does without any consciousness of hurting anyone. It is very important for Austens to attempt to be honest and open about their feelings and to tell their partners when they are upset. It is equally urgent that Beaus be aware that Austens are more sensitive and vulnerable and try to be vigilant in regard to areas where their spouses may feel hurt or rejected. It is a good exercise for Beaus to try to actually verbalize through role playing what the other person is experiencing. If both partners remember to keep communications open; not to lash out at each other, but to honestly describe their feelings and perceptions, this problem is imminently soluble.

Average Austens tend to be somewhat rigid and dogmatic in their beliefs and actions. *"People should do this. You mustn't say that. That isn't the way to do it."* These statements are irritating to flexible Beaus who are willing to bend their responses to the needs of the situation. Austens can be embarrassed, even shocked by pragmatic Beau responses which do not meet the criteria of their belief systems. These beliefs can be formal and traditional, such as, people should attend religious services on a weekly basis; or informal and based upon their own family of origin experiences, such as, men should be able to make home repairs, women should be able to sew.

The vital point at issue here is that Austens overcome the belief that their perspective represents some basic truth of society at large and see it as one possible view of many in a heterogeneous society. Once they can do this, they will be able to hold a dialogue with mutual respect and honesty. The other half of this picture is the fact that average Beaus can be too pragmatic, sacrificing the means to the end and riding roughshod over those around them. They must learn to acknowledge that there are limits to pragmatism if it is healthy, and that it is useful to have Austens around to remind them of the demands of conscience and society.

Beau personalities are naturally aloof. They are very extroverted and friendly, but it is difficult for them to speak deeply and intimately with a friend or partner. This detached quality is difficult for Austens to understand. Austen personalities are eager to engage anyone close to them. They love to share their perceptions and the details of their days. They like to explore their own thought processes on issues and agonize over their decisions with others. They can easily experience Beau detachment as rejection. Average Beaus are not in touch with their feelings. This is an area where the couple can help each other. The Beau needs to work on letting down the mask of casual friendliness and poise in order to discover the genuine feelings that lie beneath it. The Austen needs to learn that others do not find each nuance of feeling as interesting as they do. If the Beau starts to identify emotions and share them and the Austen learns greater selectivity in what is shared, they will have helped each other to become healthier more interesting people.

Beaus are quite competitive and often enjoy confrontation. Naturally cooperative, fearful Austen personalities tend to withdraw from heated disputes and feel uncomfortable when they are in disagreements. In domestic arguments the Beau can be unnecessarily mean and nasty as a method of winning. The Austen is likely to be both frightened and hurt by such Beau ruthlessness. The disparity might seem to produce a situation in which Beaus always get their way in controversies with Austens. This is not true in real life, as Austens do get angry, feel badly used, and tend to become passive-aggressive, achieving by indirect means those goals which they feel unable to fight for more directly. In this situation the relationship will be the loser. It is better for the Beau to realize that ultimately always winning and getting one's own way is an unrealistic goal only achieved by marrying a marshmallow. It is healthier to rein in that over-sized competitive drive and start learning the art of compromise. Austens must strive to be honest about what bothers them and about what they want in various situations. Then as the Austen becomes healthier and ceases to be afraid of disagreeing openly, both partners can participate on an equal footing in decision-making.

Ingratiating behavior can be a problem for both partners. Beaus tend to flatter and play up to those they consider important or useful to them in some way. Average Austens are less discriminating and more likely to use ingratiation as an automatic response to those around them. Both partners should work on being aware of this tendency to be too nice, too flattering and work toward greater honesty in relationships.

Average Austen personalities tend to have many fears and anxieties, which appear trivial and overblown to Beaus. This can create problems as the Austens talk at length about whatever is bothering them and Beaus can appear quite callous and disinterested in their partners misapprehensions and worries. It is essential to find a middle ground in this area of functioning, with the Beau attempting to listen patiently and to help and reassure the partner instead of brushing off the concern. As the Austen learns to confront fears and not be held back by them, the quantity of fears will diminish. It is the responsibility of

Austens to work on doing this, rather than allowing these apprehensions to immobilize and handicap their lives.

Infidelity can be a problem in some Beau-Austen relationships. Average Beaus want the appearance of a good marriage, but are not above dalliance on the side as long as appearances are preserved. This is certainly not acceptable to the home loving, security-conscious Austen personality. If this is a problem, the Austen must confront the partner on this issue and seek professional help in preserving the marriage if necessary.

GREATEST DANGER SIGNAL: Beaus are pragmatic people, drawn to the most advantageous situation. If the home-loving, family-centered Austen fails to measure up in maintaining an active social life, the Beau is likely to start looking elsewhere for social stimulation. Austens need to remain self-aware, and work at being active participants in the couple's social life to guard against this situation. Beaus, who realize that they are deserting their partners emotionally, should seek professional help in dealing with this issue.

PRIMARY FOCUS: Both Beaus and Austens enjoy projects. One of the best ways to keep this relationship strong and growing will be to work together on joint interests, such as gardening, planning a vacation, or redecorating a room. Whatever the focus, accomplishing things together is a great method of establishing greater bonding and cohesion and can keep the relationship stable and satisfying for both partners.

THE BEAU-MOZART RELATIONSHIP

George's work demands that he take clients out to dinner once or twice a month. When they were first married, Gini had no objections to playing hostess on these occasions, but now, the novelty had worn off and she has become increasingly reluctant to give up an evening to talking business with people whom she often finds to be dull.

The situation finally reaches a boiling point when George arranges an evening with the same client for the third time in a couple of months. "I'm not going, I've had enough of them. If I see them once more, I'll die of terminal boredom."

George tries to be conciliatory. "I know they're pretty grim, but they're also pretty important to me. Don't see them as people, see them as a new car and you'll feel better."

"I'm sorry George, but no. I've had it. I'll do without the car, thanks."

"Come on, Gini—this is important to me. I really want his business. Once more and then no more?"

"Wheedling will get you nowhere. Tell them I have pneumonia. Tell them I'm in Tahiti on business. You don't need me. You all talk job, job, job and I have nothing to contribute. You'll do just as well without me and I'll do a great deal better not being there."

George is angry, but as Gini is adamant, he goes alone, claiming that Gini is home in bed with a virus. Having freed herself of this chore, Gini is actually out with friends at another restaurant, which would have been fine, had she not been spotted by the client's secretary while there.

George did some fast talking when he learned of this, and the deal did not fall through, but he is furiously angry with Gini, for behavior that he views as irresponsible, and childish.

Gini is unrepentant. "I don't care. I didn't tell you to lie. You chose to lie and your lie caught up with you. All you had to say was that I wasn't available to join you. You were the one that wanted to smarm up to them by having them think that I had to be at death's door to want to miss an evening of their enchanting company."

George seems to be living in an earlier time frame in this scenario. His expectation that Gini will always be available to meet his business needs is unrealistic. On the other hand, there may be occasions when her presence is a real asset. He needs to reassess his demands and make them more reasonable. He must balance: *"These people really want to go out for a night on the town, please come with us,"* with *"This is essentially going to be a business meal where we're negotiating terms, so you'll be bored, don't come."* Gini, a Mozart, must come to terms with the fact that marriage is a partnership and that sometimes we do things for the other person because of their need even if we don't particularly enjoy the situation.

As George, the Beau, becomes healthier, he will be able to identify those demands that have more to do with status seeking than real need and to abandon them. Few clients will forego a deal because they don't have dinner with your wife. He will understand that his need to emphasize position and status springs from his feelings of insecurity and that such displays are unnecessary. His genuine ability and poise are his true assets, rather than his adherence to an artificial code of behavior.

Gini, as she grows emotionally healthy, will learn to channel her impulses and accept the reality that she must sometimes postpone immediate gratification. It is simply not possible for any of us to experience constant happiness. It is paradoxical, but true, that when we try, we are generally operating in a self-defeating manner. In this case, the price was certainly too high. Living with George's anger and reproaches for several days canceled out any pleasure she may have had in going out for the evening with friends. The pursuit of happiness is an important and worthwhile goal, but it must be balanced by the acceptance of limits and responsibilities. Healthy Mozarts take pleasure in what they are doing and attempt to find enjoyment in all aspects of their lives rather than trying to spend their days in perpetual search for the maximum source of immediate amusement at each moment.

The mutual appeal of these personalities is natural and readily understood. They are both adventurous and have high energy levels. They are interested in a wide range of projects and activities. Both Beaus and Mozarts are usually physically attractive.

As they get to know each other better, they will discover that even though their interests may be similar, the motivations behind those interests are quite disparate. If Beaus play tennis they want to work on improving their game and to fuel their strong competitive drives. Winning is important. They also use the game as a networking opportunity, meeting people and cementing relationships. Mozarts play tennis for fun. If a Beau-Mozart couple are partners in a doubles game, the Beau may become irritated by the Mozart failure to concentrate and even to talk or joke in the middle of the game. The Mozart will be impatient with the intensity of the Beau and protest that this is supposed to be fun not work. When they go out to dinner, the average Beau will want to choose a fashionable restaurant catering to the "right" clientele. The Mozart will have no objection to this sometimes, but on other occasions may prefer a neighborhood restaurant where the food is good, or a lively pub that attracts a fun crowd.

This difference in goals may be harmless when it comes to diversions, but it is more seriously reflected in such areas as career decisions, choosing large-scale purchases, and friendships.

An on-going problem for this couple will be the disparity between the natural self-control of the Beau and the difficulty experienced by the Mozart in governing impulses. Understanding and supportive Beaus can be helpful to their partners in this area, talking to them about strategies for gaining greater control, and praising their successes. Anger and condemnation are unlikely to be useful tools in creating change. It will be more effective to attempt to provide some degree of structure. The Beau might say, *"Next time you feel you really need to buy an expensive item, could you call me and talk to me about it first?"* or *"I know that you like to snack right before dinner, so I've put out some celery and carrot sticks for you. I know they're not your favorites, but I bet you'll be able to make it without a candy bar if you try them."*

Mozarts are usually aware that they have less impulse control than those around them do. The hard part of becoming healthy is actually creating change. It is up to Mozarts to seek out structures that will aid in the battle to regulate those proclivities and whims that often seem to override their judgment. Viewing areas to be changed systematically can heighten their awareness. What are the specific temptations that I regularly succumb to? How can I help myself to remember not to do it? A timer by the phone may help the marathon telephone addict, a picture in a bathing suit on the refrigerator door may deter the snacker. People who leave their credit cards at home unless they are going out to make a planned purchase may find their monthly bills considerably reduced.

The Mozart spontaneity and sense of fun, while often liberating and amusing, can also be embarrassing to the more conventional Beau partner. It depends on specific circumstances. Since Beaus care deeply about self-image, any action that might cause them to appear as less important or less worthy of respect will be upsetting to them. Mozarts need to be aware of this aspect of the Beau personality and curb their high spirits in circumstances where they are likely to be upsetting to the Beau partner. Beaus, at the same time, need to loosen up a bit and realize that their self-esteem is unlikely to be permanently lessened by a little showing off or silliness on their partners' part.

Both Beaus and Mozarts have the propensity to look elsewhere if they find a relationship unfulfilling. Preserving the marriage will require both partners to be alert to trouble signals and to deal with them through honest discussion. A therapist can be extremely helpful in sorting through the problems and enriching and strengthening the relationship.

Control will be an issue in this marriage. Beaus are uncomfortable when they feel their lives are out of their control in any way. While Mozarts don't feel as strongly about keeping everything in their own hands, they don't respond well to someone else being in control. They will become angry when they feel thwarted, and will usually be quite successful in eluding Beau attempts to structure them arbitrarily and without their consent.

Discussion of this issue is the first step toward keeping it from becoming a major concern. Beaus who can talk in terms of their own needs will meet a more receptive response than those who try to meet those needs dictatorially without exploring them with their partner. Mozarts must then evaluate and respond, Sometimes they will be able to say: *"That seems reasonable, I'll try to accommodate you"* In other cases, they may feel*: " That is stepping on my toes unnecessarily,"* or *"This is my decision and I will choose how to handle it."*

Both Beaus and Mozarts have the potential to be explosively angry. This can lead to bitter confrontations if ground rules are not set in place early in the relationship. The basic rule is that either partner can call time out when he or she is about to lose control of anger or perceives that the other partner is out of control, and that this will be unquestioningly respected by the other person. Other important rules are: no name calling, focus on the behavior, not the person, no yelling—keep voices down. These rules are protection not only for the relationship, but also for the children and the neighbors. Beaus and Mozarts in no holds barred combat have the potential to do permanent damage.

Children can present problems in the relationship as Beaus and Mozarts tend to have different goals for children. Mozarts think of children as delightful, something akin to a new toy. They can make good playmates, but tend to have little interest in the downside of parenting, whether diaper changing or disciplining. Mozarts are wonderful while focused on the child, but if they shift their focus to something else, the child can be dropped summarily and without explanation.

Beaus have high expectations for their children. They see them as extensions of themselves and it is important to the Beau parent that they be attractive, intelligent, well mannered, etc. If a child is so fortunate as to meet the criteria of such parents, they will be doted upon, but pity the child who is unable or unwilling to meet Beau standards.

In a Beau-Mozart partnership, the Beau will demand achievement from the children and feel unsupported by the Mozart partner, who usually doesn't think perfect table manners and straight A's are what childhood should be about. The Mozart may forget to come to the school play if something more amusing is on offer, while the Beau will have far too much to do to devote a week-end afternoon to a Monopoly game. If the partners can come to the understanding that they are both providing important components of parenting and that they supplement each other's contributions, these differing strengths can become positive assets and balance each other out.

Mozarts often have a problem in the area of commitment. They are so interested in the new, the different, the unexpected, that they can experience a continuous relationship as monotonous even when they love the partner dearly. The wise Beau will be aware of this problem and attempt to bring enough energy, new ideas, new people, and fresh experiences into the relationship to provide the Mozart with continued novelty and excitement.

Beaus, with concerns for status and upward mobility, will have second thoughts about any partner that does not appear adequate in terms of career, interests, or appearance. Mozarts who value their marriages will do well to keep this fact in mind and act accordingly. Naturally, as both partners become healthier, they become less demanding about having specific needs met.

The Mozart potential for any addictive behavior that would jeopardize career, social life or appearance will be anathema to most Beaus. This is somewhat paradoxical as many Beaus used cocaine in the 80's when it was considered an "in" drug and believed at the time that they could function better on it. Some Beaus may find marijuana acceptable with the same rationale. Thus, it is not what you do, but how socially acceptable what you do is that will be at issue in the Beau-Mozart relationship.

People do not function well on drugs or while engaged in any other addictive behavior, obviously, and if either partner appears to be addicted, they should be confronted and asked to seek help. It is also important for the non-addicted partner to seek help whether the addict agrees or refuses to do so.

Both Beaus and Mozarts have the potential for over-spending. Beaus need high-visibility status items with which to impress others and signal their superior status and life style. Mozarts just want to have fun, but their fun often carries a high price tag. If one or both partners are over-spending, they will need to seek a financial counselor to help them get their priorities in order and set some limits on their purchasing habits. It is essential that Beau-Mozart couples face this issue honestly, before every credit card they possess has reached its maximum and all of their loan sources have dried up.

GREATEST DANGER SIGNAL: The greatest danger to this relationship lies in the failure of the two partners to compromise on their needs. Both personalities are focused on their goals and are strong-willed. If they are tenacious in refusing to modify their needs and demands, the relationship will be doomed.

PRIMARY FOCUS: The primary focus in this relationship should center on good listening skills. Both of these personalities are better talkers than listeners and this marriage will only grow through both partner's taking the time and making the effort to genuinely hear and empathize with the other person's needs.

THE BEAU-CAESAR RELATIONSHIP

Evelyn, a Caesar, is a vice-president in charge of marketing. She has had a recurring problem with another woman in her office, who has been dismissive of her projects in meetings several times, and whom she believes is behaving unethically in relation to certain client accounts. Evelyn is planning a major showdown, which she believes will lead to the woman's dismissal from the firm.

When she tells George that she is going to do this, he is appalled. "Do you know who her husband is?"

"Of course I know. Do you think I'm stupid?"

"He's a very prominent lawyer and heavy in local politics. If you do that, it won't only backfire on you, it's going to effect me as well."

"So, I should let her get away with this, because she's married to someone you think is important? I'm sorry. That's not the way I work.

"It is the way life works, all you'll end up doing is making enemies that neither of us need."

"I would never have mentioned it, if I had remembered what a social coward you were. This is strictly my business and I'll handle it my way. When people try to take advantage of me, they're going to get hurt, regardless of who they are or know or marry."

"Be reasonable, Evelyn. There are better ways to handle this. I'm not saying you shouldn't be angry or shouldn't put a stop to her behavior. Just find a way to do it that isn't so likely to have unfortunate consequences."

"I don't want to handle it a better way. I **like** the way I'm dealing with it."

Inevitably, Evelyn pursues her own path, as she will do repeatedly throughout the marriage. Whether George's fears are reasonable or groundless, the clash between his desire to negotiate and hers to barrel ahead will take its toll on the relationship.

When Evelyn, who is a Caesar, becomes emotionally more healthy, she will become less pugnacious in her dealings with others and rely more heavily on negotiation. George, a Beau, on the other hand, will begin to consider his responses to situations less in terms of the status of the other person and more in simple human terms.

Their interaction would have had a more successful conclusion if both partners had listened with open minds to the other's ideas rather than focusing on doing things their own way. Finding the middle ground, between the excessive pragmatism of the average Beau and the damn-the-consequences approach of the average Caesar, is a more functional way to approach most problems.

In this case, the result of compromise might have been that Evelyn would have first confronted the woman privately on any ethical problems that she felt should be addressed, to give her a chance to correct the problem. In the same meeting, she would have made an attempt to clear the air regarding their personal conflicts, and set some firm limits. Only if these measures failed to correct the problem, would she seek other redress. Beaus who want the approval of everyone they respect, are likely to come into repeated conflict with Caesars, who want to say and do what they please in most instances without undue regard for the opinions of others.

The Beau stance can appear hypocritical and shallow, sometimes just plain dishonest, to the more blunt Caesar. Beaus, for their part, will often be aghast at the destruction that Caesars can achieve as they barrel their way through life. In a good marriage with plenty of ongoing dialogue, both partners will help each other to modify their approach and both will profit from finding a middle ground.

Beaus and Caesars have many common goals. Both have strong drives and are oriented toward achievement. Beaus are especially likely to be physically attractive and they tend to be poised and self-assured. They are responsive to the ideas and concepts of the people around them. These traits will appeal to the Caesar. Beaus will be drawn to financially successful Caesars who are generally shrewd and capable in managing their affairs. They can be charming companions as well and are persistent and focused in their attention to a person they find attractive.

Since both partners are competitive and heavily invested in getting what they want, it is almost inevitable that they will have serious clashes relatively early in the relationship. Even when they agree on a common goal, Caesar directness and Beau diplomacy and expediency are likely to dictate quite different paths to achieving their ends.

Beaus and Caesars can both be extremely confrontational. In the average range of emotional functioning, it is quite likely that there will be many issues on which both partners will take a position and refuse to back down. Obviously, this can lead to either an unhappy marriage or a divorce. As Beaus become healthier, they will rein in their competitive drive and act less ruthlessly. Healthier Caesars will come to accept the reality that people living in relationships cannot have their own way all the time and will also learn to compromise. Learning the art of negotiation is essential to the health of this relationship.

The struggle over the need to control, a prominent feature of both personalities will present another difficulty in this marriage. It will be especially necessary in this relationship for both parties to admit that they cannot give orders to the partner and to develop the mutual respect that allows both of them to function autonomously within their separate spheres.

It is probably best to agree to divide up the tasks that must be done and the choices that must be made at home and then to agree that each partner has the right to make the decisions in regard to the tasks they perform. If Evelyn is in charge of paying the bills, then she must make the decisions as to whether to pay revolving accounts in full or carry over charges without second-guessing from George. If George has taken charge of getting the kids to camp and says that after the long drive, he wants to stay at a motel rather than drive back the same day, it's his call.

The childcare issues between Beaus and Caesars can be of two kinds. The more easily resolved is the one of who will be there for the children at specific times. Both partners are likely to have heavy schedules with demanding work commitments. Good childcare help will relieve the undue strain that will otherwise take a toll both on the couple and on the quality of their relationship with their children. The important thing for both parents to remember is that good childcare does not relieve them of their obligation to spend quality time with their children.

The second problem area in childcare occurs because Beaus and Caesars are likely to have different desires and expectations for their children. Beaus tend to want their children to be high achievers. It is important that they get good grades, look attractive, and get along well with others. They will certainly encourage them to take up one or more areas of specialized achievement as well: piano playing, tennis lessons, art, dancing, etc. Caesars are likely to perceive too much of this type of programming as pretentious and unnecessary and may mock it or attempt to sabotage it.

Caesars can be unduly demanding in a different way. They will often expect unrealistic standards of obedience and compliance from their children and be unduly punitive when their demands are not met. They may be deeply disappointed in a child who fails to conform to their notions of appropriate childhood interests, such as sports, and respond by ignoring or rejecting such a child.

In healthy marriages, dialogue between the partners will help both Beaus and Caesars to keep their own needs and demands in proportion in relation to their children. Beaus can help their partners to modify unrealistic standards and respect the varied strengths and weaknesses of all of their offspring. Caesars can remind their Beau spouses that children need time for unstructured play and that their lives cannot consist of unending lessons, however worthy the goal.

Some Beaus and Caesars can have a problem with long-term marital commitment. If this is a problem in the marriage, it is wise to seek professional help. It is essential to acknowledge this situation as a joint issue and to realize that there are difficulties in the marriage that need to be addressed by both partners.

Money is important to both Beaus and Caesars. Beaus need money to finance their many purchases and to create the life style that accords with their self-image. Caesars are much less concerned with outward show, but money is important to them because of the power it can exert. It is often the key to the successful pursuit of many of their goals. If there is enough cash available, Caesars will be generous and uncomplaining in regard to the Beau's many consumer needs, but if the couple's financial situation becomes strained, Caesars are likely to be quite insensitive to the strength of the Beau's needs for luxuries or status purchases. In this situation it is vital that some discretionary income, however small, be allotted to both partners, with its use deemed off limits to the criticism of the mate.

GREATEST DANGER SIGNAL: Anger is the primary danger to this relationship. Both partners are confrontational and both can fight unfairly. In the heat of anger, it is very easy to say the most hurtful thing that comes to mind, and minor disagreements between these partners can quickly reach major conflict proportions with both refusing to back down. This is a relationship that demands a cooling off period whenever both partners start shouting.

PRIMARY FOCUS: The focus for this couple should be fun. Both personalities have high energy levels and both are capable of enjoying a wide variety of experiences. There will always be disagreements and clashes between them, but if they can have fun together, the cohesion built on vacations, tennis courts and dance floors will sustain the relationship.

THE BEAU-GAUGUIN RELATIONSHIP

Mike and Joan are generally a congenial couple, but when Joan sat down to start paying the bills for the month, she began to feel her customary anger. The withdrawals from the cash machine added up to far more than she had budgeted for. When she asked Mike about it, he was vague. "I didn't realize I'd taken out that much. It sure mounts up doesn't it?"

"You've got to stop this, Mike. We can't afford to have that much money just vanish on us every month. What did you do with it all?" Slowly and painfully she elicits from him the record of the special lunches with friends, the poker debt, the minor car repair, and the impulse purchases that added up to most of the missing cash. A bit of it remained unaccounted for, he just couldn't pin down where it had gone.

Faced with her anger, Mike became defensive. "All of this doesn't come to as much as you're spending on the new patio furniture and the party we gave last month," he countered.

"Can't you see the difference? That party included a lot of my business associates and a lot of people that we owed invitations to. That was a necessary expense, and we could hardly entertain anyone except our relatives this summer if we didn't get rid of that old furniture."

Actually, Mike, who is a Gauguin, doesn't get it, and he never will. He doesn't care about impressing friends or having the newest and the best. He knows these things are important to Joan, but the motivation behind them is so foreign to him that he has difficulty remembering it. On the other hand, he is more impulsive than Joan in most areas of daily life, and she has difficulty grasping his failure to control casual spending impulses.

The best thing that Beaus and Gauguins can do about their finances is to create a budget and both agree to stay within it. If a certain amount goes into saving toward big-ticket items, new cars, patio furniture, etc., then when the specific savings goal is reached, Joan can go out and acquire the things that seem to her necessary for a gracious life style. If Mike will agree to leave the credit cards at home and stay within a weekly cash budget for expenditures on lunches, poker games and miscellaneous expenses, then there will be no surprises at the end of the month.

These personalities are often attracted to each other and they have a good potential for a successful marriage. The Beau finds the Gauguin nurturing and supportive. The Gauguin ability to sit back and relax is the antithesis of the consistently striving Beau. The Gauguin is in good hands with the Beau, who is a natural manager and sees that bills are paid on time and that the couple's other obligations are met. The Beau models ways of taking on added responsibilities and facing tasks with an optimistic gusto which can provide a revealing insight to the Gauguin. The problems in the relationship tend to revolve around the differences in perception in the areas of money, responsibility, and status.

Gauguins are flexible easy-going people and their willingness to go along with a crowd, to agree to other peoples demands, sometimes to their own detriment, is another difference in style that is difficult for the Beau to understand, and another occasion for conflict.

When asked, Mike readily agreed that he and Joan would go to his brother's house for their mother's birthday, despite knowing that Joan had been planning to give this party. When she remonstrated, his response was: "Think of all the work it will save you. What difference does it make?"

It did make a difference. Joan had wanted to give the party, and viewed Mike's easy acquiescence to his brother as a failure to support her.

As Gauguins pay attention to the way they effect the people around them and become more alert to their potential for going along with other people's agendas to avoid conflict, they can inhibit this automatic nice guy response. *"I think that Joan had planned to give the party for Mom. Why don't you check with her before we make anything definite,"* would have been just as acceptable as the automatic okay that came so easily to Mike.

Joan, for her part, needs to be aware of her strong need to control situations and to remember that holding on to control at the expense of family harmony and friendships can be a mistake. If both partners are aware of their respective tendencies to take charge or to unthinkingly acquiesce in regard to these issues, they can begin to modify their response styles, which will be emotionally more healthy for both of them. Being over-rigid or over-flexible are both mistakes and the healthy reaction, as in most areas of human activity, is the middle ground.

Both Beaus and Gauguins have strong desires for the approval of others, but these needs are actually quite different. Beaus want to be commended for succeeding, at the job, at the marriage, at childcare, or at home furnishing. They are goal oriented and the achievement itself is extremely important to them. The Gauguin is nature's good guy, easy-going, pleasant, noncontroversial. Gauguins want to please people, while Beaus want to achieve results that will be perceived as pleasing accomplishments. While these results include interpersonal interactions, there is profound dissimilarity between the two agendas. Beaus will consciously behave in ways that will result in the admiration and esteem of others. Gauguins are just inherently pleasant and easy-going and go along with others without giving any real thought to how they are perceived.

Beaus have a strong need to control and can take charge of decision-making in the relationship in ways that infringe on the autonomy of their partners. As long as control issues are limited to home decor, childcare, and social scheduling, most Gauguins are reasonably comfortable handing over the decision making. The greatest conflict often rises over Gauguin career decisions. Gauguins are not workaholics. They generally do their work competently, but they are not out to climb the corporate ladder to the top. Some status-conscious Beaus have problems with this and begin to pressure their mates. Pushed too hard, the Gauguin can become passive-aggressive and begin to sabotage his career by constant lateness, frequent absences and long lunch hours. It is important for Beaus to realize that this is a battle they cannot win and to back off. They must provide structure when it can be done unobtrusively, give advice when asked, and accept their mate's career choices.

It will be easier for the Beau to back off in this regard if they can put the situation into the overall context of their relationship. They were probably attracted to the Gauguin in the first place because Gauguins are so easy to get along with, so willing to compromise, to see the other person's point of view. This is not an operational style that creates the highly competitive personality. Beaus are much more comfortable in a relationship with Gauguins than fighting daily turf battles with more combative personality types. Accepting this reality, Beaus may be better able to come to terms with the fact that if they want power, status and money, they must seek it for themselves, and allow the Gauguin partner to pursue the less ambitious course that is comfortable and acceptable to that personality.

GREATEST DANGER SIGNAL: This relationship is in danger when the Beau partner becomes altogether dominant in the marriage. If the Beau starts to take advantage of the more easy-going Gauguin, making all the decisions and setting all the agendas, the Gauguin is very likely to stage a covert rebellion against the one-sided arrangement. The rebellion can take the form of merely hanging out with buddies and not coming home on time, or it can be an addictive pattern with drugs, gambling or alcohol, perhaps even seeking out another relationship.

PRIMARY FOCUS: The primary focus for this couple should be on spending time together. They truly enjoy each other's company, but it is easy for them to lose track of this reality and allow other commitments to become priorities. As long as they remember to make their family the priority, this should be a strong relationship.

VII

The Shelley in Relationships

For the Shelley-Emerson Relationship—Go to the Emerson-Shelley Relationship.
For the Shelley-Nightingale Relationship—Go to the Nightingale-Shelley Relationship.
For the Shelley-Beau Relationship—Go to the Beau-Shelley Relationship.

THE SHELLEY-SHELLEY RELATIONSHIP

Greg has recently completed a novel, which has received mixed, but predominantly negative reviews. He is devastated by any bad press and has become moody and depressed. Jean was extremely sympathetic for the first few weeks, reassuring him of the worth of his work and trying to coax him into a more balanced view of the role of the critic in the creative process. However, her patience is beginning to run short as he has continued to mope, declaring that he will never write again, and that his life is useless both to himself and to the world at large.

After a particularly hard day, when she returns home to find the sink littered with a day's supply of coffee mugs and Greg curled in a semi-fetal position on the sofa, she says, "Look, I'm sorry that you got some bad reviews, but it's not the end of the world. I've been very sympathetic, but you're not making any effort to help yourself. Lying there wallowing in your own pain is not a particularly healthy way to proceed."

"I don't perceive myself as wallowing, I do seriously doubt that I'll ever be able to write again which does concern me. I have no alternate form of employment to fall back on."

"I'm not minimizing your pain, Greg, but I can't help but be aware as a therapist that you're making yourself worse by the way your handling it."

"If I want a therapist, I'll find one, thank you; preferably one that has an understanding of the creative process. In the meantime…" Greg walks out of the room.

This incident is not discussed further. But both Greg and Jean relive it privately and each feels rejected by the other. While nothing is said, it creates a wedge between them that begins to grow wider by small increments, as each perceives a slight from the other and withdraws a bit more.

The failure to talk is at the basis of this rift. The allied problem is the failure to understand that all empathy must eventually reach limits if pushed far enough. Greg needs to acknowledge that Jean is not the crass insensitive being of his depressed fantasies, but a concerned wife. Jean, for her part, should acknowledge Greg's response as momentary irritability, rather than a serious rejection of her professional abilities. This confines their spat to a normal moment of tension in a relationship, instead of making it the backdrop for mutual withdrawal of affection. As both partners become healthier, they will begin to live less exclusively in their feelings and learn to accept the give and take of marriage.

Healthy people confront the person they are angry with and discuss what happened in real life, rather than in their daydreams. Greg might have said, "When you said I was wallowing in pity, I heard something to the effect of 'You're pathetically over-dramatizing your situation.' I think that I was already afraid on some level that I was doing just that, and when you said it, it made me more depressed and angrier with myself. I *just couldn't handle it so I lashed back at you. It seemed to me that you made the situation inside my own head infinitely worse."*

Jean could have responded, *"Obviously that wasn't my intention, but I can see that it was a moment of insensitivity on my part. You have no idea how difficult I find it to live with you when you get depressed and stay that way for so long. I just can't handle it myself, and that makes me irritable. However, when you zinged me back, I became very upset. I have always felt that you respected by abilities as a therapist, and suddenly, your remark put that very much in doubt. I was really hurt."* This is a discussion with the potential for healing and strengthening the relationship. The failure to have this discussion leaves a lingering misunderstanding with potential to create further harm.

Since the heightened sensitivities of both partners can create serious misunderstandings on occasion, it is important for both of them to remember that their high degree of emotional reactivity causes bad feelings to be disproportionately heightened and brooded over. They must learn to monitor the, often disproportionate, sense of hurt and violation that they experience.

Shelley personalities are attracted to each other by their mutual sensitivity. They feel that they have suffered more than most people in the course of their lives and relish discussions about emotional and spiritual issues. Feeling a strong aversion to intrusive personalities, they can relax together, safe in the knowledge that they will respect each other's need for space and privacy. They will have many similar interests and enjoy going to the same places and doing the same things. In many ways they see the other as a mirror image and have a sense of both understanding and being understood that is particularly affirming because it is a rare experience for them.

Problems in the relationship will grow from the same sensitivity that was initially experienced as so seductive and affirming. When either partner experiences some slight or lack of understanding on the part of the other it will be felt as greater and more devastating just because the other person has previously been so attuned and discerning. The instinct to withdraw when hurt, which will also be mirrored by the partner, will then intensify the anger and pain.

The avoidance of confrontation is a major problem for the Shelley personality. This is true both in their relationship with each other and in their dealings with the outside world. If a Shelley is in a relationship with someone who is more willing to talk when angry, the Shelley is inclined to step back and let the other person handle any joint human relations problems that require confrontation and limit setting. When a marriage contains two Shelley personalities, there is no one available to take on the role of limit setter, which can create major difficulties. There is no one to tactfully tell Jean's mother that she can't come to visit when it is going to cause major inconvenience. There is no one who will feel comfortable speaking to the teacher if something is happening at school that is effecting one of their children adversely. Clearly, one or the other or both of the partners must steel themselves to these tasks, but it is done with an unnecessary degree of emotional strain and is an ongoing problem in the Shelley-Shelley relationship.

An allied problem that springs from the partners possessing the same strengths and weaknesses is that of attention to detail. Shelleys are not very good at noticing that the screen door needs to be repaired, that the chimney needs cleaning or that someone should call the plumber about the leak in the toilet. They are considerably better about cosmetic detail, the house will be painted, the rooms will be well decorated, the garden will be beautiful, but the basic structure may well be crumbling. It is important that Shelleys in a relationship make a list of the types of basic repetitive household upkeep chores that need doing and either agree to devote a certain amount of time to getting them done or get someone else to do them.

Reaching out to friends is another Shelley problem. Shelleys genuinely like their friends and enjoy being with them. They just often forget to make the arrangements necessary to do this. If the couple discuss this mutual reluctance to reach for the telephone, they can divide the responsibility, each agreeing to remember to touch base with their share of the list.

GREATEST DANGER SIGNAL: The primary danger for this relationship is that when adversity strikes, both partners will tend to go into depression. Such depressions can feed off each other and intensify to the point at which the couple and the relationship itself are in serious emotional difficulty. It is important to seek immediate help from a skilled therapist if this happens.

PRIMARY FOCUS: The primary focus for this couple should be countering the intensity of their relationship through frequent lighter interactions with friends. They will spend a great deal of time talking together and exploring their feelings, but this mutual involvement can obscure or negate any correction of their joint perceptions. It is important to remember to go outside the relationship to balance the somewhat hothouse quality that can exist in it.

THE SHELLEY-EINSTEIN RELATIONSHIP

Jean has been quite depressed recently. Her best friend died six months ago and another friend has been in a serious accident. On top of this, she is experiencing personality conflicts with her supervisor at work. She has tried to talk to Arthur about how upset she feels and he has listened sympathetically and said he was sorry she was unhappy, but instead of sitting down to explore the situation with her in greater detail, he has usually gone off to put on the television. At first Jean felt hurt and rejected by what seemed to her a lack of concern, but at this point, she has become less hurt than irritated by Arthur's seeming indifference, and has begun to turn to a co-worker when she has needed to talk to someone.

Arthur has assumed she was feeling better since she stopped complaining about things to him. He felt helpless to deal with her unhappiness and thought she was overreacting to some degree and should do something constructive to take her mind off her problems.

Jean did not say anything to Arthur about his relatively disinterested response to her emotional issues. She quietly brooded over it for weeks, and reluctantly concluded that Arthur was not the kind supportive husband she had believed him to be. She began to wonder if they should separate.

A few days later in a momentary lapse from her resolve to steer clear of emotional issues with him, she spilled out the heated dynamics involved in a disagreement she had with a friend. Arthur replied that she was very sensitive, maybe too sensitive and should stop agonizing over such trivia. This was too much for Jean. "Our marriage isn't working Arthur, maybe we should separate."

Arthur looked at her as if she had suddenly turned purple, "What in the world are you talking about? We have a perfectly happy marriage, what's wrong with you, Jean?"

"You have a perfectly happy marriage. I am a woman and we live in the same house and that's good enough for you. It satisfies your job description. Well, it doesn't satisfy mine. I want someone who can be there for me and you clearly can't. I don't blame you, I think it's just beyond you, but I can't live this way any longer."

Arthur was bewildered. "What do you want me to do. I know you've been mad at me, but we can work it out, whatever it is."

"I would like to work it out Arthur, I really would, but I don't think we can. It just isn't working for us. It's not anything you're doing as much as it's who you are and you aren't going to change that."

What has happened to Jean and Arthur is a clash of sensitivities. Arthur focuses on his work and on intellectual issues, as a method of handling pain, anger, and disappointment. He has always been afraid he might seem foolish if he expressed too much emotion and has kept most people at a distance in terms of feelings. He prefers to focus on intellectual issues in conversations or at least to intellectualize the discussion of emotional subjects.

People and relationships are important for Jean. She is invariably fascinated by personalities, and how they interact. She can happily spend a great deal of time analyzing emotional interactions and the dynamics between people. She is quite reserved and would not share deep feelings with casual friends or acquaintances, but her emotional life is intense and it is important to her to be able to talk at length with her intimates.

If Jean and Arthur are to work things out, it will be important for both of them to understand the natural psychological predisposition of the partner. Such understanding will allow Arthur to try harder to support Jean when she needs to talk about something, and Jean will be more tolerant of Arthur's limited response if she remembers that often it is the intensity of his feelings that frighten him away from such discussions.

Shelleys may feel a kinship with Einsteins because they are both sensitive and introverted, creating feelings between them of empathy and bonding. Both Shelleys and Einsteins fear intrusive personalities and the fact that they give each other adequate space is very attractive to both of them.

Introversion may also prove to be a difficulty for the couple in that they tend to reinforce each other's tendencies toward social withdrawal. They may be quite happy in this situation, and will not necessarily perceive it as a problem in the relationship. However, over time they may find their social lives becoming more and more limited as their failure to reach out to friends and to be socially available isolates them.

While both Shelleys and Einsteins may seem aloof in casual encounters, the Shelley is quite emotionally intense beneath the surface. The Einstein also has deep and complex feelings, but the fear of too much intimacy is a strong component of this personality type, so that as the relationship deepens, the Shelley expectations of greater and greater closeness may be experienced as increasingly threatening. Einstein attempts to set boundaries or to back off for emotional protection can be interpreted as rejection by the sensitive Shelley.

Einsteins can often seem patronizing in their response to emotional demands. They can give the impression that they consider such concerns immature and beneath their notice. This is not the case. It would be more realistic to say that they actually have considerable empathy, but the idea of delving further into someone else's pains and anxieties is too painful, and that they flee more in self-protection than disdain. This stance is often misinterpreted and Shelleys are particularly sensitive to being patronized. They do not forgive it easily. It is important for Arthur to be aware that the desire to avoid strong emotional material is not a strength, but a deficit in his makeup. He will be a stronger, emotionally healthier person if he learns from Jean how to stay with and fully experience all of his feelings instead of repressing or denying them.

Jean must overcome her natural inclination to go off and brood when she is angry. Withdrawal is not a healthy way to handle anger. While they can generally deal in impersonal confrontations, such as political controversy without difficulty, it is hard for average Shelleys to confront people close to them when they are upset. Einsteins have a similarly unhealthy avoidance of confrontation. Their method of handling anger is to become lost in their work and even more withdrawn and out of touch with those around them, while nursing their grudges. Learning to articulate anger and to forgive past affronts is an indication of growth for both partners in this marriage.

There may be sexual issues in Shelley-Einstein relationships based on differing levels of desire and passion. If this is a problem, it is wise to seek help from a reputable therapist in dealing with it.

Both Shelleys and Einsteins can be relatively anxious. Shelleys tend to respond to undue anxiety by becoming depressed, while Einsteins may project their feelings onto others and when unhealthy, may show signs of paranoia. Talking about the situations and concerns that are causing anxiety is a helpful way of venting some of the stress. This is very natural for the Shelley, but difficult for some Einsteins. Shelleys can help their partners by questioning them and drawing them out about situations occasioning stress. Long-standing feelings of intense anxiety probably require professional help to overcome.

Money can be a problem in this relationship, as Einsteins tend to be relatively frugal and to have difficulty spending money for ephemeral pleasures. Money is relatively unimportant to Shelleys. If they don't have it, they will manage without. However, when it is available, they generally enjoy spending it, and this may create conflict with the Einstein partner. Compromise is necessary in this situation. If quarrels over money are frequent, it is best to work out a budget covering necessities and then to divide the remainder of the money, allotting a portion to the Einstein for saving and a portion to the Shelley for spending.

GREATEST DANGER SIGNAL: The danger to this relationship is likely to come from outside the couple. Neither partner is good at remembering to attend to the small details of daily life. It is important that they sort out the tasks that must be accomplished and divide the responsibility for them, lest plants go without water, green mold pours from the dishes in the refrigerator and the taxes are not filed on time. These tasks left undone can create chaos and mutual recrimination, undermining the quality of the relationship if not destroying the marriage.

PRIMARY FOCUS: The primary focus for this marriage should be on mutual intimacy. The danger here lies in the natural tendencies of the Einstein to need large amounts of solitude. The Shelley, who also appreciates some time alone, can still experience excessive pursuit of solitude as rejection and withdraw in turn. As long as both partners are aware of this possibility, they can guard against it. The Einstein can remember to articulate a need for space rather than disappearing, while the Shelley can remember to communicate any feelings of rejection instead of swallowing them.

THE SHELLEY-AUSTEN RELATIONSHIP

When they were first married, Jane took on many of the joint family responsibilities for Greg. She enjoyed the idea that she was taking good care of him. If the car needed to go to the garage, Jane was the one who took it. She painted their bedroom to save money. Despite her nine to five job, she did all the grocery shopping, and was the primary cook. She ran to the cleaners, the drug store and the bakery as often as necessary. She straightened up the family room before they went to bed every night. Now Greg simply expects that she will do these things and she finds that she gets no extra thanks or appreciation for her time and effort. If they have a dinner party, Jane plans, shops, cooks and does most of the cleaning up. Greg helps if asked, but rarely takes the initiative in any of the mundane chores that are necessary to run a household.

Jane is troubled by Greg's failure to appreciate all of her work and devotion. He takes her for granted and seems to enjoy the company of his friends more than that of his wife. When his friends come over, she feels that he ignores her contributions to the conversation, cuts her off when she says anything, and generally treats her in a patronizing fashion.

When they are alone, he is silent and moody much of the time, pointedly leaving the room or putting on the television when she tries to talk to him. When she asks questions about his day, he is unresponsive. "I wrote. That's what I do. There's not much to be said about it."

"But did you have a good day writing?"

"I never have a good day writing. Writing is hard miserable work; I had a terrible unproductive day. Let's leave it at that."

Jane has begun to feel increasingly taken for granted by her husband and has begun to complain about all that she does for him. She has also begun forgetting to do some things that he asks her to do, his library books are not returned, the bill that she promised to pay turns up with an overdue notice the following month.

When Greg questions her about what is happening, she denies feeling angry or upset, but she does mention that he doesn't appreciate what she does do, he's so busy complaining about her minor oversights. Then she walks away crying.

Greg stops her. "Wait a minute, why are you crying. I said you forgot to pay a bill. Was that an accurate statement? What is there to cry about?"

"You don't love me. You don't want a wife, you want a maid and a secretary."

"Look, I don't mind paying the bills if you don't want to pay them. You don't have to do it. I thought you wanted to."

"I do. But…"

"But you seem to keep forgetting to do it lately."

"Yes, but…You don't understand. I do so much for you and you don't seem to even notice."

"So, do less for me. Just tell me what you don't want to do, so I can make alternate arrangements."

"No, I want to do what I do."

"Then what's the fuss about? I don't get it. Just tell me what you want me to take over and I'll do it, but stop messing me up. My life is hard enough without having a temperamental wife whining and bursting into tears every time she makes a mistake."

What is happening in this relationship is that Jane is trying to please Greg by taking care of him and has the expectation that he will respond with gratitude and love. She is oblivious to Greg's dislike for being fussed over and continues to do those things that she believes, in the face of strong contrary evidence, will please him. Ingratiating behavior is rarely appreciated, and Shelleys find it particularly aversive. Greg's response is to withdraw more and more from Jane and this in turn, keys the passive-aggressive "forgetting" that average Austens tend to use when they feel unappreciated.

To turn the relationship around, Jane must become aware of her need to please the people around her, often at her own expense and often without reference to whether the kind things she does actually meet the needs of the person they are done for. It is really necessary at this point for Jane and Greg to sit down together and talk frankly about what she is doing that she thinks Greg wants her to do and what he actually wants from her. She may be surprised at the diversity between his needs and what she has believed he wanted. Jane is doing more than her share and feeling resentful about it. She needs to become aware of this and be frank about what she wants to do and what she would prefer Greg to handle.

Greg must learn to confront Jane when she is irritating him rather than withdrawing and feeling angry with her. Because they put a great deal of energy into being precise and discerning about feelings and perceptions, Shelleys can conclude that expressing their feelings on minor issues is too much trouble and that it is far easier to simply get away from what bothers them. This is not healthy in a marriage, and Greg needs to make a genuine effort to communicate with Jane and include her in his life, but to be able to include her, he must be honest about the things she does that bother him and tell her about them. Austens want to be agreeable to the people around them, but they need feedback if they are to do this successfully.

Jane needs to learn to hear what Greg has to say without turning it into an argument, a common negative dynamic in this marriage. If Greg describes a gut-level feeling or perception, it is often countered with an argument by Jane, explaining why he should not feel the way he does. As Greg is coming from raw feelings, unreachable by logical explanation, he becomes further irritated by this, since it seems totally irrelevant to him. At other times when he explains that he finds what she has done annoying, she bursts into tears and recriminations. Both of these reactions confirm Greg's natural inclination not to bother with feedback as it only creates more trouble. It will not be easy for Jane to learn to listen to what her husband has to say and think about it without trying to change his perception, but it will strengthen the emotional bond between them, which is an important goal for her.

Shelleys are attracted to Austens because they perceive them as sensitive and caring. Often the desire of Austens to please and make themselves agreeable to others will be initially seen by the Shelley as indicative of a natural affinity. Austens will find the decisiveness and empathetic qualities of the Shelley very attractive.

The moodiness and irritability of the Shelley and the indecisiveness and failures of intellectual honesty of the Austen will mark the downside of this relationship. Average Austens often confuse their desire that a situation be as they would like it with the assertion that it is that way. Austens with abusive, neglectful parents swear that they have had happy childhoods. They can claim to have no anxiety about situations that are visibly driving them into nervous frenzies. They can describe as nice, someone who they've just crossed the street to avoid. All of this is maddening to Shelleys who consider a lack of intellectual honesty and self-awareness to be unforgivable.

Austens faced with the demand to tell it like it is, can feel cornered and miserable. They are much happier adding a slight sugarcoating to life and don't see why the Shelley needs to make such an issue of it. They may begin to perceive the Shelley as cruel.

Another problem in this marriage will be the average Austen's tendency toward rigidity in thinking which is in direct conflict with the strong distrust of authority that is natural to Shelleys. Austens want to do what is expected of them and the Shelley's refusal to respond with unreasoned compliance to public opinion can be upsetting to them. This is an appropriate area for compromise. If the Austen worries about what the neighbors will think if the house is a mess and the Shelley doesn't see what difference it makes, it is sensible to talk about it and achieve some level of agreement.

Jane might say, *"Don't ask people over on Monday when I haven't cleaned up from the week-end. It really bothers me if you invite people over when the kitchen sink is overflowing with dishes."*

"Providing you don't expect me to wait until you've done a major clean-ing to have the guy next door over for a beer," could be Greg's response.

Shelleys have an instinctive distrust of authorities and tend to be cynical about pronouncements from them. Austens tend to believe that respect for authority is necessary and beneficial in all well-run societies. The instinctive automatic respect they grant to the likes of doctors, elected officials and religious leaders is puzzling to Shelleys. This is the same problem on a larger scale as conforming to what the neighbors think, and can be resolved by the same approach.

With a reasonable degree of good will, compromise is possible. It is important that Austens be aware of the difficulty with flexibility inher-ent in their personality structure. Its hard for them to let go of their positions because of all the "shoulds" in their heads, but the result will be worth it in terms of an improved relationship.

Another area for scrutiny in this partnership is their differing under-standings of the meaning of companionship. Shelleys don't always enjoy making small talk. They just don't see the point of it. They are perfectly happy to sit in the room with someone else and read a book or to go for a quiet walk with someone, each thinking their own thoughts. Austens relate by talking. Silence is indicative of lack of togetherness to them. If you have a relationship, you tell each other everything: who you saw at the grocery store, what topic was on the talk show, what you said to your boss at lunch. The need to confide this relentless accumula-tion of trivia is incomprehensible to Shelleys. Who cares? Why would anyone want to know?

If both partners understand this inherent difference in approach, it will be less painful to both of them. Austens can attempt to tone down the amount of information they disseminate, and Shelleys can make an attempt to communicate some of the day's happenings. As long as Shelleys realize that the Austen needs to feel related and achieves this through small talk, and Austens realize that it is uncomfortable for

Shelleys to do this, both personalities can be more understanding of the amount of conversation the other is comfortable with.

Decision-making styles between Shelleys and Austens are at opposite poles. Shelleys are extremely decisive over just about everything. They know what they want and how they want it. Given a choice, they will consider pros and cons and make a quick decision. Austens are nature's fence-straddlers. They are cautious and hate to make mistakes. They can spend a month agonizing over a choice that a Shelley would make in five minutes. Shopping expeditions for the Shelley-Austen couple can go one of two ways. Either the Austen succumbs to the Shelley certainty and goes along with it (after all, if it's wrong, it will be the partner's mistake) or the Austen refuses to concur. The second situation could put some severe stresses on the relationship.

"Which sofa do you think we should get?" Jane asks.

"The white one, it will look really great in the den and I like that style," *Greg says.*

"But it will show the dirt a lot more than the blue one."

Greg is easy, "If you really think it makes a difference, I can live with the *blue one."*

"But I think you're right, I like the white one better too."

This conversation would continue for days, except that Greg leaves it after the first fifteen minutes and refuses to participate further, which is indicative to Jane of his lack of support and understanding, and leaves her in an even greater state of indecision.

The problem for average Austens is that they believe there is a right answer to questions that are merely matters of personal preference. Greg needs to help Jane to remember that there is no correct choice, and that, even more difficult to grasp, it really is all right to make honest mistakes. Jane needs to leave the cognitive decision making modality that works for intellectual and ethical decisions, but is flawed as a model for small daily options. Instead of asking, "What is right?" she needs to ask "What do I want to do?" or "What do I want?" She must confront and overcome her fear of making wrong choices. After all, most of these decisions are just not worth the mental agony that Austens subject themselves to in making them.

GREATEST DANGER SIGNAL: If the Austen in this relationship fails to curb dependency needs, it will endanger the relationship. Austen's need reassurance, and they need the closeness they experience when they share the trivia of their day with a partner. They often need help in decision-making. This can be experienced by the Shelley as clinging, whiny behavior. It is important for Shelleys to identify and discuss what is happening if they begin to feel oppressed by their partners needs. Once the situation is identified, it can be amended by compromise and understanding. If it is not dealt with, it will seriously impair the relationship.

PRIMARY FOCUS: The focus in this relationship should be on mutual understanding. It is hard for the Shelley to remember and take into account the need of the Austen to appear conventional and to be like everyone else. It is equally hard for the Austen to grasp the absolute need of the Shelley for individuality and uniqueness. Continuing dialogue about these differences will keep either partner from failures of sensitivity toward the other.

THE SHELLEY-MOZART RELATIONSHIP

Jean and Bruce decided to grow their own vegetables last summer, a big step, having in previous years planted no more than a couple of tomato plants and some herbs. Bruce was particularly enthusiastic about the plan. He bought several books on vegetable gardening and was eloquent in describing the pleasures they would experience when they sat down to wonderful meals of their own produce. Jean became increasingly committed to the idea as she listened to him talk about it.

They went to the garden center together in early spring and purchased a large variety of garden tools, fertilizer and seeds. On the first warm spring

Saturday, Jean was ready to get started. Unfortunately, Bruce had sched-
uled a golf game and was unable to participate in soil preparation. Jean
decided to go ahead and do the work alone as it was important to start get-
ting the seeds planted. During the week, she made extra trips to the garden
center for supplies, and the following Saturday was ready to start planting
in earnest. Bruce was unable to join her once again; he had completely for-
gotten about a commitment he'd made to his friend. He'd promised to help
him move some furniture that day.

The next week, Bruce had a really bad cold and was afraid that going
out and working on what turned out to be quite a damp day would make
him worse. Jean reluctantly agreed that he was probably right.

On the day the first green shoots were visible, Bruce rushed out to exam-
ine their work. He was tremendously gratified, "Look at that, they're really
coming up. This is great. Aren't you excited? It's going to be more work
from now on, but we'll do it."

Jean seemed a bit subdued as Bruce enthused, reminding him, "We're
going to have to keep after the weeds and to water if it doesn't rain for a few
days if we're going to get vegetables out of this."

"Absolutely. Look, I know you've done more of the work up to now, but
I'm going to do my share. I just had a run of stuff I couldn't get out of."

The following weekend Bruce does go out and check on progress and he
pulls every hint of a weed, but there doesn't really seem to be too much to
do. Jean is somewhat encouraged by the fact that he's gotten into old
clothes, however, and tries to reinforce the need for effort in the coming
weeks.

The following week-end, Bruce is busy again, but it doesn't matter
much as an hour of weeding and some additional planting seems to be all
that is required. The weeks that follow are the bad ones for Jean. She comes
to realize that she has planted a vegetable garden and that she is devoting
about three hours a week to tending it. She feels anger and resentment, but
keeps them to herself. What is there to say after all? She is happy with the
garden and has already harvested and enjoyed a few early vegetables from

it. Without Bruce's early enthusiasm and energy, she would never have begun the project. She's glad she has it, but even so, she's very irritated over the gulf between Bruce's early enthusiasm and his actual participation.

Bruce is marginally aware that Jean seems somewhat withdrawn and quiet, but he is so busy with several new projects he's organizing that he hasn't really focused on her moods too much.

This is a pattern in their relationship that leaves issues unresolved. Jean has been upset and angry over the years about Bruce's failure to keep commitments to her, but she has never confronted him about this. Her reasoning is that it won't change anything and that it's her own fault really for being such a fool that she doesn't learn from experience. Bruce wants to believe that Jean doesn't really mind when he gets so overbooked that he doesn't do his share. If it bothered her, she'd say something after all. He does wonder why she sometimes seems to have withdrawn from him, but he really has so many other things going on that he doesn't give it much thought.

Both Jean and Bruce have contributed to this situation and both need to make conscious efforts to change if they want their relationship to improve. Jean finds Bruce's enthusiasm stimulating and likes the fun of being with him in his upbeat moods. She needs to come to terms with the fact that while they can be very hard workers over a short span, faithfulness to long-term projects requiring systematic attention is not a general characteristic of Mozart personalities. The wisest course on her part would have been to plant a smaller garden, using Bruce's enthusiasm as a stimulus and recognizing that it was going to be basically her project. Then if Bruce felt in a gardening mood one day and wanted to join her, it would have been an unexpected plus. Her summer would have been passed in quiet enjoyment of her garden and its produce without resentment.

While he wants to follow through on his plans, and believes that this time he will, when he agrees to something, Bruce needs to learn to recognize his limitations and not make commitments on the spur of the moment to projects requiring substantial long-term effort.

As Mozart personalities grow emotionally, they do learn more long range planning skills, but probably the best way to test this is in rather small doses. *"I'll help you next Saturday afternoon",* may be followed through on, and is thus a better contract than an overly ambitious commitment of a whole summer. They need to start small and work up to making longer-term commitments as they gain staying power and are able to follow through.

Jean needs to tell Bruce that she is irritated with him when she is. Shelley personalities tend to harbor resentments out of a sense that voicing them is useless. This is not true and it is important for the relationship that Bruce realize when he has irritated her and that she not allow cumulative grievances to mount over time until she is overwhelmed with the aggregate stock of minor annoyances.

Shelleys are attracted to Mozarts because they are upbeat and amusing, their enthusiasm and energy are contagious. Mozarts find Shelleys intellectually stimulating. Mozarts are always seeking new and different experiences, and Shelleys often seem to offer new perspectives in thinking and to have unusual theories and ideas. The Shelley sensitivity can be interesting and appealing to Mozarts. Problems in Shelley-Mozart relationships tend to center on their differing understandings of commitment, the difference in energy levels, and on extrovert vs. introvert issues.

Another problem area for the Shelley-Mozart relationship is in the difference between the self-controlled Shelley and the impulsive Mozart. Shelley personalities do not have much sympathy for a lack of impulse control. They tend to view it as childish, if not a major character flaw. This becomes serious when the impulse affects not only the Mozart, but has implications for the Shelley as well. *"You said we'd do what next weekend?"* or *"How could you have bought that without talking to me first?"* screams the enraged Shelley. The explanation that it sounded like fun in the first instance and that it was too good a bargain to pass up in the second generally does not prove to be an acceptable explanation. Mozarts must learn to consult their partners before impulsively doing things that will effect them. Shelleys must learn to be more accepting of minor impulsive acts that do not affect them. If a Mozart spouse eats a candy bar on the way to the restaurant, it may be foolish, but it is not actually a major character defect.

Impulse control becomes a more serious problem in Mozarts who develop addictions. Shelleys are less likely than many personalities to develop co-dependent behaviors, but they can be deeply hurt by the addictive behavior of a partner. Addicts need to get professional help. If the partner refuses, it is important for the Shelleys to seek a support group and learn to handle living with an addictive personality with a minimum of damage to themselves.

There is a major difference in stamina level between most Shelleys and Mozarts. Mozarts are extremely high-energy people, and if they expect Shelleys to keep up with them, they will probably be disappointed. Shelleys need to realize that Mozarts will keep going, after they have collapsed for the day and not respond resentfully if the Mozart chooses to leave them behind and go on to another activity when they have elected to collapse with a book and a cup of tea.

Childcare can be a problem area in Shelley-Mozart relationships. Healthy Shelleys are good parents who know how to nurture their children without being intrusive. Mozarts are adoring parents, but the relationship tends to be out of mind when out of sight. There are just so many things that Mozarts want to do and so many places they want to be that the tedium of daily childcare can overwhelm them.

They are more fun on trips to the zoo than the Shelley is, but not so good at providing milk and cookies every afternoon of the school year. Shelleys can be resentful of this, seeing the Mozart as cashing in on the good parts of the parent-child relationship and leaving the drudgery to them. It is necessary for the Shelley to be relatively philosophical about this. Children are going to love both parents for being themselves, if they are good and loving parents, and, as they grow up, they will see and appreciate the strengths of both.

GREATEST DANGER SIGNAL: The greatest danger for this couple lies in the pronounced difference in energy levels between them. If the Shelley constantly pushes to keep up with the Mozart, it will not be long before fatigue breeds resentment. If the Mozart fails to understand and accept what is basically a physiological difference between the partners the resulting tensions can create unnecessary dissension in the relationship.

PRIMARY FOCUS: The primary focus for this couple can lie in their ability to bring their separate strengths together for their mutual enrichment. The Mozart pursuit of joy and happiness can keep the Shelley tendency toward depression at bay, while the Shelley can provide a depth and intensity of feeling in the relationship that will bring a new dimension of enjoyment to the Mozart.

THE SHELLEY-CAESAR RELATIONSHIP

The computers where Jean banks seem to have lost a sizable amount of money from her checking account. She is both annoyed and depressed by this. The necessity of dealing with the situation is more upsetting to her than the lost cash. She is feeling miserable by the time Bob gets home that evening.

He shrugs off her worries. "We ought to think about changing banks if these jokers can't keep their act together, but it's nothing to worry about. Just get your bank statements and deposit slips and canceled checks for the last three months together and go down to the bank in the morning and straighten it out."

After dinner, still depressed, Jean goes to her desk and attempts to follow Bob's suggestion. Unaccountably, two deposit slips and a statement seem to be missing. She searches with greater and greater misery, dreading having to admit to Bob that she doesn't have all the information.

When she finally has to acknowledge that she seems to have lost some of the material, her fears are confirmed. Bob explodes: "What is wrong with you? Any fool knows you have to keep track of this stuff. What do you mean you don't have it?"

"I do try to keep it all together. I thought I had it. I can't imagine what happened. I try to be careful with anything I get from the bank. I know I didn't throw it away, but I can't find it."

"I don't know what I expected. This is par for the course with you. You know everything there is to know about stuff that doesn't matter, but when it comes to your own business, you don't even have enough sense to file it."

"Look, I'm sorry, I didn't do it on purpose. Yelling at me isn't going to make it better. I didn't make the mistake, the bank did."

"I made the mistake when I set up a joint account and let you handle some of the money. Well, that's about to change."

"If you don't want a joint account, it's fine with me, we'll each have our own."

"So you can foul it up and not tell me about it? Oh, no, from now on, I'm taking over the finances, period."

"I hate to mention a small detail to you, but I make my own money and if you think I'm putting my pay check at your disposal, you've lost touch with reality. Forget that one." Jean stalks out of the room.

The next morning at the bank, Jean finds they are able to straighten the situation out despite the missing deposit slips and she leaves the building feeling vindicated but still furious with Bob. Since the problem has been solved, Bob promptly forgets about the whole thing, but Jean doesn't. The previous evening's quarrel and dozens of similar confrontations are alienating her and weakening their relationship.

Clearly Jean had no intention of losing the banking material, but the loss points up an ongoing problem for Jean. She pays very little attention to the small details of life and for that reason things such as bank statements often seem to vanish. While she considers it contrary to her nature to focus on the trivia of daily existence, these problems will persist until she acknowledges the necessity of doing so.

It is understandable that Bob is irritated by Jean's carelessness, but his punitive response does not achieve any worthwhile goal. Clearly, he has no authority to unilaterally take over the couple's finances and his threat is doubly misjudged, since Jean can immediately pinpoint its empty nature, while at the same time feeling miserable and angry about his desire to hurt her.

When the couple achieve greater emotional health, such scenes will be minimized, as Jean works on behaving more responsibly in those aspects of life that she finds uninteresting. Then when mistakes do occur, Bob will be able to act with more empathy. He needs to realize that Jean is genuinely intimidated by aspects of daily life that seem matter of fact to him, and to try to help her structure such activities in a way that will allow them to be handled with minimal chance of error rather than humiliating her for her mistakes. He will also acknowledge that making mistakes is a common aspect of human existence and not some aberrant behavior exclusively reserved to the most incompetent among us.

The Shelley and Caesar have certain traits in common. In their ways both are free spirits with a strong sense of themselves. They dislike being in situations where others are in charge and telling them what to do and both have little tolerance for conventional pieties. Caesars can be touched and somewhat mystified by the Shelley's understanding and empathy toward themselves and others. Shelleys admire the directness of Caesars and prize their easy coping skills.

Both Shelleys and Caesars are very strong willed, and often refuse to bend to plausible compromises, so that when they do clash over an issue, it can be extraordinarily difficult for them to achieve any resolution. Shelleys are likely to experience their Caesar partners as crassly insensitive and even brutal when they are in conflict with them, while

Caesars often find Shelley vulnerability irritating, and still often take advantage of it.

The differences in sensitivity level in this relationship are probably greater than between any other personalities. This means that both the alacrity with which Jean experiences hurt and the depth of her pain are very difficult for Bob to take seriously.

It is equally perplexing to Jean, for whom empathy is built-in radar equipment, to comprehend that anyone could fail to pick up on the feelings of a person they care about. It is important that Jean give Bob adequate feedback about exactly how she feels and why she feels that way when he hurts her. It is equally necessary for Bob to tell her how he would have responded in her place. Reverse role-playing, with each taking the partner's role and stating the partner's viewpoint may help them to understand each other better.

The Shelley personality has an exceptionally strong need to feel loved and valued. Caesars are often unaware or neglectful in this respect, seeing such demands as frivolous and unnecessary. Shelleys need to overcome their diffidence about asking for what they need and learn to tell their partners when they are feeling neglected or unloved.

Caesars are naturally confrontational and can enjoy the surge of adrenaline that comes with conflict. They may even create disputes to dispel unpleasant emotions such as anxiety, so that when they begin to feel anxious, they often react by becoming pugnacious.

Shelleys hate conflict. At the same time they are innately unable to avoid it by backing down on issues about which they have strong feelings. They tend to withdraw in the face of marital disagreements, stubbornly going their own way while refusing to discuss the issue. This strong distaste for confrontation, leaves basic conflicts between the couple unresolved and is guaranteed to arouse frustration and anger in a Caesar partner.

If the Caesar can present their differences in terms of problems to be resolved rather than angry collisions of will, the Shelley will be better able to stay with the discussion and work toward a resolution of the problem.

A tactful approach is also a great asset when disagreeing with Caesar partners. They are much more likely to respond positively to someone pointing out that there is a specific problem with what they want to do than blunt refusal of their desires. Shelleys as they become healthier manage to stay with disagreements when they arise, and to handle confrontation more assertively.

Differences in energy level can be a problem in this relationship. Shelleys are hardworking, but when they become energy depleted, they need to stop. If they push themselves beyond the limits of their stamina, they become run-down, depressed and irritable. Caesars with their strong drive often do not understand this difference and try to push Shelley partners to do more. A great deal of strain will be eliminated from the relationship if the Caesar learns not to push and the Shelley remembers to call a halt when tired.

Caesars have strong impulses to control the people around them. Shelleys have little desire to control the actions of others, but they have extremely strong negative responses to any attempts to assert control over them. As Caesars become healthier, they acknowledge that it is inappropriate to give peremptory orders to their partners and work on fighting their natural inclination to do so.

Discussing this issue frankly provides the only hope for creating change. The Shelley will need to gently remind the Caesar that it is fine to make requests, but not acceptable to give commands. The Caesar will have a natural inclination to lash out at such reminders, but the health of this relationship is dependent on such reminders since they are a necessary component of creating change.

Caesar anger can be quite disproportionate to its causes and can frighten the average Shelley. It can also create a serious breach in the relationship, as Shelleys hold grudges for a very long time and seldom forget an affront. When Shelleys become healthier, they learn to let go of old hurts and concentrate on what is happening in the present. Caesars need to find strategies such as regular physical exercise to help them ventilate anger safely and to regulate and control disproportionate responses. If they cannot find methods that work for them, it is time to seek professional help.

Shelleys need commitment in their relationships. Any failure by a partner will be seen as abandonment. This does not mean that Shelleys themselves are never unfaithful, but when they are it is usually an indication that they have already jettisoned the partnership emotionally. Shelleys entering relationships with Caesars should be explicit about their needs in this area and avoid forming alliances with anyone unable to accept such constraints. In Shelley-Caesar relationships where problems of infidelity exist, a good therapist will be invaluable.

Making money is much more a focus for Caesars than for Shelleys. If the Shelley patronizes the Caesar for this innate personality component, this could become a problem. As Shelleys have no problem in enjoying the results of their partner's focus, they should be doubly cautious about minimizing its importance.

Even given this understanding, Shelleys will rarely comb the financial pages of the paper or become fascinated by investment strategies, and Caesars will usually be more than willing to accept the fact that financial planning for the family is going to be largely their responsibility.

GREATEST DANGER SIGNAL: Uncontrolled anger is the greatest danger in this relationship. Caesars often use anger as a weapon to get their own way without regard for the long-range consequences of their actions. This will not work well in the Shelley-Caesar partnership. Although often internalized, Shelley anger tends to be intense and to smolder and build until it reaches a point of no return for a relationship. The danger to the marriage is that this point of no return can be reached without the Caesar being aware of the possibility that simple anger could have such serious consequences. It is important for Caesars to realize that bullying is simply not viable in this relationship and for

Shelleys to be clear about the depth and intensity of their feelings in this regard early in the marriage.

GENERAL FOCUS: The focus in this relationship should be on mutual respect and understanding. There are a number of areas in which these personalities show a marked resemblance. Both have only disdain for the good opinion of those they do not respect and a willingness to say what they think without regard for the conventions. But, they are likely to hold widely divergent views in many other areas and it is important that they do not allow these strong beliefs and opinions to lessen mutual respect for each other within the marriage.

THE SHELLEY-GAUGUIN RELATIONSHIP

Linda and Greg have an on-going quarrel over visits to family members. Greg sees his family about four times a year and has been known to remark that this is three times too many. Linda has a warm relationship with her parents and brothers and sisters. She is genuinely fond of them and enjoys their company. This affection reinforces her belief that it is a matter of filial duty to visit her parents regularly.

These disparate filial styles have precipitated the usual conflict as the week-end approaches. "I'm not going to your parents this week, so forget it. Go if you must, but count me out," Greg declares as soon as the subject is broached.

"But they want to see you too, they really care about you," Linda assures him.

"I don't know what makes you think so, but in any case, people don't get the pleasure of my company just because they want it. There has to be some mutual benefit in the arrangement for it to work. Leave it, Linda, I'm not going. I can't stand your brothers and their childish desire for physical contact sports and if your mother says that she made chocolate pudding especially for me one more time, I'll stuff it down her throat."

"But she does, she's trying to please you, can't you see that?"

"No, I only see that she thinks she has to butter me up. Go ahead and go there, enjoy. I honestly don't mind."

"But I do. I want to be with you on Sunday."

"Then, don't go. Please yourself."

Poor Linda is genuinely torn apart. She goes to her parent's for a few hours, awkwardly fielding questions on her husband's whereabouts, and then rushes home feeling vaguely miserable, only to learn that Greg has gone out with a friend and won't be home for dinner.

This situation will improve as both Greg and Linda become healthier. Linda needs to listen to Greg and accept what he is saying. He really does not mind if she visits her family and he really does not want to accompany her. A part of the problem has been Linda's difficulty in seeing the situation from Greg's perspective and accepting these two pieces of information at face value. She must then make her own decisions about how to handle this information. Perhaps her mother's assumption that her children will come over for a meal every week is unrealistic and she needs to begin to wean her from this expectation and set up a new pattern for interaction between the families.

Greg is responding to Linda's expectations out of his own exasperation and it is possible that he is projecting his cool relationship with his own family on to Linda's in an unwarranted manner. He needs to explain to Linda that he is feeling imposed upon by her family, and that he experiences such intrusive and demanding behavior as intolerable. What Linda has experienced as his intransigence and bad temper might more accurately be viewed as the self-protective response of a vulnerable, over-sensitive person who fears being engulfed.

If he feels better understood, he might be better able to recognize that some of his response has been over-kill and make a conscious effort to modify it. Linda's family is making a genuine effort to be friendly and include him. While he does not need to respond to their every demand, he is an adult and must come to terms with the reality that his current stance puts Linda in an embarrassing quandary and that relationships involve mutual obligations, which can be honored even when they are not our preference. An agreement that he will join her in visiting her family once a month might become a compromise they could both live with.

Shelleys are attracted to Gauguins by their low-key, unpretentious easy-going style and Gauguins find Shelleys sensitive and empathetic. There is a mutual respect for each other and a lack of intrusive behavior that both members of this relationship find reassuring.

The average Gauguin does not want to or even know how to engage in the search for self-understanding and self-awareness so important to Shelleys. The average Gauguin's comfort with conventional ways of feeling and acting can be shocked and affronted by the Shelley's tendency to be anti-authoritarian and by their, often blatant, disregard for convention. Shelleys can be cruel in their honesty, and their constant drive to present a totally candid assessment of their feelings and reactions can appear mean and callous to a Gauguin who cringes from unpleasant emotions.

The disparity in the couple's emotional perceptions will be an area of difficulty in this relationship. The Shelley has deep feelings and enjoys analyzing and discussing them. Human behavioral foibles and interactions are a continuing source of interest to most Shelleys. Average Gauguins tend to resent any attempts to demand that they focus on unpleasant or negative incidents or people. When the Shelley says, *"Why do you think she did that?"* the Gauguin is likely to shrug in response. *"Who knows? Why do you care? What difference does it make?"*

This unwillingness to speculate and probe is likely to be perceived as either personal rejection or intellectual dullness by a sensitive Shelley.

As Gauguins become healthier, they feel less intimidated by such discussions and will be more willing to participate in them, but will probably never reach the level of interest that will totally satisfy the Shelley partner. Shelleys need to seek out a sympathetic friend to dissect their feelings with, probably another Shelley or an Austen, and resist the impulse to make unreasonable demands on the Gauguin partner in this area.

Both Shelleys and Gauguins tend to avoid confrontations. Shelleys know that conflict makes them anxious and they find it upsetting. Gauguins believe that few things are worth making a big fuss about. This would seem to be a point of mutual agreement and appreciation, but it can backfire. While Shelleys don't like to fight, they are easily irritated, and their failure to address what is bothering them means that the annoying behavior will inevitably continue. At some point, when they can no longer tolerate it, the Shelley will then explode or say or do something cruel out of pent-up anger, to the pain and astonishment of the partner. Gauguins tend to turn to food or drink to compensate for their failure to confront. This is an equally unhealthy response, both physically and emotionally. Part of the task of becoming healthier for both partners is to work on speaking up promptly when they don't like something rather than allowing it to fester.

The Gauguin potential for addiction can create a problem in the relationship. Shelleys should be quick to look for help if this situation occurs. The general reticence of the Shelley is a great advantage in this case, as they will not usually respond to the discovery of addiction by becoming overtly censorious or rejecting. The resources of the various 12-step programs and/or a therapist skilled in working with substance abuse will be helpful to the Shelley with an addicted Gauguin partner. Finding a sympathetic friend to turn to for additional support is also wise. Because Gauguins are so intimately bound to their mates, it is generally possible for the Shelley through patience and empathy to encourage Gauguins to deal with this problem in a healthy and responsible way.

GREATEST DANGER SIGNAL: Failure to address and resolve disagreements is the greatest danger to this relationship. Both partners tend to retreat from confrontation, leaving important differences unresolved. The negative result of this apathy can be devastating to the marriage over time.

PRIMARY FOCUS: This is a relationship where the focus should be on getting things done. This requires planning activities and creating a structure, with each partner assuming a share of responsibility for those minor tasks and errands that can otherwise be neglected. Both partners have a dislike for dealing with the petty detail of everyday life. The tendency on both of their parts to procrastinate and overlook things that must be done can eventually create trouble for the marriage. This is a tendency that can be overcome, but it must be recognized, discussed and actively combated through planning and structure.

VIII

The Einstein in Relationships

For the Einstein-Emerson Relationship—Go to the Emerson-Einstein Relationship.
For the Einstein-Nightingale Relationship—Go to the Nightingale-Einstein Relationship.
For the Einstein-Beau Relationship—Go to the Beau-Einstein Relationship.
For the Einstein-Shelley Relationship—Go to the Shelley-Einstein Relationship.

THE EINSTEIN-EINSTEIN RELATIONSHIP

Arthur has been offered a remarkable job opportunity in a neighboring state. He is very excited by the possibilities it presents. Marion is happy for him and there is no question in their minds that he should take advantage of this situation. They agree that it would be extremely difficult for Marion to find a job in Arthur's new location, which would be commensurate in salary and prestige to the one she currently holds, and that she must stay in her present situation. They further agree that this will not present a difficulty. They will be only two hours from each other and can take turns commuting on weekends.

Arthur makes the move and their plan works well for the first month. At that point, Arthur calls to say that while it is his turn to visit Marion, some things have turned up and he is going to have to miss the weekend. Marion totally understands. It is not a problem, but she has already made commitments and will be unable to go there. A few weeks later, problems rise again when professional commitments interfere. Again, neither of them is angry or demanding, they both understand.

As time passes, both Arthur and Marion make friends to whom they are able to turn for entertainment when they can't manage to get together. At this juncture, they sometimes agree to stay in their separate residences, not out of necessity, but from choice. Now Arthur is talking about the possibility of going on a fishing trip on his vacation time. Marion doesn't enjoy fishing and thinks she may go to Italy with a friend if those are his plans. There is no thought of a formal separation and neither of them is angry or unhappy with their circumstances. Only a few of their friends really notice an underlying sadness inherent in the fact that their marriage has just about ceased to exist.

Some Einsteins reading this scenario are likely to wonder if there is a problem at all. The perception of a difficulty must rest on the assumption that intimate human relationships are valuable and worth cultivating. If Arthur and Marion are to become emotionally healthier, they must realize that something important has inadvertently occurred to their marriage and take steps to remedy the situation. They can then make a firm commitment to spending weekends and vacations together if this is all the time that will be available to them. Both of them need to take responsibility for making this a time of intimacy and shared experience, not just a situation in which they go their separate ways from the same living space.

Shared interests are likely to provide the momentum behind the relationship between two Einsteins. It is natural for a consuming interest in a subject, whether a branch of science, a theory of history, stamp collecting or rock climbing to evolve first into friendship and eventually into romance. As they get to know each other, Einsteins will also be grateful and relieved that their partner is not too demanding in terms of time or attention. They do not need to fear intrusion or emotional effusiveness from a fellow Einstein.

Problems in the relationship are likely to occur through sins of omission rather than overt difficulties. Both partners can become over-involved with work, theories, and projects, leaving no one to take care of the relationship. Good marriages need attention. They do not flourish through benign neglect rather they stagnate and lose cohesion. This is likely to be a major difficulty in the Einstein-Einstein relationship.

It might be said that lack of confrontational style is a problem in the relationship of many Einsteins. They have such a strong natural tendency to withdraw and make do with whatever the situation may be that they rarely address the issues that bother them personally. The same person who defends research findings to the death will suffer personal discomforts and inconveniences in total silence. This means that in a marriage, even those situations that can easily be remedied may be allowed to grow and fester. It may be an effort to say, *"I don't really like boiled eggs, please don't make them for me," the* first time, but compared to a lifetime of eating boiled eggs, it wins hands down.

The other point for the Einstein to remember here is that with practice it becomes easy, particularly with a partner sharing the same personality style, who will neither have hysterics, nor become irrationally angry at the information provided. Breaking through the communication barrier that probably got erected in childhood is difficult, but with repeated forays into making this type of contact, it will become easier with satisfying results for both.

Sexuality can be an area of difficulty for Einsteins. In a continuum of sexual drive and arousal, they are often at the low end of the scale. This can be compounded in some instances by the Einstein tendency to theorize. It is easy to formulate elaborate theories concerning sexuality and hundreds of them have been devised over the centuries:

when it is appropriate, what positions and behaviors can be used, or what are suitable settings in which to pursue sexual activity. Einsteins, who often neglected to reference them to reality, have created many of these theories.

Clearly, such theorizing is the enemy of passion, which demands that we turn off our analytical brain cells to experience it. Einsteins who become victims of their own cerebral inventions in regard to sex are often difficult to dissuade. If this occurs, to the detriment of the relationship, it will probably be necessary to seek therapeutic help in restoring the partner to a healthier sexual perspective.

The failure to deal with the details of daily living is a problem which frequently surfaces with an Einstein couple. Many, though not all Einsteins, have trouble remembering to set aside time to clean out their closets, throw out the old magazines, or mow the lawn. If no one deals with these petty concerns, they eventually can get quite out of hand. It is probably wise for an Einstein couple to make a list of these minor details that must be dealt with and systematically allot an hour or two a week to handling them.

The children of an Einstein couple are often quite angry with their parents. The complaint that they are not like other families is likely to be true in this case. While lives of conformity to some artificial norm are manifestly undesirable, it is genuinely hard on children when their peers view them as having overtly eccentric life-styles.

The problem comes in two pieces: living space and rules. In regard to living space, the children of most Einsteins learn early that if they want to have friends over, and they care about appearances, they had better clean the house before extending the invitation. This is a problem that can be handled. When they make a concerted effort, even Einsteins find that it is possible to put their books, newspapers and other clutter away, or contain them in studies and bedrooms.

Parental rules can also create obstacles for the children of these couples. There are two disparate possibilities that can create problems.

Average Einsteins love to theorize and may then attempt to project their theories into their daily lives and those of their children. This can result in children who are told such rules as: *"Television is a waste of time and you may never watch it; we are vegetarians, you must be careful never to eat anything containing even a flavoring of meat;"* or *"Learning something or other is extremely important and you must sacrifice your after school time to classes in this area."* Such rigidities can have unfortunate results in any circumstances, but when it is foisted on children, it isolates them from their peers and can be devastating to them.

An equal possibility exists at the opposite end of this continuum. Einstein parents can become so caught up in their own concerns that they fail to notice that their children are suffering from neglect. They forget to wash or iron clothes, and don't notice that the size seven sweater no longer reaches their son's wrists. Their children can appear to teachers and neighbors as neglected little waifs

Einsteins tend to be economical, sometimes downright penurious. In a relationship between two Einsteins, there is no one to modify this tendency and it can be carried to an extreme by the couple. It is important for both Einsteins to be aware of this potential in order to keep within the bounds of moderation. It is fine for them to decide that they don't want to be up on the latest fashion, but if they are wearing shoes that need new heels, and the wardrobe they acquired in their teens when they reach thirty, they are overdoing it.

GREATEST DANGER SIGNAL: The danger for this relationship is that both partners in their need for time alone and their preoccupation with their own interests will fail to devote enough time and attention to the marriage to keep it cohesive and growing. They should cultivate a mutual awareness of the importance of having joint pursuits and spending time together.

PRIMARY FOCUS: The focus should be on finding stimulation through friends and family. Two Einsteins together can be extremely insular, staying home, forgetting to call friends, and forgetting to make contact with the outside world apart from their jobs. This is a mistake. Everyone needs outside stimulation and it is important to seek it and leave time for it.

THE EINSTEIN-AUSTEN RELATIONSHIP

Arthur has come up with a hypothesis involving a breakthrough in computer electronics. He is very excited about it and feels that he is finally putting his theoretical knowledge into a practical application. He has kept this idea very much to himself up to this point, but it will take a significant bite out of their savings to market his concept, so at this point he sits down with Jane and explains to her what he wants to do. He is sure that the money he will use will be substantially repaid when the implications of his work are acknowledged.

Jane is aghast when Arthur suggests that he wants to put half of their combined savings into promotion of this project. Arthur is usually financially extremely conservative, and she would never have expected him to propose such a thing. Her response to his proposal is automatic and extremely negative. While Arthur rarely discusses his work with her, and she is frankly not very interested in a lot of what he does, the suddenness of the proposal creates an added dimension of uncertainty and anxiety for her.

Arthur begins to have second thoughts himself as Jane talks to him about the dangers involved in the possible loss of money targeted toward the children's college and their own retirement, but his primary emotion is hurt over Jane's lack of trust in his judgment and abilities. He agrees to put the plan on hold temporarily.

The next day, he is quite astonished when Jane brings the subject up. She is having second thoughts about what she said to him and she is also experiencing guilt over her lack of loyalty. Maybe he should go ahead and make the investment. It could be a real financial breakthrough after all, if it is successful. Taking her at her word, Arthur begins work on the project and says no more about it.

When the next bank statement arrives, Jane opens it and is horrified to see that half the money in their savings account has been withdrawn. She is in a state of near hysteria by the time Arthur gets home. He is confused, "You told me to go ahead with it. You said it could be a great opportunity."

"I know I did, but now that you've done it, I'm scared. I didn't know you'd do it all at once like that."

Arthur tries to soothe her. Things are going quite well. The odds that everything will be fine are greatly in their favor. She remains agitated. At this point, she wants guarantees, certainties. The knowledge that every-thing seems to be progressing well is not enough. Arthur is both confused and angered by her reactions. His realization that she doesn't trust him and doesn't understand the importance of what he is doing is a blow to his self-esteem, but her vacillation over the project is even more disquieting as it leaves him off balance and undermines both his own self-assurance and his feelings for her.

A better understanding of each other's basic dynamics would have been extremely helpful to Jane and Arthur in this situation. Jane has a strong gut-level need to feel safe and secure that is far beyond any rational control on her part. When she thinks her future is threatened, she cannot suppress the anxiety that she experiences. If Arthur under-stood this, he would realize that her lack of trust was not directed at his good judgment, but at the unknown and anything that could not be predicted and structured to provide a guarantee of safety.

If Jane had understood Arthur better, she would have grasped the fact that he uses his intellectual competence to shelter himself from the world, that he considers his ideas and theories his protection against an environment that might at some point prove hostile. He is still the same fiscally conservative man he has always been and far from squandering their savings, he believes that he is securing their future by this move. She would probably still be apprehensive, but she would not be angry and would be less likely to feel that her life was spinning completely out of her control.

As Arthur becomes healthier, he will be less secretive about what he is doing. He will want to share more of his plans with Jane as he goes along, if not in technical detail, then in a general conceptual sense. He actually does trust her, he has just gotten into a habit of keeping his work to himself. If she felt more a part of the project, through watching it develop and listening to Arthur talk about it, Jane would not have reacted with the same degree of alarm at Arthur's original proposal.

Arthur knew that when Jane said, maybe he should go ahead with the project, she was wavering, not giving full consent, but he also correctly surmised that checking back with her could spell an end to his dream. As he becomes healthier, he will continue the discussion, rather than pretending to believe that her indecision is tantamount to approval.

As Jane becomes healthier, she will feel less anxious and fearful. She will come to realize that life is always going to include risk and that there are very few firm guarantees. In this instance, instead of first responding with horror and than wavering out of loyalty, a healthy Austen would begin to ask questions to get a better grasp of the situation, make an honest attempt to understand conceptually what Arthur was proposing, and then engage him in a more in-depth discussion regarding the degree of risk versus the degree of potential in what he was doing. As Jane becomes healthier, she will find herself less conflicted over choices in general. She will think through decisions, making the choices that are right for her instead of responding out of anxiety and then backing down because she has overreacted.

The natural kindness and sensitivity of the Austen will be appealing to Einsteins. Austens will respond to similar qualities in the Einstein personality. There will be many mutual interests to draw the couple together. Neither personality seems overbearing or threatening to the other, creating an atmosphere of safety and security in the marriage. Difficulties will occur when the Einstein's minor quirks and eccentricities meet head to head with the conventionality of the Austen. One of the first areas of disagreement may be a superficial one. Einsteins are not very concerned about outward appearance and conventional Austens may have problems with certain clothing eccentricities or just with the disheveled, quickly thrown together appearance of the partner. This issue is likely to be the tip of the iceberg. Beneath this superficial disregard for style, lies a roving mind filled with theories and concepts to challenge pieties in every area: politics, religion, medical advice, or family custom, all questions capable of disturbing or embarrassing a more traditional person.

Austens are constantly doing things: they clean out cupboards, organize filing systems, make scrapbook albums or chauffeur children who are old enough to take the bus. Einsteins are intensely involved either in their chosen career or in some extracurricular interest outside their work, but are generally uninterested in household projects. This can be a problem in the Einstein-Austen relationship as the Austen feels imposed upon, doing all of the small daily tasks alone, and the Einstein responds that the dresser drawers don't need to be rearranged again when such projects are suggested as priorities. Austens need to stop to assess what they are doing and perhaps decide to cut back on their own constant fussing over details. Einsteins, in turn, should make the effort to assume a realistic degree of involvement in household tasks.

Both Einsteins and Austens can be rigid. This might seem an area of agreement, but in fact the Einstein rigidity is an intellectual stance. It occurs when the average Einstein tries to insist that reality fit into preconceived theories. This is no problem in purely intellectual areas, but when the theories intrude into household management or joint areas of concern, major problems occur. This is a difficult situation for most Austens to surmount. Head-on confrontations will usually only strengthen the partner's original opinion. It is possible often to find newspaper or magazine articles from respected sources that present other viewpoints. An additional way to break through is to ask questions that present problems with the theory, as posited, without directly challenging its overall truth.

The final recourse when a theory is too far-fetched is one of limit setting. *"I know that is your theory, but it is not mine, and I simply do not have the time or energy do what you would like in this case."* This may seem to go against all prior admonitions to compromise and seek a middle ground, however this is advice specifically tailored to this couple. The Austen, who is generally willing to compromise, must recognize when that strategy, far from resolving the issue, simply creates further elaboration of a situation that is already a problem. As the Einstein grows healthier, this situation will cease to arise. Healthy Einsteins understand that theories must be put into practice in real life and that they must be modified to meet the demands of daily living.

Austen rigidity tends to be a by-product of conventionality and family custom: *"Beds must be made in the way my mother made them. What would the neighbors think if they saw Jimmy's room? My father always did household repairs himself."* Healthy Austens learn to transcend these old beliefs. They discover that the world does not end if a bed is unmade one day and that sending for the plumber solves the problem adequately. Einsteins whose partners have not reached this stage of growth can help things along by firm gentle reassurance and by promising to share responsibility for the outcome of the problems. Much of the Austen dependence on precedent comes from a fear that doing things differently will be a mistake and that something untoward will occur. If the Austen is absolved from total responsibility and guilt on this score, they will probably find it easier to let go.

Austens have a great need for closeness and reassurance. One way they seek reassurance is through tactile contact. They like to be touched, stroked and cuddled. Einsteins tend to want space and can be quite aloof and withdrawn, especially when preoccupied with other matters. This is an issue that can be partially resolved by both partners becoming more aware and communicative about their respective needs. Austens must learn to say, "*I would like to be held,*" or "*Please come and sit with me for a few minutes and hold my hand.*" Einsteins should feel free to verbalize their need for space equally openly. "*I need to be alone for an hour or two to get myself focused, but I'll come hang out with you later.*" If the couple are aware that both of them have legitimate requirements in these areas and are able to respect each other's needs, this difference will not become a major issue.

Austens want the approval of the people around them, not merely the family, but the neighbors and the wider social circle. Einsteins can be relatively oblivious to the implications for themselves in their partner's concerns. The Einstein has no objection to visiting friends and relatives, but the Austen feels it both a duty and a necessary source of pleasure to touch base with people. The average Einstein, who can be rather quiet and withdrawn in many social settings, can be irritating to Austens who want people to like and approve of their partners. As Einsteins grow healthier, they become more socially adept and begin to appreciate their partner's viewpoint.

As Austens become healthier, they understand that their Einstein partner's silence is not motivated by hostility, but most often by the feeling that they have little in common with the people they are with and that they therefore have little to say that would interest them. Austens can often help their spouses on this score by making suggestions about ways to approach specific people: "*My father would really be interested in that book you were reading, why don't you tell him about it?*" "*When you see Doris, remember to talk to her about your ideas on that.*"

Both Einsteins and Austens tend to avoid confrontation. This should make for a peaceful marriage, but it can, in fact, become a difficulty in itself. Issues between them can be avoided by both partners until the anger and disappointment has festered and become deeper than was necessary. It is important for both partners to address concerns as they occur instead of leaving them and hoping they will go away. When issues do occur, Einsteins must be aware of their tendency to rationalize partner's complaints: *"There is no reason for that to bother you because..."* while Austens must be equally on guard against the tendency to deny that a problem exists.

Communication can become a problem in this relationship. Austens like to keep those they care about informed of the trivia of their lives. They are absorbed in the day to day details of living and like to talk and hear about them. Einsteins are abstract thinkers. In a typical interaction, the Austen will say: *"I ate lunch at the little Italian restaurant we like so much. It was wonderful,"* and proceed to list the menu. The Einstein will respond. *"Oh, that's nice."* Then, when the Austen attempts to prolong the conversation by asking, *"So where did you eat?"* the response is likely to be a monosyllabic one.

These interactions are quite unsatisfactory to both partners. They bore and irritate Einsteins, who can't imagine why anyone would want to relate the fine points of their daily routine, while the Austin feels rejected by the terse response. As both partners become healthier they will come closer to a middle ground, with Austens limiting themselves to talking when they actually have something to communicate, and Einsteins pushing themselves to expand their conversational repertoire. If the couple can discover areas of mutual interest, it will be helpful in providing common ground for conversation.

GREATEST DANGER SIGNAL: The danger for this relationship is centered in the need for solitude of the Einstein juxtaposed to the need for frequent reassurance of the Austen. Austens can easily interpret the need for space of the Einstein as rejection and become upset and angry. Expressing anger may trigger further Einstein withdrawal, with the result that the marriage can spiral down into difficulty. Communication about things that anger, irritate or upset either partner is the key to prevention of this impasse.

PRIMARY FOCUS: The primary focus for this couple should be on bridging the gulf between the conventional Austen and the partner, who while not intentionally unconventional, finds many conventional responses outside the framework of Einstein reference. This is far from a petty difference. Austens really worry about what other people think and need to convey the depth of that concern to their partners. If Austens seem troubled, yet fail to address what bothers them out of a dislike for confrontation, Einsteins would do well to inquire whether they are inadvertently doing something their partner perceives as upsetting or embarrassing.

THE EINSTEIN-MOZART RELATIONSHIP

Bruce wants to have friends over on Saturday night for dinner and bridge, and Marion agrees to this. It is always important to Bruce to have his weekend full, so he then proposes that they arrange a picnic in the country with some other friends for Sunday afternoon. Marion objects at this point. "I have some work from school to get done. You've got to leave me some time to do it."

"Don't worry, you've got plenty of time. I'm going to the gym after work on Friday, so I won't be home until late. I'll bring take-out, so you won't have to cook. You can do what you have to all of Friday evening."

"I really want more time than that. I'm willing to entertain on Saturday, but that's really my limit for the week-end."

"So we'll just sit around like a couple of sticks all day Sunday? Come on, Marion, get with the program. I didn't get married to spend my days in a rocking chair on the back porch."

"I don't think you need to worry," Marion responds with some exasperation. "Do what you want, Bruce, I don't care if you go on a picnic, in fact I would enjoy having the house to myself. But I can't go with you. I have a responsibility to my students."

"Do you know how it looks to our friends when you never want to see them or do things with them?"

"That's not fair. I'm doing something on Saturday. I just can't devote my whole week-end to pleasure."

"Is that an accusation? I work damn hard all week and I deserve to have a little fun on the week-end." Bruce has begun to get huffy at this point, but he is also ready to abandon the argument. One part of his mind is saying, "I'll probably have more fun if Marion doesn't come. I can ask some people that I like, who I think are uncomfortable with her." He stalks off as an expression of his displeasure, but is soon at the telephone, happily arranging the picnic.

This is a fairly typical picture of this marriage. Bruce finds his wife mildly irritating, but he plans his life to meet his own needs and bullies her into some degree of participation when necessary. Marion goes about her work, glad that Bruce isn't under foot too much as she finds his noise level distracting. She has no serious complaints and has learned not to expect much more in the relationship.

The reality is that they are going their separate ways and if Bruce finds someone who is there for him and is more fun, he will probably leave her. She will be initially surprised and upset, but she will not be devastated. If he develops another relationship while remaining in the marriage, it will sadden her, but she will probably do very little about it.

As Marion is uncomfortable with action, she may theorize about what has happened, but she will not make an active attempt at finding a solution. If Bruce wants to create change in the relationship, his best hope is to encourage Marion to go into therapy. As Einsteins become more healthy, they modify their fears of emotional interaction and become more capable of deep involvement with others.

The Einstein-Mozart pairing is a rare pattern, as they would seem to be at opposite ends of the spectrum in terms of needs and interests. When such a relationship occurs, it will truly be a case of the attraction of opposites. The introverted cerebral Einstein can find the Mozart ability to cope energetically with day to day life appealing. Mozarts, always attracted by something new and different, could easily fling themselves headlong into some Einstein intellectual pursuit or project as a new frontier to be conquered. Einsteins will realize that this enthusiasm is one of a dozen diverse interests of the Mozart partner at any current moment.

Mozarts will find the Einstein's knowledge and their intense commitment to their projects and concepts attractive. Anything new and different is fascinating to Mozarts and they will be genuinely enthusiastic and eager to learn about whatever field the Einstein is involved in. Two months later, they will be equally enthusiastic about something completely different and the Einstein preoccupation may then seem tedious to them.

The difficulty over the long haul will be a philosophical one, the Einstein will have difficulty in understanding or condoning the hedonism of the Mozart, while the Mozart, once the novelty has worn off, may find the Einstein boring.

The difference between Einstein self-control and Mozart impulsiveness may be a problem in this relationship. It is difficult for Einsteins, who seem to have less material needs than most other people, to comprehend the urgency behind Mozart desires. The absolute need for new clothing or jewelry, the intense yearning to see the new play or go to the new restaurant, is so far outside the Einstein range of experience as to seem truly alien. Thus, the purchases Bruce brings from the mall are liable to be perceived as sheer self-indulgence and mindless consumerism by Marion. Intelligent budgeting presents a solution to this problem. Bruce needs a fixed amount that is his to do with as he chooses, without meeting with reproach from his wife. Marion needs the assurance that he will confine his impulse purchases to his own spending money.

Mozarts can be confrontational, either from conviction or sometimes purely for the pleasure of creating a fuss. Einsteins are inclined to find this unnecessary and embarrassing. Here, the Einstein tendency to withdraw should be accepted by the Mozart. The expectation that the Einstein mate should stand by and cheer while Mozarts mount picket lines or joust with headwaiters is unrealistic. It's not going to happen.

When both partners let go of their unrealistic expectations and accept each other for who they are, then the Mozart can go into battle unimpeded by Einstein restrictions and the Einstein can retire gracefully without fear of later Mozart reproaches.

The extroversion of Mozarts does not usually bother Einsteins. It is even viewed as an attractive quality when not carried to extremes. Mozarts, on the other hand, often misunderstand introverts and view their naturally more quiet inclinations critically. It is important for Mozarts to grasp the reality that it is simply impossible for Einsteins to turn themselves on and sparkle in the way that Mozarts find so simple and natural. It is not mean-spirited, party-pooping or antisocial for Einsteins to be quiet, it is simply their nature and will remain a constant whether Mozarts rail against it and make everybody miserable or decide to accept this difference in style and stamina for what it is.

Differences in sexual need may be another aspect of this difference in energy. If there are marked differences in degree and frequency of arousal levels between them, frank discussion of the problem is imperative. They will need to work together to find ways that will allow the Einstein to accommodate the sexual needs of the Mozart partner. If the situation does not show considerable improvement, then it is time to seek outside help.

Average Einsteins and Mozarts do not have strong parenting skills. Einsteins are preoccupied with work and intellectual issues, and Mozarts are likely to be wonderful playmates, but to be too distracted by their many other interests and pursuits to be consistently available to children. This couple will probably find that their children will flourish best if they place some reliance on outside resources for child care, while including in their daily schedules, a time that they can allot to giving the children their total attention.

Commitment can be an issue in this relationship. If Einsteins do not work on meeting their Mozart partners halfway, they are likely to lose them. It is necessary for the Einstein to face this issue and realize the importance of being available, talking and doing things together. Unlike Einsteins, Mozarts are unlikely to merely sit back and feel mildly depressed if they feel neglected or under-stimulated. They will leave the relationship, if not in body, certainly in spirit.

Average Mozarts have a potential for addiction. It is easy for Einsteins to lose themselves in their work and ignore danger signs. Einsteins who perceive tendencies toward addictive behaviors in their partners need to seek help through 12-step programs or a therapist.

GREATEST DANGER SIGNAL: This relationship will be in danger if the Mozart gets bored. Mozarts need stimulation and new challenges and if they cannot find them within the relationship, they will almost certainly seek them elsewhere. It is imperative that Mozarts convey the urgency of their needs to Einsteins and that Einsteins take these messages seriously and respond to them.

PRIMARY FOCUS: This marriage represents the temperamental extremes of personality types. They are the furthest apart in terms of introversion-extroversion and energy level of all the personalities. The need to meet each other half way will be an ongoing challenge to this couple. They must focus on compromise in terms of activities, friends, and spending patterns. Ongoing communication and awareness of their pronounced differences in personality are essential for them.

THE EINSTEIN-CAESAR RELATIONSHIP

Evelyn and Arthur have decided to do some renovation on their house. They want to add an additional bathroom and have a screened porch built off the kitchen. Evelyn has had three contractors over and received estimates and is now ready to make a choice. "We should go with the man from Main Street, don't you think, Arthur?"

This is a rhetorical question; she expects Arthur to ratify her decision. In this case, however, he demurs. "Why that one? Isn't he the most expensive?"

"He's only slightly higher than the guy on Spring Street, and the third estimate was so much lower that there has to be something wrong with it."

"Not necessarily, why don't we have the other two come back and talk some more?"

"It will be a waste of time. Trust me, Arthur. We can afford Jason's and they'll do the best job. I have a sense of these things. Believe me, I wouldn't take them if I thought they were jacking up the price. I think they're giving us more for our money in the long run."

Arthur begins to dig in his heels. "I want to have the other two back. This is a big decision, we shouldn't make it off the top of our heads."

"We're not. We've spent a month getting estimates. Spring is coming. I want the porch on the house before the summer. There's no point wasting more time getting started on this," Evelyn says with mounting exasperation.

"I'm just not comfortable with that. Another few days won't make any difference."

"This is ridiculous. It's not another few days, it's another few weeks. This is the real world. Every time you make an appointment with a contractor, it takes a week at least before he'll come and they've already given estimates, they won't be eager to come back for a second round. You don't do any of this, you just sit back and throw curves into the process. I'm the one that's actually doing it, so I'm the one who should make the decisions."

Arthur says no more, and Evelyn assuming that his silence denotes consent signs the contract with Jason's the next day. Arthur discovers that Jason has the contract when he shows up to start work two days later.

When he remonstrates with Evelyn, she responds with exasperation, which quickly turns to belligerence. "You didn't say anything else, so I assumed you agreed. Anyway, we'd have come down to this in the end, you were just going to waste more time before we got started. Frankly, I didn't have the patience to wait any longer.

"It's my money too, Evelyn, and I like to be in on the decisions about how I spend it."

"The bottom line is that you're cheap. I don't care how hard you squeeze your pennies on yourself, but when it's something that involves me, I want it done right. Drop it, Arthur, you're dead wrong and we both know it."

Arthur resigns himself to the situation, but he feels hurt and angry and is unusually cold and withdrawn with Evelyn for several weeks. This is a recurring pattern in their relationship. Evelyn wins the battles by the simple expedient of taking independent action, but she loses in terms of her bond with her husband, who becomes increasingly cold and aloof.

Communication requires hearing what the other person says, not just talking. This is often a problem in the Einstein-Caesar marriage. The Caesar waits while the Einstein speaks, but discounts what is said, while pushing ahead with the Caesar agenda. In this instance, Evelyn needed to accept Arthur's desire to double-check as legitimate, however irritating, while he needed to hear that she was satisfied that she had examined alternatives adequately.

The resolution in this case is relatively straightforward. Evelyn could have said, *"I feel satisfied with my choice, and unwilling to waste more time on the project. If you want to go back and talk to the other contractors again, by all means, do so. Here are the specifications from Jason in terms of material and work. If you get prices that sound better to you, be sure that you lock the other person into providing the same materials and labor. Once you do that, I'll be more than willing to double check at that point before we go to contract."*

Evelyn is probably right that she's made the best choice. Caesars are generally more skilled than Einsteins at this type of interaction. The difficulty was that she was disregarding Arthur and his concerns, and however correct her position might have been in terms of getting the job done, it was incorrect in terms of good human-relations skills

Arthur was not blameless either. He is uncomfortable dealing with contractors and workmen, and wanted no part in the negotiations he criticized. As he becomes healthier, he will concede that it is necessary to deal with such situations even though they are not in his range of expertise, and that if he is dissatisfied with what his wife negotiates, he will have to take the plunge and try to come up with a better solution rather than criticizing and second guessing her choices.

Caesars admire accomplishment and an Einstein personality with impressive credentials in an intellectual sphere would arouse the admiration of most Caesars. Einsteins would admire such a partner's ability to organize and accomplish and might also find the Caesar's goal orientation and sense of direction a great asset, providing motivation for them to become more productive in their own fields. An added advantage in such a marriage would be that neither partner would make excessive demands for closeness and intimacy. Each partner would have an engrossing interest allowing them to give each other adequate space.

Joint decision-making can be an area of difficulty in such a match. The Caesar personality likes to take charge and accomplish and has little patience with delay. *"This is the situation, here is my solution, end of problem."* This approach is likely to upset and intimidate the more cautious Einstein, whose reluctance to move from thinking about what to do into actual task performance will infuriate the action-oriented partner.

The sensitivity of the Einstein personality is in strong contrast to the relative toughness of the Caesar. This can be a problem in this marriage, as Caesars can simply forget or ignore this aspect of the partner's nature as irrelevant to whatever the situation they are dealing with. This is going to damage the relationship if it happens often. It is necessary for Caesars to work to understand their partner's feelings and to remember to take them into consideration. Einsteins can help this process by giving their partners feedback. *"I don't think you meant anything when you said such and such, but the way I understood it, it hurt my feelings."*

Caesars honestly enjoy a battle in most situations, they look upon it as a chance to flex their combative skills and it is their experience that they usually win, at least in the short term, which provides a powerful reinforcement for using such techniques. This makes arguments difficult for the Einstein who hates conflict and avoids it except on purely

intellectual levels such as chess games. It is human nature to take ad
tage of one's skills in such a circumstance and in unhealthy Ca
Einstein relationships, the Caesar wins the majority of the conflicts
the Einstein retreats more and more from meaningful involvement
the bullying partner.

As Caesars become healthier, they begin to realize that this is n
feasible way to conduct a marriage. It is easy to yell louder and to
because you'll do whatever it takes to win. It is simple to take advant
of the partner's distaste for conflict. The more difficult task is to b
off, and decide not to win by coercion, but to hear the other side of
story and to try to understand the thinking of the other person. Heal
Caesars can become just as proud of these skills as they originally w
of their ability to force their decisions on the family by fiat.

Einsteins will become healthier as they learn to set limits for the pa
ner, and to refuse to be bullied. The acquisition of assertive skills h
multiple pay-offs on the job, and in social settings, as well as in the ma
riage. There are many books and courses on assertiveness availab
today, and a short course in assertiveness training would probably l
very worthwhile since it will provide group support and role-playing
reinforce new skills.

The amount of time and attention the couple will give to socializir
is another area where considerable compromise and adjustment will
necessary for them. If the extroverted Caesar expects the introvert
Einstein to entertain extensively or to socialize frequently in busine
settings, for example, there is likely to be a problem. These situatio
can be torture to the Einstein partner, who often feels awkward, out
place or bored by such occasions.

If this is a problem in the relationship, Caesars need to re-exami
how great a priority Einstein participation in such social occasic
actually is. Considered realistically, the physical presence of a part
who feels awkward and uncomfortable adds very little to most gath
ings. It is both considerate and sensible to limit the Einstein partn

participation to those occasions where it is truly mandatory for one rea-son or another. As Einsteins become healthier, they acknowledge that appropriate social behavior is a skill that can be acquired, and that it is worth some effort to learn. Short-term therapy can be extremely valu-able to an Einstein in over-coming shyness and polishing social skills.

A high energy level generally results in a high sex drive and as most Caesars have far greater stamina than most Einsteins, this is an area that requires honest open discussion. If there is a disparity in frequency of arousal, which is not acknowledged and addressed, this will certainly generate an on-going anger in the Caesar, which will spill over into other aspects of the relationship. There is a strong likelihood that an unsatisfied Caesar personality will seek satisfaction elsewhere. When both parties talk openly about their feelings and needs, they will be bet-ter able to work on practical solutions without endangering the mar-riage. Seeking a sex therapist is often the most efficient approach to resolving this situation.

Children can present problems in the Einstein-Caesar relationship. While there are Einsteins professionally involved in child psychology, infant behavior, or pediatrics, who will be extremely absorbed in their children, those who are not in such a field professionally, may take only a sporadic interest in child care issues. Most Einsteins love their chil-dren, but don't find them very engrossing.

Caesars may be more involved, but expect to be in control and when children disregard or defy their wishes, the temptation is toward mas-sive retaliation. They can become rigid, over-punitive disciplinarians. In addition, they will generally be too busy with careers for day to day hands-on parenting.

Since neither Einsteins nor Caesars are temperamentally suited to the task, it is probably wise for them to seek competent full-time child-care. However, the parents must be alert to the dangers involved for them in such a choice. They do not want to relinquish the parental role through over involvement in their careers. Healthy couples will make a

point of spending time in mutually rewarding activities with their children when they come home.

Infidelity can become an issue in some Einstein-Caesar marriages. Unhealthy Caesars can see a second relationship as a challenge or as just another perquisite of their success in life. The problem is likely to become magnified by the easy distraction of the Einstein partner who simply may not notice on the one hand or by the somewhat paranoid response that can also be a part of the Einstein personality on the other. If infidelity is an issue, it is best to seek professional help quickly.

GREATEST DANGER SIGNAL: The greatest danger for this relationship is the inherent possibility that the Einstein's relatively weak social and fashion skills will come into sharp conflict with their mate's needs to make a statement about his or her prestige and power. This demand on the partner's part can be very specific. For some Caesars, physical appearance will be the criteria, for others it will be social skills and the ability to entertain well or to be an amusing dinner partner or it may be a demand that the partner achieve a level of success within his or her own sphere. For the Caesar, a partner who can present the desired appearance becomes an important asset, and sheer lack of ability to comply adequately is unlikely to be an acceptable excuse. Einsteins should get whatever help they may need from friends and professionals to attain the facade that will keep their marriage on track, while Caesars with Einstein partners need to help and encourage them in this area.

PRIMARY FOCUS: Decreasing the distance between the couple should be the focus in this marriage. Both partners can become over-involved in their own concerns, finding little time to spend together. While they may both be content with this situation, the marriage will suffer from their failure to cultivate mutual interests that will create cohesion between them and refocus their attention on each other.

THE EINSTEIN-GAUGUIN RELATIONSHIP

Marion is working on a research project that takes an enormous amount of time. She has been working ten hours a day for the past few months. Mike raises no objection to this. She is often gone by the time he gets up in the morning and he generally has dinner ready by the time she gets home at night. When she arrives, they have a pleasant low-key meal and after they clean up, Marion often feels exhausted and goes straight to bed. Mike watches television until he is ready to join her. Sexual intimacy has become less frequent as they are seldom awake at the same time when they are in bed.

On occasion, Marion has attempted to discuss her research with Mike, but it's obvious that he has little interest in what she is doing. He smiles and says how proud he is of her, then turns back to his television program. She feels sad that he has no interest in her work and senses he is not there for her in the way she would like him to be, but feels that there is nothing she can do about it.

She has turned increasingly to colleagues at work for support and understanding. There is no sexual element in these friendships, and she certainly has no intention of leaving Mike, but he has come to figure less and less in her thoughts and plans. Mike has also begun to turn to others for pleasure and friendship. He makes no complaints about his marriage, but he has more and more golf dates and fishing trips scheduled to fill up the time when Marion is preoccupied with her work. If these conditions continue without some change of direction, their relationship will begin to resemble that of friendly roommates more than husband and wife.

The first step in creating change for this couple is for both Mike and Marion to acknowledge that there is a problem. Marion needs to evaluate how much she values her marriage and if it is necessary for her to accomplish her research goals with a speed and intensity that will endanger her marriage. It is possible for her to put in long hours and work hard as long as she also remembers to put aside time for Mike when she can genuinely be with him. This means listening to him and seeking out areas of mutual interest and pleasure in their relationship, not merely giving him a run-down of her accomplishments and concerns,

Mike genuinely loves his wife, and he has accepted her assessment of her work requirements unquestioningly. He needs to take responsibility for not challenging her workaholic behavior. By placidly accepting Marion's absence from his life without protest, he has inadvertently given her the message that minimal contact between them is acceptable to him. Gauguins long for closeness with the loved partner. They thrive on shared intimacies and time spent together. Mike wishes that Marion were around more and spent more time with him, but it is hard for him to make demands and challenge her needs. He must begin to do so if the relationship is to grow and remain healthy.

This is likely to be a relationship where the partners appreciate what the other one doesn't do as much as each other's positive traits. Neither partner will try to control the other unduly. Neither one will act intrusively or demand an excessive amount of attention. There will be a mutual agreement to live and let live that both will find attractive.

An excess of this virtue can create its own problems, since no one is taking responsibility for the relationship or giving it any special care and attention. There will be few scenes or confrontations, but there is also likely to be less effort given to deepening the relationship. Einsteins may be very much aware of this and worry about it, but still take no initiative to correct the situation. Average Gauguins will probably not experience it as a problem and may wonder what the fuss is about if their partners try to discuss it.

Many of the areas of stress that are present in other marriages will not be a problem for this couple. They are both introverts, neither enjoys nor encourages confrontation, neither will try to dominate the other. This sounds like an ideal marriage, but there is a very real problem inherent in this mutual lack of combativeness.

When the plumber doesn't call back for three days or the teacher fails to intervene when the school bully is harassing Jimmy, no one steps in to address the situation. As the house gently drifts into decline and the newspapers pile up higher and higher, no one *says "We have to do something about this."* Marion occasionally experiences some guilt about these omissions, but then refocuses on her research without addressing the problem. Mike hardly notices that anything is amiss. If Jimmy complains that he really needs help, he assures him that it will pass and returns to practicing his golf stroke.

The children of this couple are likely to be very angry, because they feel uncared for. They lack many of the problems that other children experience in warding off parental control and supervision, but they also lack the security that comes from being the focus of parental attention. They may not have a curfew, or if they do, there are unlikely to be consequences to overstepping it. They are never admonished to clean their rooms, as their rooms tend to resemble the rest of the house, or to be islands of neatness within the general chaos. Sometimes they assume the role of cleaning person for the family, as they feel ashamed to have friends see the clutter in which they live.

If they are angry about their circumstances, these children may have the added problem of feeling guilty about their anger. It is quite understandable to be angry with a dictatorial father or an intrusive mother. It is much harder to conceptualize the source of one's misery when both parents are kind, gentle and non-intrusive.

Money may provide the one source of overt conflict within this relationship. Einsteins tend to be conservative spenders. Gauguins are relatively easy-going and while they do not seek extravagance or overt display, they do like to meet their own material needs and often have little concept of sensible limits in this regard. They may make a habit of stopping at neighborhood bars or diners, buy too many books and records, or run up credit cards unduly. This will trouble the Einstein, who is likely to believe that financial ruin will be the inevitable result.

The best solution to this problem is for the both partners to agree to a reasonable amount that the Gauguin can spend unchallenged. It is then up to the Gauguin to remain within the limits, and for the Einstein to let go of concern over this issue.

GREATEST DANGER SIGNAL: The danger for this relationship is that it will become too bland. Neither partner will challenge the other one to do new things, go new places, or think new thoughts. The relationship between them can fall into a deep rut of complacency and routine. This is not the worst possible outcome, but it means that the relationship has ceased to grow and deepen. It is important to be aware that this can happen so that both partners can actively work to avoid it.

PRIMARY FOCUS: The primary focus in this marriage should be on the necessity of attending to the small details of everyday life. The Einstein can easily put off the practical problems and the Gauguin can fail to notice them. Eventually if the house isn't painted and the children don't get to the pediatrician, something bad can happen, with mutual recriminations all around. It is a matter of remembering that the small stuff really does have to get done and making a schedule for doing it, with one or the other partner accepting responsibility for getting each task done.

IX

The Austen in Relationships

For the Austen-Emerson Relationship—Go to the Emerson-Austen Relationship.

For the Austen-Nightingale Relationship—Go to the Nightingale-Austen Relationship.

For the Austen-Beau Relationship—Go to the Beau-Austen Relationship.

For the Austen-Shelley Relationship—Go to the Shelley-Austen Relationship.

For the Austen-Einstein Relationship—Go to the Einstein-Austen Relationship

THE AUSTEN-AUSTEN RELATIONSHIP

Childcare is a major source of friction between Jane and Dan. Jane has read many of the current books on raising children and tries to follow their recommendations rather closely. Dan acknowledges that his wife is a good mother and appreciates her nurturing abilities, however, he becomes critical when the children deviate from his recollection of his own childhood norms or when they do anything that embarrasses him in some way. He and Jane quarreled repeatedly over her refusal to toilet train the oldest child as soon as he thought appropriate, and he frequently criticizes her for being too permissive.

Visiting Dan's parents for the weekend can bring this conflict to a boil. Jane has always allowed the children to use the VCR by themselves. They do this competently at home, although Dan remains uncomfortable with it. Dan has arbitrarily decided that seeing a seven-year-old operating their electronic equipment will upset his parents and tells the children they are not to touch it at grandma's house.

Jane is indignant. "Did your parents say they didn't want the kids to use their stuff?"

"No, and they wouldn't, but I know them, they'll keep it to themselves, but Dad will be a nervous wreck."

"I see no evidence of that. Your father is an adult. He can speak for himself if it upsets him. You always walk on eggs when you're around your parents and it's a disservice to them. You act like they're monsters. I'm going to ask them if they mind."

"I don't want you to do that. They'll say no, but believe me, that won't mean it doesn't upset them."

Jane ignores Dan and does ask his parents if it will bother them. The children are duly allowed to run their own videos, but Dan remains angry about it, and when they become noisy and silly at dinner, he orders them from the table.

Jane is furious. "Your parents are very sweet, but you become a monster when you're around them. The kids weren't doing anything terrible. They're going to hate visiting their grandparents if you don't let up on them."

"You could have intervened first if you'd wanted to, you don't say anything, and then when I take over, I'm criticized."

By the time they leave for home, three more incidents have occurred, Jane has accused Dan of child abuse, and they drive off in stony silence.

The difficulty for this couple is easy to understand in terms of their similar personalities. Both rely heavily on authority, they are simply referring to different experts. Dan is looking back to his own childhood, and expecting that his children should be raised with similar constraints, while Jane is reading the advice of psychologists and other child-care authorities and adopting the more permissive stance which they recommend.

The first step toward family peace is for both parents to understand that there is no absolute code of right and wrong in these matters. As long as they perceive their individual positions in terms of morality rather than preference, they will remain locked into them, and compromise will be difficult or impossible. If they can reach agreement that they are discussing preferences, Dan may be able to admit that he is dealing from his own early memories in conjunction with a fear of losing control of his children's behavior. Jane will be able to concede that the same childcare books that speak highly of understanding children's needs also recommend setting limits and that she may be reading selectively and relying heavily on those chapters that support her own views. Once these concessions are made, it is much easier for both parents to become more pragmatic in their approach to childcare. Jane is not going to let the children "run wild". Dan knows this just as Jane knows that Dan is a loving father who is not going to evolve into a punitive martinet from whom she must protect the children.

Austens are friendly and sociable people. They are likely to find that they share many similar values. Family and tradition are important to them. They like to please others and want the good opinion of the people around them. It is not surprising that they should enjoy each other's company.

Problems that are likely to occur in this relationship will often be due to one partner being more emotionally healthy than the other, but can also occur because families of origin have stressed different values or because the partners consider disparate people or institutions authoritative on some issue. There can be a surprising diversity in outward behavior between two people of this personality type. While both

Austen's underlying issues will include strong safety needs, and a high degree of anxiety over coping with life's problems, and, there are marked differences in the responses these feelings elicit. While some Austens respond to situations by acting extremely tough and aggressive, confronting perceived dangers and handling them, often in an impulsive manner, most Austens are rather cautious and try to avoid and deny problems. The tough Austens are generally referred to as counterphobic. They respond to whatever scares or upsets them by plunging ahead with it, in order to get past the anxiety they are feeling.

Average Austens tend toward rigidity. When two of them become adamant over their positions, they can get into a total impasse. The escape hatch for this situation lies in moving from the area of moral imperative, which is almost always questionable when it is examined, into a more pragmatic approach, admitting that the argument is over preference rather than right and wrong. *"It really bothers me when I see the cat walking over the kitchen counter."* is easier to hear and respond to than *"You want to live in unsanitary squalor and we're all going to come down with bubonic plague if I don't stop you."*

Austens need the approval of others and when they are in a relationship together, there is no one to say, *"Who cares what the neighbors think?"* or *"It's time for a change of pace."* It's important that the couple remember that too much conventionality is the enemy of spontaneity and imagination. They need to watch themselves when they start to automatically assume that *"Of course we will do it this way, we always have."* This is true whether it's joining a club because friends expect you to, or going to the same vacation cottage for the third year in a row.

While there are occasions of overt disagreement, most Austens hate confrontation and there is likely to be quite a bit of tip-toeing around issues and avoiding discussions for fear of creating conflict in this marriage. Far from improving the relationship, this behavior creates problems. The anger generated when people don't say what is bothering them, doesn't just disappear, it goes underground and returns in numerous unexpected and inappropriate ways. Austens must learn to speak up about minor irritations, but to do so in a non-judgmental, matter-of-fact way.

The problem for Average Austens is that they tend to hold their minor annoyances and hurts inside themselves and let them accumulate until they are extremely angry before they speak. *"Could you please turn the television down a notch, it's distracting me,"* is not a rude or offensive statement. *"Shut that damn thing off. Can't you see I'm balancing the checkbook?"* is. This may seem quite elementary, but it is surprising how often the distinction is overlooked.

The key to family peace in this area is to speak from one's own innate feelings or needs rather than from some abstract moral or ethical principle which the partner may not share or may not think applicable. *"I get really anxious when you start urging Terry to have another drink. I'm pretty sure it upsets Donna because she's been after him to cut back,"* is not an offensive statement. *"Why would you push more liquor on Terry when you know he verges on alcoholism?"* on the other hand, suggests lack of judgment and willful misconduct and is almost guaranteed to start an argument.

Because they lean either toward the Einstein or Mozart personality, Austens can be quite dissimilar in the areas of introversion vs. extroversion and in terms of energy level. Some Austens are extroverts and have the high energy level typical of the Mozart, while others are lower energy introverted people similar to Einsteins. In the same way some Austens verge toward the impulsivity of the Mozart while others display the control of the Einstein. Since both partners are basically Austen personalities, the traits will be less pronounced than in those who are of that primary personality type, but to understand more about these dimensions of Austen-Austen functioning, consult the chapter on the Einstein-Mozart relationship.

Average Austens have strong dependency needs; they like to turn to someone they trust for advice and support. We all need a support system, but with this personality the need can be more intense and insistent, and the fear of making mistakes may cause the couple to jockey around to avoid ultimate responsibility in situations. This problem will be particularly likely to surface at times of stress or crisis. In such cases, both partners must be alert to the need to be there to listen and encourage each other. They also need to remain aware that there are limits on their partner's willingness and ability to shoulder mutual responsibilities. As they become healthier, Austens will become more independent and these needs will diminish.

GREATEST DANGER SIGNAL: Both partners in this marriage dislike confrontation. Both of them are more comfortable sulking for a while and then going on without discussing what happened. These unresolved conflicts create mounting anger and resentment, which will eventually undermine the relationship. Both partners must remember to talk about what is bothering them and not allow themselves to retreat from conflict. Disagreements are a necessary component of a good relationship.

PRIMARY FOCUS: The focus for this couple should be on remembering to do new things, meet new people, and try new experiences. Austens are home loving and they tend to create routines and get comfortable in them. This is fine. We all need structure in our lives, but with two Austens intent on becoming more and more comfortable and secure, the daily routines can become stifling and monotonous. Some novelty will add excitement and zest to the marriage and help the relationship to grow toward greater fulfillment.

THE AUSTEN-MOZART RELATIONSHIP

Dan comes home from the office tense and worried. There has been talk about potential cutbacks in staffing, and while, realistically, he thinks he's safe, he's still feeling threatened and upset. He is eager to share his concerns with Gini. He expects to find her at home, and is irritated to find that she hasn't returned from work yet. As time passes, irritation gives way to concern and then to apprehension. When she breezes in after an hour and a half, he's really angry. "I wish you'd call me if you have to stay late, you know I worry when you don't get home on time."

Gini shrugs, "I didn't work late, I stopped off for a quick drink with Donna. She has a new boyfriend and I wanted to hear all about him. He sounds gorgeous. We went to that new cafe near work that I told you about—really great ambiance." Gini starts for the bedroom to change into casual clothes.

Dan follows her, "Then I wish you'd call when you're going out with Donna." Dan momentarily pushes aside his anger as his desire to discuss his concerns is paramount and he launches into a detailed discussion of the rumors of the day.

"That's terrible, I'm really sorry to hear that, but luckily it won't affect you," Donna starts to walk away again as she speaks.

"Where are you going now?"

"To start dinner, I have things I need to get done tonight."

"Great, that's terrifically empathetic. If I lose my job, you aren't going to feel so light-hearted about it."

Gini's impatience begins to show: "You're not going to lose your job and you know it. You have loads of seniority and are one of the hardest workers they have. You can't possibly really feel worried, so I don't know what you're carrying on about."

Dan knows on one level that Gini is right, but he is still uneasy and feels that he wants to talk about it more. As he persists in analyzing and dissecting the situation, Gini leaves the room and when he follows her to the kitchen, she explodes.

"Look, we've said everything there is to say. I'm trying out a new recipe and I can't think what I'm doing with you droning on and on about your non-problems. Just stop and let's enjoy our evening instead of wasting all this angst crossing bridges before we come to them."

They do not enjoy their evening. Dan sulks and worries silently and Gini gets disgusted with him and goes into the bedroom for a long telephone conversation with a friend. He can hear her laughing through the open doorway and this makes him feel even more hurt and angry.

This disagreement may seem rather petty, but over time the repetition of what Gini thinks of as Dan's whining and what Dan considers lack of empathy and consideration on Gini's part can add up to serious conflict.

While certainly there are attractive facets to his personality, Dan needs to honestly look at his image; he has allowed himself to become an instant whiner, a constant complainer, someone for whom the cup is always half empty. His conversation has become laced with his anxieties.

He must begin to monitor the obsessive nature of his fears and complaints. He has a right to his feelings, but he needs to ration the number of them that he presents to Gini. If he needs to talk about some of his less realistic concerns for his own peace of mind, he may need to find an alternate outlet, perhaps writing about them in a journal, or talking to a sympathetic friend. If his anxieties are too disproportionate, he should seek a therapist to help him regain a sense of balance. At any rate, he needs to accept the fact that reeling off a regular list of complaints and worries to Gini is not making him attractive to her and is not good for his marriage.

Part of Dan's problem is timing. Austens tend to feel a terrible sense of urgency in communicating whatever is happening to them. This often makes them oblivious to the agenda of the person they are talking to. Seeking an appropriate time to talk and waiting until the other person is not preoccupied will make it easier for the partner to hear what the Austen has to say.

Gini needs to learn to control the impulse to immediately dismiss Dan's concerns and to make a greater effort to respond with some degree of sympathy to the problems that he does choose to bring to her. If they are both aware of this interaction as a temperamental difference between them and stay aware of the other person's perception of what is happening, they can both modify their natural inclinations and behave in ways that are more acceptable to the other person.

Thus, if Gini had called to say she'd be a bit late, but should be home by 6:30, Dan would have started the evening with less tension and anxiety. Then if Dan had allowed her to come in, change her clothes, cook dinner, and waited to talk about his problem until after they ate, he would probably have found a more receptive audience. If he had kept the story in proportion, *"It's only a rumor and realistically I know it doesn't effect me, but I can't help feeling a bit of anxiety,"* he might have gotten a more sympathetic response.

Austens find Mozarts attractive they find them stimulating and fun to be with. While Mozarts enjoy the kindness and willingness to accommodate others that is a part of the Austen personality. They often introduce Austens to new experiences and pleasures and bring added zest and energy into their activities.

Problems between the two personalities are likely to come from an excess of the same qualities that initially attracted them. The Mozart wants to go places and have new experiences most of the time. The Austen is essentially a homebody with strong nesting instincts who likes to be at home, puttering, doing home improvements, watching television, relaxing. The difference in energy levels between Austens and Mozarts is likely to be pronounced. Austens do not have Mozart stamina. They run down and go to sleep while Mozarts are still dancing.

The Mozart prefers an upbeat atmosphere and people who are positive and optimistic most of the time. The Austen can become pessimistic, anxious or fearful. This inclines Austens to a type of self-concern that often seems excessive to other personalities. Austens when they have a headache, generally tell everyone around them that they have a headache first, seek their advice, worry a bit, and only then, look for something to alleviate it. They like to share their worries and concerns. The Mozart response, when they perceive this as overdone, is likely to range from disinterest to irritation, hostility, or even worse, mockery.

Sensitivity is generally going to be an issue between Austens and Mozarts. Austens are easily hurt, vulnerable people. Mozarts are much more pragmatic. Most of them believe that crying over spilt milk is not a good solution and that it only prolongs the misery.

Self-observation is the key to handling this temperamental difference. When Austens feel rejected and misunderstood, they need to talk themselves through their hurt feelings first and then to talk to their Mozart partner about why it bothered them. The Austen, who leaves the room or starts to sulk because the Mozart makes an insensitive remark, has made the situation worse. The Mozart is likely to label the behavior moodiness and to dismiss the partners concerns more completely as a result.

Mozarts need to remember that Austens are truly more sensitive and that they often take literally and exaggerate the seriousness of what is said to them and honestly do get their feelings hurt rather easily. This does not mean their partners must swallow their irritation or refrain from exploring differences, but it is better to do this with the reassurance that this is a solvable problem and that any anger is focused on the behavior, not the person.

Mozarts are impulsive, while Austens tend to be self-controlled. This difference can be a problem over much of the relationship. Mozarts may make impulse purchases that destroy the family budget, engage in romances and affairs, embark on impulsive projects without considering the cost in either time or money or feel an absolute compulsion to pursue a new hobby with an expensive start-up cost. Austens can be quite lacking in enthusiasm for any of these projects and deeply hurt and angry over the selfishness and lack of consideration of their partner.

In these circumstances, Austens must learn to set limits, which is difficult if they are feeling insecure and indecisive. It is important for both partners to remain aware of Austen dynamics in these situations. Austens have a natural tendency to feel afraid of confrontation, and to be indecisive about whether to say anything. If they elect to remain silent, it does not mean that the Mozart is home free. Austens, who do not say what is on their minds, usually become passive-aggressive; which is more destructive to the relationship in the long run than letting their partners know that their behavior is not acceptable. It is important, therefore, that Austens confront and overcome their fear of the partner's anger or disapproval and deal with responding to the impulsive action, saying that such unilateral decisions are not acceptable.

Mozarts need to acknowledge that this is a problem area for them and that gratifying every impulse is not realistic. Furthermore, since it can only be done at a tremendous cost to the relationship, it does not bring happiness in the long run. If they value the marriage, they must learn to postpone some of their desires and to negotiate and compromise on others. Their demand for immediate gratification has unacceptably strong consequences in the real world.

Both Austens and Mozarts want the approval of others, but this desire springs from such different motivations in these personalities that it can still cause conflict for them. Austens want to please, sometimes to the point of ingratiating behavior. They want to do what their parents, their neighbors, and the community expect of them. They are natural conformers. Such an outlook is meaningless to Mozarts who simply want to do what will make them happy. The Mozarts desire for approval is more akin to applause. They want to be appreciated for being so much fun to be with, but not at the expense of missing out on something exciting or being bored. When Austens want to go to the PTA meeting, because the school expects parents to attend, or worries about what people will think if their partners do not conform to some community shibboleth, the couple are on different planets.

The sensible solution is to realize that these differences are going to be there throughout the marriage, and to relax about them. Austens must learn to say, *"No we can't both come, but I'll be there,"* without expecting to be judged and condemned for their failure to produce the partner on demand. The Mozart must understand that fitting in is a genuine concern to the Austen and curb any blatant public display of irreverence for parental or neighborhood standards in order to save the Austen partner from embarrassment or humiliation.

GREATEST DANGER SIGNAL: The danger for this relationship is that Mozarts, by constantly pushing for the next new and exciting experience, will cause the Austens to feel pressured and to retaliate by digging in their heels and becoming rigid. Austens can become extremely stubborn and refuse to compromise out of fear of being pushed too far. If both partners are aware of this dynamic, the Austens can tell their partners when they are feeling unduly pressured and Mozarts can become sensitive to the strength and force of their desires which can to cause them to pressure others too far and frighten their partners.

PRIMARY FOCUS: Learning to compromise should be the primary focus in this relationship. Both partners need to remain sensitive to the very real differences in their personalities and take responsibility for meeting each other half way.

THE AUSTEN-CAESAR RELATIONSHIP

Bob and Jane's son, Tommy, has been having some trouble in school and has brought home a note from his teacher asking for a parent-teacher conference. Jane talks to Tommy about what he's been up to and decides that it is not very serious. He basically gets in trouble for talking in class and has had a couple of minor run-ins with two other boys. She decides that the evening will be much more pleasant if Bob doesn't see the note, so she sticks it in her purse and tells Tommy she'll call his teacher the next day and that she expects him to work harder at behaving himself.

Everything is under control when Bob comes home. Then, at the dinner table, Tommy, whose poor impulse control was what got him in trouble in the first place, starts to talk about what happened at school and intimates that Mommy will get the teacher off his back. Bob glares at Jane and let's Tommy know quite definitively that he does not want to have any more notes coming home and that there will be serious consequences if Tommy doesn't shape up.

After Tommy goes to bed, Bob explodes: "You weren't going to tell me about that note at all, were you?"

"I didn't want to upset you, you get these things completely out of proportion. He has a very strict teacher this year and her expectations are really unfair. I was going to deal with it. I already talked to Tommy."

"Yes, the results of your talk, were that Tommy believed he had your permission to carry on as before. Luckily the boy has more integrity than you and wasn't afraid to tell me about it."

"What do you mean more integrity? That's a terrible thing to say to your wife."

Well, it's pretty terrible to have a deceitful wife, in my book."

Jane starts to cry. "I knew this was the way you'd act, that's why I didn't want to tell you."

"Look, I'm not mad at you that the note came home. I'm not even mad at Tommy. I've dealt with him. What I'm mad about is the way you try to keep things from me."

"You didn't handle it well, you threatened him. He'll probably have nightmares tonight."

"Tommy doesn't have nightmares and he didn't look scared to me. He knew he was wrong and he expected me to straighten him out."

"You don't know. I used to be terrified of my father when he said things to me like you said to Tommy."

"Well, if you were acting up in school, which you weren't, you would have needed a little terrorizing. But Tommy isn't you and he can stand up to a bawling out without going all to pieces. That's part of your problem, *you treat him like he was some fragile little wimp and he's not. But, he is learning that he doesn't have to shape up when his mother's in charge. Anyway, I want to be definitive; I am to be counted in on any decisions about Tommy and school. I won't have you keeping things from me, do you understand?"*

Jane nods and goes off to watch television, but she is still fuming inside. The next day she has a number of work-related projects on her mind and totally forgets to drop by the school to see Tommy's teacher. She also forgets that she promised to pick up Bob's dry cleaning on the way home. She is totally unprepared for Bob's question about the conference when he comes home that night. "Oh my, I forgot all about that."

Bob is instantly furious. "I can see how seriously you take your son's school behavior."

Jane responds with a description of how busy she has been all day.

Bob's sarcastic rejoinder is, "The only other thing you had to do outside of work was to pick up the suit I need for tomorrow—that must have taken at least half an hour." One look at Jane's face gives him the information that the suit is still in the cleaners. "You are clearly totally incompetent. I will stop at the school on my way to work tomorrow and deal with the issue. Do you think you can possibly handle the cleaners or will I need to do that to?"

"Yes, but you don't understand…" Jane is unable to complete her sentence as Bob has walked out the door.

The dynamics fueling this scenario are simple and explicit. Caesars are strong, controlling, determined people. It's one of the things about them that Austens particularly like when they meet them. In the early stages of the relationship, they are usually dominating *other* people however, and things look very different when the person getting those Caesar orders is the Austen.

Average Austens tend to be easily frightened and intimidated and it is very difficult for them to stand up to Caesar anger. Average Caesars know this and use the knowledge to get what they want. It is very tempting to yell if you know that it will create immediate acquiescence.

This does not mean that Caesars have things all their way. While Austens have problems confronting angry people, they become angry themselves when faced with demands they believe are unreasonable or when they feel pushed around or taken for granted. Austens may not yell as quickly, but they use the classic weapon of the weak against the strong, passive-aggression. *"I won't stand up to you, but I won't do what you've asked me to either."*

This is what Jane did to Bob. She was unwilling to tell him about Tommy's behavior because she disagreed with his anticipated handling of the situation, so instead of arguing with him about how to discipline Tommy, she simply didn't tell him. She viewed this as the easy way around a difficult situation and saw nothing wrong with it. To Bob, failure to keep him informed was both a basically dishonest action and a personal affront since it took the situation out of his control. He was probably harder on Tommy than he would have been if he had not been angry with Jane for what he considered her deceptive conduct.

The next day Jane was still upset by Bob's harsh words, and did what upset Austens frequently do, she forgot to deal with an unpleasant situation. She often gets even in this fashion. On some intuitive level, she felt that forgetting the suit at the cleaners underlined just how upset and angry she felt. Her actions said, *"You can yell at me, but you can't control me. This will pay you for the way you acted."*

The passive-aggressive response is inadvisable per se, and has the added disadvantage of creating unforeseen consequences. The last thing Jane wanted was for Bob to have a solo conference with Tommy's teacher where he failed to explain extenuating circumstances.

Jane and Bob are locked in a conflict that has the potential to spiral down further with undesired results both for their own relationship and for their son. Bob needs to become aware of the power his anger confers on him in this relationship and of the basic unfairness of using that power as a method of intimidating his wife. He has created a situation in which Jane feels she can never win in a straight forward argument, and has thereby driven her to the passive manipulative ploys that he finds intolerable. He needs to stop shouting and blustering, and to rule out displays of temper as effective ways to achieve his ends.

Jane needs to confront and overcome her fear of Bob's anger and begin to stand up to him. Granted, it will be very difficult at first, but if she says *"I disagree with you"* whenever she does disagree or *"I don't want to do that,"* or *"I think you're really wrong in this situation,"* she will soon learn that saying what you mean does not destroy a marriage, and that Bob's anger is a temporary phenomenon that can be weathered without permanent damage. There is an exception to be made to this advice; some Austens are married to physically violent Caesars. An Austen in such a relationship needs help from a professional in dealing with this situation. Do not excuse your partner or put off seeking help. Get in touch with a self-help organization or a therapist immediately.

For those couples who are working on their marriages and who both want to improve their interactions, the Caesar can encourage the Austen to speak up, by saying *"Don't just say yes to please me, what do you really think?"* The Austen can remember that noise is a battle tactic and treat it as such, reminding the Caesar that yelling is a strategy of intimidation not communication.

Jane could have talked to Tommy about the note and then reminded him that he would also have to show it to his father. A different, but equally mistaken course pursued by some Austens is to totally cede the disciplinary role to the other parent: *"Wait till your father comes home and you'll be punished."* In this way Jane could remain the perennial pal and good guy to the children, but at the price of seceding from her parental role. She needs to give Tommy a clear message that she and Bob are partners and will both be informed of anything important relating to anyone in the family.

Bob as a healthy Caesar could have kept his anger in check over the situation and both parents could then express their concern over Tommy's behavior and their expectation that he would shape up. This could happen without undue belligerence on Bob's part and without Jane glossing over the incident and leading Tommy to believe that she would take his part in any discussion with the teacher.

They might then either have decided to go to see the teacher together or that only one of them would attend the conference. The expectation would be that even if only one person attended the conference, substantially the same message would be conveyed to the teacher, and the other partner would get accurate feedback of what was said.

Neither of them would be angry, so the passive aggressive behavior that Bob triggered in Jane would not come into play and as an added bonus, he would probably have received his suit from the cleaners on time.

It is easy to understand the dynamic behind this bond. It is a very common mutual attraction. The Austen views the Caesar as strong, capable and self-sufficient, very desirable qualities. *"Here is someone who will take care of me, someone I can depend on,"* says the Austen. Caesars experience Austens as obliging, flattering and agreeable. They notice that Austens look up to them and depend on them, and are duly complemented by their respect and trust. During the early stages of the relationship, Austens seldom disagree, contradict or argue, which Caesars find very pleasant, and the relationship is off to a fine start.

Naturally, this degree of harmony is too good to last, and as the relationship progresses, Caesars find that when Austens say yes, they often mean, *"I don't want to argue,"* and when they say maybe, they may mean, *"I can't stand up to you about this, but I deeply disagree."* As this recurs, the relationship can begin a pronounced downhill slide.

Another dynamic to be aware of with this couple is a marked difference in sensitivity level. Caesars see themselves as tough, capable of giving and taking both verbal and physical knocks. Even as young children,

Caesars enjoy schoolyard give-and-take. They jump up and keep going after bumps that send young Austens running to their mothers in tears.

As adults, Austens are still quite vulnerable, easily hurt, and apt to brood over minor aches and pains. What may be a genuine difference from the partner in pain thresholds, is often coupled with the tendency to give a detailed report on whatever minor symptoms they might have. If Caesars perceive them as cosseting themselves, they are likely to find it irritating and to mutter darkly of hypochondria. This response to physical pain is mirrored by their lower tolerance for emotional upset. This difference in sensitivity needs to be respected on the part of both partners.

Caesars can feel pain too and Austens sometimes forget this, feeling that they are free to say anything, no holds barred to a Caesar partner since they don't get an overtly pained response. Caesars, when they have been hurt, are very likely to counterattack as strongly as possible, so the momentary pleasure of making the most cutting available retort comes with a high price tag.

Once Austens feel unfairly attacked, they retreat into wounded animal behavior and any genuine exchange between the partners becomes impossible, so, in their own interest, Caesars should stay aware of the greater vulnerability of Austens when they disagree.

Civility in disagreement is the only safe solution for this marriage. One method of promoting this is to choose a cue word that may be said by either partner as a signal that things are getting out of hand. The rule might be that all conversation stops, after the cue word has been said, for five to ten minutes, giving both sides a chance to cool down and think through what they want to say and the best way to say it.

Austens and Caesars often have different energy and stamina levels; Austens usually tire more quickly and require more relaxation and sleep than Caesars. If this is the case, it is important that both partners acknowledge it. Unless they understand that this is a physical fact, Caesars tend to resent their partner's desire to stop while they are still at full speed. Some Austens tend to push themselves to exhaustion to please Caesars, which has the result of leaving them over tired and irritable. Once it is accepted as a simple reality of the relationship, it is less likely to be an issue.

Austens need the approval of others: family, neighbors, friends. This almost inevitably becomes an area of conflict. With the exception of their concern over appearing strong and self-sufficient, Caesars do what they want to do and feel little concern for what others may think. A compromise must be negotiated here between Austen conformity and Caesar need for autonomy and relative disregard for the opinion of others. This is mutually advantageous as both sides can probably gain by modifying their standpoints, and behaving more moderately.

Austens are concerned over the minutia of daily life to a degree that baffles Caesars. This sounds like a trivial problem, but it can often come to loom disproportionately large in their marriages. Austens like to talk about what they did at work, who they had lunch with, and what the lady in the checkout line at the grocery store said to them. Caesars see this as totally pointless and truthfully don't pay that much attention to such things, so that they would be unable to make this sort of chitchat even if they tried. Austens tend to perceive failure to respond in kind to a detailing of the day's events as secretiveness, rejection, or cruelty, while Caesars are driven wild by the recital of trivia when they are attempting to concentrate on something else.

A reasonable amount of give and take on this issue can bring both partners to an acceptable compromise. Austens need to edit the length of their reports and try to present them at an appropriate time, rather than in the middle of the TV program that the Caesar has been waiting to see all week. They will have to come to terms with the fact that they will not receive a return report of equal length and may not receive one at all. Caesars just don't find the small details of life as absorbing as Austens do.

The final problem that may arise in the Austen-Caesar relationship is one of commitment to the relationship. Some Caesars have affairs, or even take on a permanent extra-marital commitment, certainly not acceptable behavior to conventional, home-loving Austens. Austens facing this problem need to get professional help. If it is at all possible, they should involve the partner in the counseling relationship, but it is essential that they get the help whether the partner agrees to participate or not. Average Austens often engage in denial when faced with problems of this nature. This is a serious mistake, since allowing the situation to slide without addressing underlying issues, can destroy the marriage.

GREATEST DANGER SIGNAL: Austens often feel deserted and abandoned by the Caesar's attention to business, hobbies or other interests, while Caesars feel irritated and angry over Austen demands for time and attention, which they perceive as childish and immature. It is important for the partners to discuss what is happening so that they can better understand each other. Austens do have dependency needs, but they can learn to keep them within reasonable bounds if they are reassured that they are loved and if their Caesar partners remember to make time to meet their reasonable needs for time and attention.

PRIMARY FOCUS: Austens must learn to abandon their indecisiveness and make a conscious effort to stick to the decisions they make. They need to combat their fear of responsibility and work to achieve greater independence and autonomy. In doing this, they will find that they enhance their partner's respect and affection. Caesars, in turn, must learn to value and cultivate greater sensitivity and relinquish inappropriate displays of anger as shortcuts to attaining what they want. It is important to remember that a good marriage is a very primary, and ultimately much more satisfying goal, than the temporary satisfaction of reducing one's partner to a grudging compliance.

THE AUSTEN-GAUGUIN RELATIONSHIP

Jane has a difficult choice to make at work, which has thrown her into a state of intense anxiety. She must either accept a new job that she has been offered at higher pay, or refuse it and stay in her current job category. She has two weeks to make a decision. Her boss is urging her to make this move, that requires the assumption of considerably greater responsibility, but she is unsure that she is up to the challenge.

She discusses the pros and cons of the situation with Mike and asks his advice. He replies that he is in no position to advise her. She must decide what she feels comfortable doing in the situation. When she points out that it will mean a large increase in salary for her, if she accepts the new position, he is unimpressed. They are managing just fine on their current joint incomes; that should not be an overriding consideration.

Jane is appalled. "How can you say that, the house needs a paint job, and I would really like to put in another bathroom. The kids are getting older, and we haven't saved anywhere near enough for their college expenses. Don't you ever think about these things?"

"We've always gotten by, I'm sure we'll continue to. We'll manage. Look, take the job if you want it, but don't take it on and then feel miserable about it. I just want you to be happy."

"But what do you think I should do?"

"Do what you want to. I don't know what you want to do. It sounds to me like you're going to be pretty anxious if you take it, so maybe you shouldn't."

"See you never want me to achieve, you always settle for second-best."

"That's not true, I said take it if you want it."

"But you're not telling me that I can do it."

"How could I do that? I don't know if you can do it."

Jane is hurt. "See, you have no confidence in me at all. My boss has more trust in my abilities than you do."

"Maybe your boss is in a better position to judge than I am. Look, I only want you to do what's best for you. Don't be mad at me about it."

Jane is mad. She feels hurt that Mike isn't able to reassure her that she can do the new job, but if he had pushed her to take it, she would have been equally upset with him about that. This is a very typical case of Austen indecisiveness meeting head on with the average Gauguin's refusal to engage in problem solving.

Obviously this is not a situation that threatens the relationship. The damage from it is minimal. Austens and Gauguins usually do get along without encountering giant rifts in their interactions. All that really needs to be done in this case is for both people to understand themselves and their partners better. Even the healthiest Austens are a bit indecisive. They have trouble making up their minds. They must work on coming to terms with the fact that it is permissible to make mistakes. All situations have pros and cons and their search for the perfect solution is fruitless. It is good to discuss the decision to be made with a partner, but it is unfair to press them to make the decision for you. Austens would like someone else to do their decision making, then, if things turn out badly, they won't feel guilty and responsible. At the same time they are unable to trust anyone else to make the right decision, so they often end up asking several people what to do and continuing to be confused by the conflicting advice they receive. As Austens become healthy, they conquer much of their fear of taking responsibility.

Gauguins don't like to admit that there are problems in their lives. They use denial to protect themselves from facing the harsher realities of the world. Gauguins need to become aware that they do this, and stop running away from difficulties. When they force themselves to face situations as they arise, they will become stronger more capable people.

Ideally, if Jane presented the alternatives to Mike, he would not have made the choice for her, but would have attempted to discuss the issue in greater depth, asking her for specifics of what she was worried about in the new job, and helping her to assess exactly how much in added buying power the raise would be worth.

Jane would weigh the recommendation from her boss that she take the job, and would consider his confidence in her as an objective measure of her competence, but she would not allow his position as an authority figure to overpower her own assessment of her position. Then she would make her own decision, with gratitude to Mike for helping her to explore the issues objectively, but without either the expectation or desire that he should be the arbiter of her choices.

Both Gauguins and Austens are friendly people with pleasant personalities. Their attractive qualities draw them to each other. Austens go about the process of arranging their lives in a systematic orderly fashion, paying attention to the small details that often escape the notice of Gauguins. Someone who can organize a closet or a checkbook may seem particularly gifted to the disorganized Gauguin, and the Austen gets a boost in self-esteem from this admiration.

Difficulties in the relationship will occur when Austens, who are natural worriers, become anxious and upset over problems, and their partners refuse to acknowledge the difficulty or to help them to deal with it. Sometimes the Austen's dependency needs become crippling to them. When this happens they can profit from a display of emotional toughness from their partners, being told to face reality and get on with it. Gauguins have difficulty doing that. It's not their style. They are happy to be empathetic, but when their partners would profit more from a dash of cold water than soft soap, the Gauguin is unable to provide it.

Average Austens enjoy being swept off their feet and like the sense that their partners will take care of them. Their dependency needs often cause Austens to seek relationships with high energy, superficially strong people. The solid, placid Gauguin is actually a better choice for Austen personalities, but they may continue to yearn for someone who will assume a firm leadership role in the relationship and sometimes resent the lack of these qualities in the partner.

Average Austens, due to their reliance on authority and tradition, often attempt to impose life styles on their spouses based on roles in their family of origin or on some authority's preconception of how people should behave. Austens, whose father's were handymen, may demand advanced carpentry skills of manually inept husbands; while Austens, whose mothers were superior cooks, may demand home-baked goodies from career-focused, time-pressed wives. Once the unrealistic aspect of these expectations is understood, they will usually not remain a problem.

Both partners tend to be conventional. But while Gauguins tend to follow the norm as the easiest way to get along, Austens are overly conscious of what the neighbors might say, what their parents would think or what their friends expect and can become stressed and anxious by perceived deviations from other people's expectations. Gauguins provide a model of a more casual acceptance of society's conventions, and can help their partners to relax, and feel more comfortable both with their own choices, and in making decisions without reference to other people's standards or values.

Austens generally have a higher energy level than most Gauguins do. This is not likely to present a major problem in itself. However, some Austens, perceiving a lack of interest or involvement on the part of their partners, take on an unfair share of household tasks and responsibilities. It is important for Gauguins to realize that they must make a reasonably equal contribution to fulfilling household responsibilities, if they are not to eventually incur resentment and anger from their partners. If this does not happen, Austens should discuss the situation and request greater participation, lest the weight of household responsibilities fall too heavily on them.

Gauguins have a potential for addiction. This is a natural result of their tendency to suppress their wishes and needs in the interest of harmony, and then to compensate for this through food, alcohol, or drugs. Austens, because of their desire to please, are natural co-dependents. If this is a problem in the relationship, the appropriate twelve-step programs, or some other professional help, should be sought.

Unfortunately, the Gauguin sometimes refuses to participate in any recovery program. It is important for the Austen to find one of the groups for the co-dependent spouse of the addict in such cases, as they must protect and strengthen themselves by learning how to abandon co-dependent behaviors.

GREATEST DANGER SIGNAL: Austens keep themselves busy. They hurry from one task or activity to the next. It is their way of keeping their anxiety under control. Gauguins love to relax and see the perpetual motion of Austens as unnecessary and exhausting. The danger in these opposite positions occurs when Austens place a moral value on their activity level and attempt to force their placid spouses to join them in wallpapering, gardening, and other strenuous activities. There is an equal chance of trouble when Gauguins decide that since Austens seem to be naturally task-oriented, it is permissible to let them do everything and resign all responsibilities for the household to them.

PRIMARY FOCUS: The primary focus for this relationship should be seeking outside stimulation. Austens and Gauguins are both home loving and tend to be focused on home and family. A relationship without any outside stimulation can become ingrown and monotonous. Here the problem is not a failure to spend time together, but rather that all the couple's spare time is spent together. It is reasonable to have some friends and interests apart in order to have new things to talk about and new ideas to share in the time they spend together.

X

The Mozart in Relationships

For the Mozart-Emerson Relationship—Go to the Emerson-Mozart Relationship.

For the Mozart-Nightingale Relationship—Go to the Nightingale-Mozart Relationship.

For the Mozart-Beau Relationship—Go to the Beau-Mozart Relationship.

For the Mozart-Shelley Relationship—Go to the Shelley-Mozart Relationship.

For the Mozart-Einstein Relationship—Go to the Einstein-Mozart Relationship.

For the Mozart-Austen Relationship—Go to the Austen-Mozart Relationship.

THE MOZART-MOZART RELATIONSHIP

Gini and Bruce are giving a barbecue for a group of friends. This is the kind of party they both love. Bruce tends bar and displays his skills on the barbecue. Gini is a whirlwind of activity, setting out flowers, making hors d'oeuvres, salads and deserts. About an hour before the guests are due,

Bruce decides that it would be fun to string up some Chinese lanterns around the patio and tells Gini he's going to run out and buy them.

"It's a great idea, Bruce, but there's not time. People are going to be here in an hour."

"It will only take twenty minutes to run to the store and back. I've got everything ready. The meat is in a marinade and the bar is all set up. I have to pick up more ice for the cooler anyway."

"Just get the ice, please. There won't be any time to string the lanterns up if you do get them."

Bruce doesn't bother to argue as he's already decided what he wants to do and has no intention of letting Gini stop him. It takes a little longer than he estimated to get to the store and when he runs into a friend, he has to stop to chat for a couple of minutes. There are two people ahead of him when he goes to get the ice, so that his return home coincides with the arrival of the first guests.

*He greets them cordially and runs out into the yard with a ladder, an extension cord and the lanterns. Gini, helping their guests to drinks, can hardly credit what she sees. "Bruce, be reasonable, it's too late to do this now, more people will be here any minute." She feels unable to say what is really on her mind, "You've got to take these people off my hands **now** and let me get back to the kitchen."*

Bruce, intent on his decorating chores, calls, "I'll just be five minutes. Come on out and supervise, folks. Doesn't this add a final touch?"

The bemused guests troop dutifully out to the patio and are soon employed in handing up lights and holding ladders. Gini stalks back to the kitchen in a rage, only to hear the doorbell ring before she can accomplish anything.

Once the lanterns are up and the party goes into full swing, there are no further problems. Mozarts are excellent hosts and when the last guest leaves, both Bruce and Gini agree that it was a successful party. Bruce has drunk a bit too much and starts to head immediately for bed.

Gini is indignant, "Where do you think you're going? There's at least an hour's worth of cleaning up to be done."

"I'm sorry, Gini, I'm in no shape to do it. Can't it wait until morning?"

"No, it can't. I've got a full day scheduled for tomorrow and I'm not going to start it by looking at this mess. There's nothing more disgusting than smelling left over food when you get up in the morning."

Bruce approaches the task ahead in a half-hearted manner. He begins by piling a tray with glasses and promptly knocks half of them over, breaking two.

Gini becomes increasingly grim and finally says, "All right, you win, you're no help anyway. Go to bed before you break something else."

This sounds like a fairly mundane interaction, nothing traumatic or devastating happened. Bruce and Gini wake up the next morning irritated with each other, but both have full schedules for the day and by the time they see each other at dinner, they don't even bother to discuss it. Such incidents still take their toll on the relationship. Gini adds Bruce's behavior at the party to the long list of times that Bruce has let her down. Bruce remembers Gini's anger at him over the lanterns and the broken glasses and adds it to his characterization of Gini as a nagging wife.

These minor mishaps would hardly be worth enumerating in many stormier marriages, Mozarts, however, have a relatively low tolerance for unpleasantness. If enough incidents of this nature accumulate in their marriage, one or the other partner will probably ask for a divorce. By the time they decide they are unhappy, it may be too late to reconsider or create change.

If they are to improve the quality of their marriage, Bruce and Gini must make some time to talk intimately to each other on a daily basis. This need not be a heavy conversation; many times they will just chat, but it will provide an opening for either of them to be honest about anything that may be bothering them. Mozart personalities have so much to do and so much to say that they have a tendency to skip over minor mishaps and irritations or even to joke about them in the interest of getting to the next item on the agenda. This would be wonderful if it meant they had really let go of what was bothering them, but too often, they merely push it aside and move on, filing it for future reference, and Mozarts tend to have long memories.

It is important to talk about what happened from a non-accusatory stance. If Gini says, *"You walked out an hour before the party, how could you have done such a stupid thing?"* Bruce will naturally defend himself and counterattack, and yesterday's fight will be revitalized. But if Gini says, *"I know I was snippy when you came back with the lanterns, but I was feeling frantic, trying to get everything ready and whether it was rational or not, I felt like I'd been abandoned,"* she stands a rather good chance of being heard. She is admitting that the problem arose from the dynamics between them. She is not making any accusations, but talking about her own feelings in response to what occurred. She has keyed off a discussion in the hope of better mutual understanding, not a mutual accusation session.

In the course of a problem-solving discussion, Bruce should then be able to take some responsibility for following his impulses without thought for the consequences. He will apologize for letting himself get into a condition that precluded helping clean up, admitting that this was not fair, and assuring Gini that he will be more prudent in the future. This kind of discussion is reassuring to both partners and can strengthen the marriage.

Mozarts love to have fun. They want to do amusing things with amusing people. They want life to be an on-going party and who could they find that would be better company at that party than a partner with the same focus? A Mozart will find another Mozart's energy level, sense of adventure and desire to have a good time naturally attractive. The problems that will develop in this relationship will occur because the partners have a different agenda in regard to what will make them happy.

Since both Gini and Bruce are impulsive, it would seem there should be no problem over money, since they will understand each other's impulsive urges. However, this understanding may help them to agree to go places, do things or make large purchases, without adequate reflection. This can ultimately add its own stresses to the relationship. Mozarts tend to charge too much on credit cards, take too many vacations and eat out too often. When the bills come in and the question becomes, "*Why didn't you stop me?*" The obvious answer is inherent in the relationship.

All Mozarts are agreed that doing what makes people happy is important, but they may still disagree on what will make them happy.If Bruce wants to see castles in Spain on their summer vacation, and Gini has her heart set on touring Alaska, neither partner will acquiesce readily to the plans of the other. Since the full range of Mozart activity encompasses constant decisions: movies, plays, restaurants, museums, and outdoor recreations; the situations which may arouse disagreement are almost limitless. The simplest solution is to take turns making such choices. While this does not work well if the partner not choosing spends the time bad mouthing the choice, most Mozarts can become enthusiastic about whatever fun experience is available.

If not, the other possibility is to opt to go separate ways whenever necessary. While an optimal choice in some situations, such a solution holds potential dangers. In the natural orientation of their personalities toward whatever is new and adventurous, the couple may drift further and further apart, as they spend more and more time on separate pursuits.

Children may have difficulties if they find themselves with two Mozart parents. On the one hand, a day at the beach, an amusement park, or a ball game will be twice the fun. But when the moment devoted to entertaining the children has passed, the parents will be off pursuing their own goals and careers wholeheartedly with little thought for the needs of their kids, often leaving the children feeling neglected and abandoned. It is essential that Mozart parents monitor their consistency in being present and available. As they become healthier, Mozarts will be able to do this more easily. They will begin to place the long-term satisfaction of loving and meaningful relationships with their children ahead of the need for immediate gratification and amusement.

Commitment can be a difficult task for Mozarts. Their natural attraction to the novel makes meeting new people fun for them and when a new person is attractive, it is natural for them to be as amusing and charming as possible. When both people in the relationship have this proclivity, the chances for infidelity double. If their relationship is important to them, married Mozarts have a responsibility to recognize this as a potential problem. Prevention is the best approach. If both partners acknowledge the possibility of finding other people attractive, and agree on strategies for minimizing temptation, and handling it when it occurs, they can control their responses and set limits on their behavior. The guiding principle here for both of them should be that true joy and contentment lasts longer than transient pleasure and it is always a mistake to endanger what will ultimately create the greater happiness.

Mozart orientation toward pleasure and trying new things makes it easy for them to become addicted to drugs or alcohol. There is a real danger in this relationship that if one partner becomes addicted, they will entice the other one into joining them. It is essential that non-addicts immediately seek the support of one of the groups such as Al-Anon or Narc-Anon and/or possibly some therapy, before the partner can pull them into the addiction.

Money is important to Mozarts as a source of pleasure. Since there are so many things to be enjoyed, and so many of them cost money, Mozarts tend to run up their bills. In a marriage between Mozarts, the bills will naturally mount twice as fast. Stabilizing this situation requires budgeting. The couple should budget to put aside an adequate amount to meet their monthly expenses and to put money in savings, and then allocate a set sum to each partner each month as spending money. If this is to work, both partners must be fair about not dipping into allotted funds, no skimping on the groceries and putting that money toward an impulse purchase!

GREATEST DANGER SIGNAL: The greatest danger for this relationship lies in the impulsive nature of both partners. Mozarts have an innate tendency to go after what they want, often without pausing for adequate reflection. This impulsivity is reined in and moderated in relationships with more cautious personality types. When two Mozarts marry, and there is no one to say no, there is a danger that overspending, over-partying or addictive behavior can destroy the marriage.

PRIMARY FOCUS: The primary focus for this relationship should be slowing each other down. The partners can remind each other and themselves that it is not necessary to fulfill every desire immediately in order to have a happy life. It is important for them to have some nights at home together alone. The fear of missing out on something is never far from the mind of the Mozart; it is important to make the effort to dispel that fear and learn to find enjoyment in relaxation too.

THE MOZART-CAESAR RELATIONSHIP

Gini and Bob have a large house that provides a perfect setting for parties. Gini loves to entertain and invites people over for at least one occasion almost every weekend. Her complaint is that she is a solo hostess most of the time. If Bob isn't actually away on a business trip, he goes into work or has a business meeting, even on the weekend.

He had promised to make it up to her with a fabulous three-week trip to France at the end of the summer. However, since he made that promise, a major business expense has cropped up unexpectedly and he suddenly finds himself short of cash. When he discovers this, he comes home and announces that they will have to change their plans matter-of-factly. It's just a temporary problem, but we're going to have to postpone the trip."

Gini is wary, "Postpone it for how long?"

"Until I solve my cash flow problem."

"Are we talking two weeks? A month?"

"Maybe until spring. Winter isn't the best time for going to Paris anyway."

Gini explodes, "In other words, we go from three weeks in France to no vacation this year in one flick of an eyelash, is that what you're telling me?"

"Try to be a grown-up, Gini. These things happen. I was looking forward to it as much as you were."

"That I doubt," Gini interrupts. "I sometimes think you're happier at the office than on vacation."

"Don't tell me what I'm feeling." Bob responds irritably. These things happen when you own your own business. There's no point in arguing about it. We're can't go and that's that."

"Maybe you're not going, but I am. I put up with your workaholic behavior all year and I'm not going to let it deprive me of a vacation as well."

"This is so typical of you, throwing a temper tantrum if you can't have your lollipop. How do you plan to pay for the air fare and the hotel rooms?"

"I'll find a way. If I have to pawn my jewelry, I'm going."

"Oh no you won't. I gave you that jewelry, and if you don't care any more than that about it, I'm taking it back right now." Bob heads for the bedroom and Gini's jewelry box.

Gini flies after him, shrieking with rage. There is a tussle as she attempts to grab her jewelry, and he snatches two pieces back in total fury. The necklaces are the innocent victims of their struggle and beads roll across the floor. Bob walks out, gets in the car and drives off. Gini scrambles around the floor on her hands and knees crying uncontrollably while retrieving her possessions.

Something went badly wrong in this interchange. First, Bob showed massive insensitivity in his matter of fact approach to the change in plans. This is not surprising. He expected Gini to respond as he himself would have. It is axiomatic with him that business needs come before pleasure, and he hasn't adequately allowed for the possibility that this is not a universally accepted viewpoint. He has also been oblivious to the extent of Gini's general irritation over his workaholic behavior, which created a background anger that made this the last straw.

Gini might have been less appalled by what he said if he had not taken her solo hostess performance for granted, if he had made greater efforts to get home when there were guests through the summer, and if he had made some explanation of what was happening to his business and discussed options instead of making a blunt unilateral announcement,

He could also have softened the blow by suggesting the possibility of some less expensive alternative. *"We can't make it to France for three weeks, but a week in Mexico is still possible, with France postponed until spring."*

Gini needs to work on learning a healthier response to problems as well. Vacations constitute necessary and wonderful interludes, but her response to Bob was aggressive and immature. She is not a little girl, being denied a treat, she is an adult woman and needs to accept the fact that temper tantrums are not only unattractive but ineffective; they certainly cannot undo a situation that is grounded in a financial reality. The suggestion that she would pawn her jewelry was intentionally provocative and had the desired effect of upsetting Bob. Unfortunately, she neglected to calculate his response to being upset.

If instead of immediately deeming Bob the enemy, she had asked questions, tried to understand what had happened and then communicated how upset she was at the change in plans, both partners could have worked together at a compromise that would be at least partially acceptable. Both of them bear responsibility for the physical outcome of their confrontation.

Both Mozarts and Caesars are extroverts with high energy levels. They tend to enjoy their work and find it absorbing, and they play hard as well. Because both are hard workers, they tend to have a reasonable amount of discretionary income, which provides them with a comfortable life style. It is not surprising that they would find the things they like about themselves attractive in a partner.

Differences in where they place their priorities can become a problem for this couple. Caesars put a great deal of time and effort into their work and into projects that enhance their prestige within their business or community. Mozarts are quite willing to work hard, but they also want to have fun and it is important to them that adequate time be put aside for pleasure. This means that the couple can find themselves in substantial disagreement over the apportionment of time and money between business and pleasure.

Mozarts and Caesars are both impulsive, but they tend to direct their impulsivity so differently that it often clashes. The Mozart is impulsive in pursuit of pleasure. They want to go places and have a wonderful time when they get there. Caesars may also enjoy vacation activities, but they are able to limit their pursuit of them if there are other things to be done. The Caesar's impulsive nature is likely to surface in the area of anger and aggressive reactions. Average Caesars, when they are frustrated or opposed, can become enraged and are likely to respond out of anger instead of giving themselves time to become more composed and think the situation through. Both partners in this relationship need to learn to stop and think before they act.

Confrontations such as the one between Bob and Gini are likely to be common in Mozart-Caesar relationships. Neither Mozarts nor Caesars are motivated to change just in order to please a partner. They both have strong needs and desires that militate against easy acquiescence to someone else's agenda, and they also have strong personality styles, which they are loath to modify. The Caesar who asks a Mozart to present a more reserved appearance on business occasions will have only very moderate success. Mozarts like themselves the way they are, and don't consider their behavior inappropriate or in need of modification. Conversely, the Caesar who is asked to forgo a business or political opportunity in the interests of family bonding will either disregard the request or find it outrageous.

Control issues will be constant and difficult to resolve for this couple. When Mozarts can't make their own choices, they feel deprived of the stimulation and pleasure they need to be happy. Caesars simply find it unacceptable and tend to become enraged when decisions and choices are out of their control.

The rational resolution to this situation would be for both of the partners to agree that the other is a free agent and that all plans will be checked with each other before any commitments are made. This will minimize the temptation toward attempting to dominate on the part of either of them. This is often more difficult than might be expected, since part of the fun for Mozarts may lie in sharing occasions with their partners, and Caesars tends to feel uncomfortable saying, *"I'll have to check in at home before I can made a commitment on that."*

A subsidiary plan might be to divide up the time the couple spend together and allot spaces of it to each. *"I'll be there for you on Saturday nights if you'll agree to be there for me on Friday nights." "I'll trade you plans for Tuesday for two hours with my client on Wednesday."* If the time together can be made a marketable commodity, with each partner having equal shares, it could become an accepted game. The flaw in this strategy could occur if some Caesars opted for spending their share of the time at work, rather than with the partner. Each couple will have to work out an individual solution in this relationship, however these samples should point the way and allow the pair to begin to dialogue about peaceful resolutions.

Both Mozarts and Caesars can get quite angry and can lose control. This is a dangerous area for them. It would be prudent to put an agreement in place early in the relationship that when either partner sees that the quarrel is getting loud or out of control, that person will say, *"Let's table this for 15 minutes, I'll be back"* and then leave the room. This is of major importance as there is a potential for emotional and/or physical violence in the conjunction of these personalities. If using this strategy does not stop either or both of them, it is time to seek professional help. They may both need to acquire better self-control mechanisms.

Childcare is often not the top priority for this couple. The Mozart typically loves children and has a wonderful time playing with them, but finds it hard to be there for all the activities that are not playtime on a day-to-day basis. They take their children to the circus, the zoo and the amusement park, but find helping with homework less enchanting. They make spectacular birthday parties, but hate routinely preparing school lunches. Caesars love their children, but their needs to control those around them and their desire to be obeyed, combine with their focus on work to make the relationship with the children somewhat difficult. These are parents, who should seriously consider finding ample help in childcare, lest the children become a source of unnecessary friction and an unwelcome responsibility.

Commitment can be a difficult issue for both partners. Mozarts, with their strong tendency toward impulsivity, can respond on the spur of the moment in ways they will later regret. Impulsivity could lead them to flirt with an attractive stranger, for example, without regard for where further impulses might lead. The same impulsive tendency can cause them to go ballistic and retaliate in major ways if a partner should engage in similar actions.

Caesars tend to have a sense of entitlement, a belief that they can and should get away with anything they want badly. Unbridled, this trait can lead to infidelity and is obviously dangerous to the relationship. To exacerbate the problem, they can be extremely jealous and possessive themselves, so that even an innocent display of camaraderie on the part of a spouse can be misinterpreted and lead to a major crisis. Both partners need to keep these dynamics in mind in order to avert unnecessary problems in this area. If either partner does become involved with another person, it would be wise to seek professional help immediately.

The dynamics between these two personalities make it unlikely that a fidelity issue between them will blow over or heal with time.

Both Mozarts and Caesars have a potential for addictive behaviors. If addiction is a problem, it is a mistake to believe that this is an issue that one or both partners can handle by themselves. Many Caesars will be reluctant to take this advice, believing that they should be able to handle their own problems and that to seek outside intervention is a sign of weakness. Attempting to conquer addictive behavior alone is not a rational decision. Everyone has areas of expertise and areas where they are less knowledgeable. To call a plumber for your toilet, or a financial planner for your investments is only sensible. Addictions can be trickier and harder to deal with than most other problems, and hard work to overcome, even with therapeutic intervention.

Mozarts and Caesars both need quite a bit of money to be happy. It is fortunate that in this marriage, both partners tend to be hard workers and there is usually some extra cash available. Unfortunately, their plans for their money are not synchronized. Mozarts want to spend a fair amount of it on pleasure. Caesars, while not adverse to pleasure, may want to use most of it for long term goals, to expand a business, or to invest. Compromise will require that each get an agreed upon share after joint expenses are taken care of and that this amount be left to the discretion of that partner.

GREATEST DANGER SIGNAL: The greatest danger to this relationship lies in the need for new and different experiences that is so much a component of the Mozart personality. Mozarts have a proclivity for harmless flirtation, even when they have no intention of carrying it further. This is a behavior that the Caesar finds threatening and intolerable. It can quickly destroy their relationship. With Caesars, the motivation to go outside the marriage comes from their sense of entitlement, the belief that they should always be able to have whatever they want badly. It is important for the relationship that both partners be on guard against potential damage and that if an incident does occur that it be discussed and defused immediately.

PRIMARY FOCUS: The primary focus for this marriage should be on spending adequate time together. Both Mozarts and Caesars have busy lives and neither partner has strong dependency needs that might place time demands on the other. This is basically a good thing, but like many good things, if not monitored, it can be carried too far. The marriage requires time for intimacy, fun and conversation, above and beyond the bedroom.

THE MOZART-GAUGUIN RELATIONSHIP

Bruce is considering giving a dinner party for some people from his office. At the same time that he breaks the news to Linda, he hurries to reassure her, "I'm not talking about anything big, just three couples. I'll do the cooking, so you don't have to worry. If you'll just help with the planning and do some of the other stuff, maybe a couple of hors d'oeuvres when the day arrives."

Linda is dubious. It sounds like more effort than she cares to expend, but Bruce is insistent and she has put him off a couple of times before; so knowing that it's important to him, she agrees.

Bruce is immediately enthusiastic. "I want to have a theme. I'll go to that great paper goods store tomorrow and get some decorating ideas. What tablecloths do we have? Maybe we should get a new one, what do you think?"

"Wouldn't a buffet be easier?"

"Maybe, but that's not the idea. There's nothing like sitting around a dinner table with a couple of good bottles of wine for a wonderful evening. I wonder if I could get the butcher to order something really unique? Quail? Do you think we could get quail?"

Linda is beginning to feel more tentative by the moment as Bruce's plans unfold. "I don't think so. I wouldn't get anything I hadn't cooked before, Bruce. Roasts are probably the safest."

"Well, that's true, but they're no challenge, I know I can do it. If it's available, what about quail for the main course? Yes, I think definitely quail. Don't worry, I'm going to take care of all the details. As long as you can be available to help put it together on the day of the party, that's all you'll have to do. I'll take care of everything."

Bruce moves ahead with the arrangements, which include getting special wines, ordering fresh flowers and making appetizers every night for three days before the party. Linda accepts the fact that this dinner is inevitable and tries not to think about it.

The day before the party, Bruce reminds Linda that they are having company tomorrow and that the house is looking rather messy. Linda protests that it's perfectly clean. He concurs, but points out that there are newspapers piled up in the kitchen, there are mounds of litter in the family room and that Linda seems to have a project of some sort on the dining room table. While she definitely feels imposed upon, Linda does deal with all of his complaints. In fact, she handles them by moving everything in sight to the spare bedroom.

The next morning, Bruce wakes up at seven and when he urges Linda to get up, she reminds him that he said he was going to take care of everything.

"I will, I told you I would, but I also said I'd need some help today. Come on, Linda, what's the matter with you? Other women give dinner parties. I'm just asking you to peel a few vegetables and set the table."

"I hate this. If you didn't make it so elaborate, I wouldn't mind. You stay up nights figuring out how to make it more work."

"But that's part of the fun, doing a really spectacular show and pulling it off. I love it."

"Well, I don't. It seems like a lot of fuss for nothing."

As the day progresses, Bruce is forced by time pressures to ask Linda to do more and more. She becomes increasingly resentful and he gets more and more irritated with her as he contrasts her minimal compliance with his own focused and sustained efforts. When he finds that she forgot to polish the silver about an hour before their guests are due, Bruce feels really angry. It's too late to do anything about it at that point, but he begins setting the table grimly. His annoyance is enhanced by the sound of Linda turning on the television in the bedroom.

When the guests actually arrive, Linda is pleasant and amusing. Bruce is on top of everything. He tends bar, cooks and serves dinner. He keeps a running conversation going at the same time, enjoying both the pleasures he has provided for his guests and his own performance as host. He has a sense that the dinner is a great success.

After the guests leave, Linda begins to grumble over how late it is and how much work it was as she washes out glasses and empties the dishwasher. Still, no serious battle ensues and by the next day the conflict appears to be shelved.

Situations akin to this one are common in this marriage and seem to be minor in comparison to some of the stormier relationships of their neighbors. However, Linda becomes increasingly reluctant to accommodate Bruce's ventures which invariably require quite a bit more effort to complete than he originally anticipated, and there is a slow erosion of Bruce's reserves of love and patience, which are further tapped each time Linda drags her feet over some minor undertaking.

There is a danger that at some point, Bruce will decide that this relationship no longer makes him happy and that by the time this happens, it will be too late for either of them to repair the damage. Linda, who has resolutely refused to face so many small problems will then find herself having to confront the large reality of a failed marriage.

It is important in this relationship that Bruce begin to understand that his boundless energy cannot possibly be matched by most of the people around him. Trying for the ultimate experience in every situation is fun for him, but Linda is never going to view it in the same light. When he sees that his plans are going to involve her, it is necessary for him to modify his more elaborate schemes to the point where they will not overwhelm her.

It is equally important that Linda realize the fact that what made Bruce attractive to her when they first met was his high energy level and sense of fun, and now it's only fair to provide a little back-up support to allow him to indulge these aspects of his personality.

As Gauguins become healthier, they begin to set limits on their inclinations to minimize all expenditures of energy. Healthy Gauguins find from experience that involvement in projects is not as unpleasant as they had feared and that the more they do, the more pleasure they can find in putting some effort into their lives. As Bruce and Linda struggle to meet each other halfway in terms of the continuum between constant activity and inertia, they will both become healthier and more attractive personalities.

Mozart vitality is attractive to Gauguins. Their energy and sense of fun are seductive and appealing. Mozarts find low-key easy-going Gauguins equally charming. They provide a soothing counterpoint to the Mozart's somewhat frantic lifestyle. Gauguins are content to sit back and let Mozarts have center stage and to enjoy the performance.

Because Mozarts have an interest in quality as well as quantity, they want the best they can afford, whether in vacations or dinners. The Gauguin's passive acceptance of whatever is easily available and causes no fuss can be infuriating to a Mozart partner. The difference in the relationship is one of temperament. The sharply observant demanding Mozarts can easily lose patience with the Gauguin's casual acceptance of the status quo. Differences in approaching problems can create some conflict in this relationship. Obstacles make Bruce antsy and when they loom, he tends to deal with them quickly and impulsively to get them out of the way. Linda tends to turn away from problems, hoping that they will solve themselves while her back is turned.

Neither of these approaches is a good option, whether the difficulty is a real crisis, such as a seriously ill child, or a minor recurrent difficulty like a leak in the roof.

Their positions are at opposite poles of a response continuum and they need to seek a middle ground. Bruce needs to stop to weigh alternatives and think about what to do before springing into action. Linda must learn to acknowledge that problems do not generally go away if we ignore them and that it is better to think about what to do in a situation, than pretend that it doesn't exist.

Again, when there is a confrontation between them, Bruce and Linda have totally opposite methods of responding to the problem. Mozarts tend to be extremely sure of themselves in controversy, at least on the surface. They have the ability to delineate the problem succinctly and to make their own response to whatever the situation may be appear rational and appropriate. This is a normal human reaction and many people might appreciate their performance, even while recognizing that their presentation of the situation is somewhat self-serving, but Gauguins at an average level of functioning are unlikely to do this. Withdrawal is a more natural response for them. Mozarts, whose presentation has not been challenged, tend to believe that they have won the argument. On one level they may be correct, but they have neglected to count the cost.

Those Gauguins, who fail to uphold their own needs and preferences out of their desire to avoid confrontation, perceive themselves as pleasant easy-going people, who gracefully defer to the needs of those around them. Deep inside, however, they are angry and their concessions are made at the price of becoming disengaged from their environment. They become less and less focused on what is going on in their lives, forgetful and easily distracted. It is as if they said to their partners, "*I will agree not to notice that you get everything your way, but, I will have to stop noticing just about everything else about you as well in order to do so.*"

If their partners understood the true nature of this bargain, they might be less quick to accede to it. As Mozarts in this relationship grow healthier, they become aware that winning the battle can be too costly and begin to control their natural impulse to use their facile argumentative skills to maneuver their partners into agreeing to their demands. As Gauguins become healthier, they begin to assert themselves and to stand up for their own needs and preferences. It is a big step toward a healthier relationship when Gauguins push themselves to stand their ground and stick up for themselves even when they find it difficult and upsetting.

With their boundless energy, Mozarts can often exhaust Gauguin spouses. It's not always even a matter of having projects and accomplishing things, they can sometimes do it just by talking. All of this energy is really great, but it's essential for them to remember that those who don't have it, can't acquire it magically by being bullied and exhorted to greater levels of stamina. When both partners understand and accept the difference in energy levels, the problem is three-quarters of the way to a solution. It only remains for the Gauguin to remind the spirited Mozart that it is simply not possible to emulate such a degree of stamina and to set firm limits when being pushed too far.

Children of the Mozart-Gauguin relationship may feel themselves neglected. Mozarts love their children, but do not always make them a priority. They are extremely loving and involved while they are with them, but then other interests and concerns surface, and the children get relegated to the first available child care option. Gauguins are more likely to remain physically present to their offspring, but, when they are less healthy, they can be emotionally absent in terms of actually paying attention to the child. The average Gauguin's concept of meaningful parental involvement is likely to be watching a television program together.

When this couple become healthy, the Mozart begins to genuinely consider the children and their needs and to make daily interaction with them a priority. Healthy Gauguins begin to communicate with their children and to listen to their concerns instead of looking vaguely beneficent, while tuning out on any meaningful level of involvement.

Commitment can be a problem in Mozart-Gauguin marriages. The difficulty is likely to be one of communication. Unhappy Mozarts will have no reluctance in mentioning their dissatisfaction to their partners, but Gauguins are often unwilling to deal with such complaints seriously. In this situation, Mozarts feel increasingly unhappy and are likely either to begin to have affairs or to seek a divorce. If this happens, Gauguins respond with anger, but without much comprehension of their role in what has taken place.

Healthy Mozarts need to spell out to their partners the serious consequences of disregarding their complaints. This is a difficult task because it is seldom wise to deal in ultimatums in such situations. The goal is to impress upon the spouse that this is a situation that must be taken seriously and dealt with before it destroys the relationship. If a Gauguin is unwilling or unable to acknowledge that a genuine problem exists and needs to be addressed, it would be advisable to seek therapeutic assistance in getting through to the partner.

As Gauguins become healthy, they learn to face difficult situations rather than disregarding or denying them. Healthy Gauguins are able to listen to the Mozart partner and ask for specific examples of what is upsetting them. Concrete examples are essential in creating change since people have a great deal of difficulty following and correcting abstract complaints. *"You never want to do anything,"* is a hard complaint to address and remedy, while *"I would like for us to spend Saturday afternoons recreationally, doing something outside the house,"* is a specific demand that can be met.

Mozarts care about ambiance, they like a romantic atmosphere. This is not a large problem, as Gauguins have no objection to romance. They simply don't make the effort to produce it. This difference is worth mentioning only because Gauguins who are alerted to this

Mozart proclivity can improve their relationship with relatively small expenditures of time and effort. Putting flowers and candles on the table, bringing home a bottle of wine, or looking for a special greeting card are the sorts of gestures that will have a positive impact in cementing the relationship.

Both Mozarts and Gauguins have a potential for addiction when they are unhealthy. If either partner has a problem, it is imperative to identify it and seek help. Mozarts will usually take steps to acknowledge and correct the situation if they find their partner is addicted. Gauguins may deny the partner's condition or just not get around to responding to it. This will only allow the problem and its effect on the relationship to become worse. Twelve-step programs are important resources for the non-addicted partner in learning to live with an addicted spouse.

There is a strong possibility that there will be monetary problems in the Mozart-Gauguin relationship. That many Mozarts spend impulsively is no surprise. Gauguin partners can easily join them in overspending, to compensate themselves for their own self-neglect in other areas. If this is happening in the marriage, the couple will need to sit down and work out a budget and agree to stick to it. Getting deeply into debt creates a powerful negative impact on any relationship.

GREATEST DANGER SIGNAL: Inevitably, the Mozart will want to pursue a range of activities that will not particularly interest the Gauguin. It is healthy and appropriate for couples to go their separate ways on occasion, providing that they remember to also schedule in adequate amounts of time for their relationship. However, in the case of this couple, it is easy for Mozarts to consistently find more compelling activities that keep them away from home and for Gauguins to shrug their shoulders and say there's nothing they can do about it. When this happens, the couple will need to recognize the danger to the marriage and make whatever compromises are necessary to create adequate time to spend together.

PRIMARY FOCUS: The primary focus for this couple must be on meeting each other half way. These partners are at opposite ends of a spectrum in terms of extroversion-introversion and activity level. If the marriage is to grow and bring fulfillment to this couple, they must make a conscious effort to find a middle ground, coming to compromises on the amount of socializing they will do, the number of times they will entertain friends, and the number of types of new activities they will explore together.

XI

The Caesar in Relationships

For the Caesar-Emerson Relationship—Go to the Emerson-Caesar Relationship.

For the Caesar-Nightingale Relationship—Go to the Nightingale Caesar Relationship.

For the Caesar-Beau Relationship—Go to the Beau-Caesar Relationship.

For the Caesar-Shelley Relationship—Go to the Shelley-Caesar Relationship.

For the Caesar-Einstein Relationship—Go to the Einstein-Caesar Relationship.

For the Caesar-Austen Relationship—Go to the Austen-Caesar Relationship.

For the Caesar-Mozart Relationship—Go to the Mozart-Caesar Relationship.

THE CAESAR-CAESAR RELATIONSHIP

Evelyn and Bob have come into a small inheritance from Evelyn's parents. They now have the task of deciding what to do with the money. Bob assumes that they will place it in mutual funds with a company that they already use for their other investments. Evelyn has other plans. She would make a down payment on a house in a vacation area, with the plan of renting it and letting it pay for itself until they are ready to use it. Both partners are adamant about their strategy.

"This is none of your business, Bob. The money came from my parents and it's my choice, so just stay out of it."

"Can you read, Evelyn? The money was left to both of us, equally. There's no guarantee that you'd be able to get a tenant and if you don't, your great idea would end up costing us money every month. I'm not going to stand by and watch you mess us up with some hare-brained real-estate scheme."

"What do you mean, hare-brained? We have most of our money in mutual funds. Any idiot knows that you're supposed to diversify. This is the first time in your life that you've expressed caution about investing and it's not about investing as much as having your own way."

The argument continues without resolution and neither partner is willing to compromise. The money remains in the bank where it accrues relatively small amounts of interest while Evelyn and Bob allow the rancor from this situation to spill over into other aspects of their lives.

It dominates the conversation at dinner and causes some extremely unpleasant mealtimes. It follows them to the bedroom and puts romance on an indefinite hold. When they agree to shelve the issue for the day and go skiing, by mid-afternoon one of them brings the subject up and both immediately start shouting.

The problem is that neither Evelyn nor Bob possess many skills in conflict resolution. Both of them believe that the best way to get what they want is to make an absolute demand and stick to it resolutely. In this instance, in order to gain the upper hand in an argument, they are in danger of losing their marriage, which is actually more important to both of them.

These Caesars must learn that their gut level instinct to hold on to their position regardless of the consequences is not in their best interests in marriage. They will have to discover how to talk them-selves down from their non-negotiable demands into the arena of cooperation and compromise. This is the key to all conflict resolution and these are skills that ultimately benefit everyone who uses them.

For Caesar personalities, this is a question of stopping to evaluate the ultimate wins and losses from holding on to their positions intransi-gently. This latent instinct always counsels them to stand tight to get what they want, so they must be alert to the destructiveness of this strat-egy if they are to create any change.

When Bob and Evelyn are healthier, they will both acknowledge that much of their conflict is centered on who will be in control rather than any specific issue, such as what to do with the money from a modest inheritance. The easiest solution would probably be to simply divide the money in half and agree that each of them will do as they wish with their half of the cash. Another solution would entail coming up with a joint investment different than either of the original proposals. In either case, they would be able to let go of this issue and get on with their lives without carrying it around as a persistent smoldering quarrel, ready to erupt repeatedly with devastating results for their marriage.

Caesars will probably be attracted to each other initially through shared mutual interests in some area. These interests can be as diverse as the stock market, white water rafting, starting a new business venture or marathon running. The element all of these pursuits have in common is competition and the participant's desire to conquer new territory. Caesars are busy people with many interests and a relationship between Caesars may be one in which they need to carve out appointments in their schedules in order to make room to spend time together. The good side of this is that neither of them is likely to feel neglected or worry that the partner is spending too much time on the job. They understand each other's needs.

It is important to the Caesar to feel in control in all areas of functioning. This could result in continued jostling for dominance in a relationship between Caesars. Both partners would also be inclined to create angry confrontations when challenged, so that such a marriage could easily become a battleground. Unless both partners are emotionally healthy people with plenty of insight into their motivations, it is relatively unlikely that this will result in a viable long-term relationship.

Caesars can be impulsive and as their impulses are far from uniform, this is likely to be an area of friction in the marriage. People of this personality type seldom stop to confer with others before doing what they decide to do. If one of them decides that they want or need something on impulse, they are likely to commit to it on the spot. If the partner disagrees on the wisdom or necessity of taking a vacation, purchasing a new boat, or whatever, the acrimony can be long-lived and damaging. As they become emotionally healthy, they will learn to delay gratifying their impulses until they've consulted with each other. It won't necessarily avert an argument, but it will be a less bitter one if it occurs prior to the purchase or commitment.

The similarity of confrontational style in this couple will continually obstruct conflict resolution in their marriage. Backing down, cooling off and trying again later, admitting that the issue is not that important, seeking a reasonable compromise are all strategies at odds with their personalities. Caesars are straightforward about what they want and expect and they are extremely goal-oriented in attaining their desires. As they become emotionally healthy, they will begin to appreciate and cultivate the skills of conflict resolution, becoming more flexible and learning to respect alternate viewpoints. If implacable confrontations are a persistent problem in a marriage between Caesars, it is wise to seek the help of a therapist in learning better methods for handling disagreements.

The Caesar need to be in control is going to create serious problems for this couple. Both partners will be extremely uncomfortable in any situation where they are unable to decide what will happen. Who will drive the car and which is the best route to their destination might well become a perpetual battle for a Caesar couple, since allowing someone else to drive can be experienced as relinquishing control.

On these issues, the first step toward handling the problem is labeling it frankly. If it is agreed that the issue between them is over their mutual desire to be the boss and not over the allegation that Bob is a careless driver or that the last time Evelyn drove they got lost, then it is easier to move on to making rational decisions about how to divide responsibilities. In this case, the obvious solution is to agree to take turns behind the wheel and to keep one's mouth shut when a passenger.

Money is very important to Caesars. It is a necessary adjunct of self-sufficiency. They are serious about having enough of it and protecting their resources adequately. Money problems will arise if either or both of them use access to funds as a method of exercising control in the relationship. Since they tend to be hard workers and realistic investors, it would be unusual for really serious monetary shortages to occur, but if cash became temporarily tight, both Caesars would probably become adamant about demanding that money be accounted for and spent as they thought appropriate. In that situation, the advice of an independent financial advisor, who could stand impartially above their battling and suggest solutions, would probably be a worthwhile investment. It would be wise, if they could bring themselves to do it, for the couple to agree in advance of the consultation to abide by his advice since one or both of them is liable to be reluctant to accept the advice proffered.

GREATEST DANGER SIGNAL: The danger in this relationship is self-evident. Both partners have strong needs to control and battles over control issues will pose a threat to this marriage. It would be wise to divide up responsibilities in advance and to devise a structure for resolving these points when they occur. Simple stipulations are a start. *"I'm willing to pay the bills if you promise not to second guess how I do it."* or *"It's agreed that when we eat in we'll take turns cooking and doing the dishes."* Rules of battle that outlaw personal attacks and irrelevant side issues will also be helpful in keeping the conflicts they can't foresee from degenerating into all-out war.

PRIMARY FOCUS: The focus in this marriage should be on enjoying recreational time together. Since Caesars are far from placid, it is unlikely to be a calm easy-going relationship. This is the reason it will be unusually important to have plenty of fun together. The conflicts will be there, but to keep the marriage on an even keel, the fun has to outweigh the strife.

THE CAESAR-GAUGUIN RELATIONSHIP

Mike needs to make a job change. He works for a small family owned firm. One son and two daughters of the owner have been promoted over him. He hasn't had a raise in three years and while he is well liked at work, there seems to be little chance for advancement.

Evelyn is moving ahead in her career at a brisk pace and now makes almost twice as much as her husband. His lack of initiative is beginning to be a serious problem in their marriage. Mike agrees that he should be job hunting and makes sporadic efforts, but they do not meet Evelyn's definition of a serious career push. He has answered four help wanted ads, called a few employment agencies and had one job interview in the last three months. When Evelyn asks him about what he plans to do next, he explains that the interview was extremely positive and he's waiting to hear from them.

"How long do you plan to wait? You had the interview a month ago."

"These things take time. They really like me, and it would be a great place to work. It's worth being patient."

"Grow up, Mike. If they'd wanted you, you'd have heard by now. They've probably decided not to fill the job."

"You don't know that. I'm better off waiting for a job I think I'll like than taking something else and regretting it."

"Hear me, Mike. My patience is coming to an end. I expect you to do something. If you can't begin to make a more serious commitment, I just may not be around much longer."

Evelyn means what she says, but if she expects it to motivate her husband, she will be disappointed. Unless both partners make some changes in their interactions with each other, Evelyn will eventually leave and Mike will feel bitter and rejected, but will not take much responsibility for the failure of their marriage.

Mike needs to begin facing his problems instead of avoiding them. This is a difficult task for someone of his personality type. He may need a therapist's help in making this change in a life-long pattern. Mike learned the technique of "forgetting about" the things that bothered him in early childhood. In some situations, where change is impossible, this is an intelligent defense, a way of avoiding undue anxiety. Unfortunately, Mike has used it too much; applying it not only in those situations where effort would be unproductive, but also in cases where problems could be resolved if they were addressed.

There is also a passive-aggressive component in Mike's current situation. Evelyn is so much stronger and more assertive than he is that it often makes him angry. His refusal to engage in a meaningful job hunt is one way of getting even with her for all the times he feels she has pushed him around.

Evelyn loves Mike, but has begun to despair of motivating him to change in ways she believes are essential to their relationship. She needs to buy a book on co-dependency and take its message to heart. She has allowed herself to get sucked into the position of feeling responsible for Mike and feeling that she should be able to guide or push him into doing those things that he avoids. It is crucial to their relationship that she relinquishes this mind-set. Mike is an adult and must take responsibility for himself. He will not change dramatically, and Evelyn must remember that the traits that are irritating her are the same ones that made him initially attractive. She cannot control him, but she can inadvertently, by prodding him too insistently, steer him toward failure.

To facilitate an improvement in their relationship, Mike and Evelyn must begin to talk, Evelyn needs to express some empathy for how hard it is for Mike to make changes and acknowledge that it is a real problem for him even though it is not for her. Empathy and understanding are more likely than pressure to help Mike to make a move.

If Mike works at it, he can become somewhat more assertive. He's never going to be a hard-driving businessman, but he can acquire a reasonable assortment of assertive skills to get him through the business day. As Evelyn becomes healthier, she will accept her inability to energize Mike to her level of performance and know that continued attempts to do so are not just a waste of time, but actually counter-productive. She will learn to control her anger, so that she doesn't lash out in ways that ultimately undermine her goals for them as a couple.

The attraction of opposites prevails in this marriage. The Caesar personality finds the placid, easy-going nature of the Gauguin inscrutable, but restful and accommodating. Caesars can envy the Gauguin's ability to turn aside from upsetting situations and to seemingly ignore or rise above anger. Spending time with a Gauguin can be a relaxing experience for a Caesar. Gauguins can be stimulated and invigorated by associating with Caesars. The energy and involvement of the Caesar is interesting and exciting to the more tranquil Gauguin. Gauguins often need to be energized and a healthy Gauguin will be grateful for the push provided by a Caesar partner.

These traits, which are attractive in initiating the relationship, can be the source of friction later. In situations where Caesars want to do something which requires the partner's active involvement, the easy-going pace of Gauguins ceases to be attractive and becomes infuriating. Gauguins who want to escape their problems and to be left in peace will find the Caesar's insistence on results and their persistence in requiring the partner's participation upsetting.

Gauguins are sensitive people. Since they often repress or deny their feelings, others may be unaware when they have hurt them. Thus, Evelyn can say cruel things to Mike on occasion and find him placidly watching television or reading a magazine a few minutes later, apparently without any anger or resentment. This is illusory. Mike does not always immediately retaliate, but this doesn't mean that Evelyn will not pay for her remarks. Gauguins often give themselves permission to engage in addictive behaviors as an outlet for repressed hostility. They can also become increasingly passive-aggressive, retreating still further into those unacceptable behaviors that are the target of the partner's dissatisfaction.

Mike needs to learn to let Evelyn know when she hits below the belt. If he says, *"That really hurts me, when you say things like that,"* he may run the risk of irritating her, but at least he lets her know that he perceives what she says as inappropriate and hurtful. By failing to set such simple limits, he is effectively giving his wife permission to speak abusively to him.

As Evelyn becomes healthier, she will develop greater sensitivity to other people's feelings and begin to monitor her responses, restraining her inappropriate remarks. The rule in this is simple and we all know it. Criticizing actions in pertinent ways is acceptable, and part of the process of being in a relationship, criticizing the person or calling names is off limits. It is permissible to say, *"When you kept me waiting to leave for work, it threw my entire morning off. I really need to leave on time."* It is not acceptable to say, *"You are the world's least punctual, most thoughtless total jerk. You're self-centered egotism is intolerable."* Evelyn knows this, putting it into practice when angry is sometimes a problem for her. She has to work on it.

Gauguins hate confrontation and avoid it when it is humanly possible. Caesars, on the other hand, consider it part of the daily round, and in many cases seem to actually thrive on it. They experience it as an opportunity to ventilate tension or a chance to demonstrate their will power and drive. It is energizing for them. These opposing positions can lead to serious difficulties in a marriage.

When something bothers Evelyn, she immediately addresses the issue with Mike. He often forgets or ignores what she has said the moment she stops speaking, or thinks of reasons that her point of view is unreasonable or impractical. He does not share his thoughts with her as this would turn an already unpleasant conversation into total acrimony, a situation he avoids whenever possible. Evelyn used to walk away in the expectation that Mike agreed with what she had said and would follow through on whatever needed to be done. She now knows better and tries to get a verbal commitment from him. This has changed things only to the extent that she is now angrier when there is no follow-through.

On those occasions when Mike does identify a hostile discussion with Evelyn as seriously troublesome, he ignores or represses his irritation, or he minimizes the annoyance or inconvenience. He may feel vaguely angry or out of sorts later, but he often does not connect these feelings with his wife's behavior or his unmet needs.

Caesars and Gauguins need to talk frankly, without attaching anger or blame, about these opposing traits. As Caesars become healthy, they will learn to listen to the partner's ideas and viewpoints, rather than automatically dismissing or refuting them. They will keep the interaction on the level of discussion, where there is a chance that they will be heard, instead of issuing fiats, only to discover that the partner's concurrence was illusory.

Gauguins will grow as they learn to pay attention to their own feelings and take responsibility not only for their words and actions, but also for their failure to speak and act. They must overcome their distaste for controversy and begin to express their objections or reservations, even if it entails an argument.

Caesars have much higher energy levels than Gauguins do. This is a physical reality. It can be a problem if they view the partner's inability to put in 16-hour workdays as essential laziness. Awareness that this is a genuine difference in stamina levels can be helpful to both sides. Gauguins need not be apologetic about a physical fact beyond their control and Caesars can learn to enjoy their own incredible stamina, without reflecting negatively on those who don't possess it.

Caesars have stronger sex drives than their Gauguin partners as a rule. This may be related to their higher energy level. In any event, it is important for the partners to get this issue out in the open and discuss it. Once it is understood as a physical variant in arousal level, it is possible to find ways to deal with it. Gauguins can find ways to gratify their partners needs when they are not feeling aroused themselves, and Caesars need not experience the partner's lack of response as a personal rejection. If there are problems in conjunction with this issue, self-help books are readily available. If they are insufficient, seek a therapist.

Caesar personalities need to be in control of their lives, and generally prefer to extend that control to any lives that impinge on theirs. Gauguins have no need to control others, and are just as happy to have someone take care of structuring their environment. This sounds like a perfect arrangement. It can be, providing the Caesar shows some restraint and does not attempt to control the partner's behavior as well. Even the easy-going Gauguin will begin to object if the control extends beyond the provision of structure into personal supervision.

Mike collects records and books, not great records and books, but current popular hits and mystery stories. This irritates Evelyn, who points out that he could get the same books from the library for nothing, and could tape the stuff he listens to from the radio. She further points out that he has a backlog of books that he hasn't gotten around to reading that will probably hold him for the rest of his life.

She is absolutely correct, but she's on dangerous ground here. It's important that Caesars give their partners a few concessions in these unimportant areas if they want them to feel good about themselves and their relationship. Too much pressure on unimportant issues tends to make Gauguins stubborn and contrary and to have a negative effect on their emotional health and wellbeing. Conversely, if their small indulgences are left unquestioned, the Caesar will usually be welcome to make the big decisions, such as finance and housing, unchallenged.

Gauguins have a potential for addiction. In the relationships of addicted Gauguins and their Caesar spouses, the Caesars have a natural inclination to address the issue by decree. *"This is not acceptable to me and must stop at once."* Not only is this an ineffective approach, but it will probably intensify the problem. The Gauguin is very likely to hear *"It must stop"* as *"I must not know about it".* The Caesar will profit from seeking out a 12-step program, such as Al-Anon, and attending some meetings. Since many Caesars are impatient with this advice and feel uncomfortable in such surroundings, a secondary resource is literature on addiction. The primary point to be grasped is that the natural Caesar inclination to meet the problem head on and demand immediate resolution will not be effective in this situation. It will cause the partner to be more secretive about the addictive behavior or to replace one addiction with another. It is a real mistake to take action prior to getting insight and understanding of addictive behavior.

Gauguins who are interested in their emotional well being, will seek their own 12-step programs, but the more usual pattern in these relationships is that spouses feel the pain far earlier than the person with the addiction. By handling the problem appropriately, they are much more likely to be able to encourage their partners to seek the help they need.

GREATEST DANGER SIGNAL: If the Caesar begins to take the Gauguin for granted, a dangerous situation will eventually develop. The placid easy-going Gauguin seems willing to fall in with the Caesar's plans so often and so easily that the Caesar can become complacent. It is easy for a Caesar to take advantage of such a situation and accept total compliance as the norm in the marriage. It is inevitable that finally a situation will arise in which the Gauguin says no or sets a limit. By the time this happens, Gauguins have often repressed large amounts of anger and Caesars have developed unrealistic expectations of always getting their own way. At that point, the resultant conflict can create major damage to the relationship. Gauguins need to set limits on their compliant behavior from the beginning and wise Caesars who see that they always get what they want without argument, will discuss the situation with their partners.

PRIMARY FOCUS: The primary focus for this couple should be on making it a balanced relationship. For the Caesar, this means being careful not to overpower the partner, and to include the Gauguin in all the appropriate aspects of the marriage. It is easy for the goal-focused Caesar to exclude the partner, while pushing forward acquiring new friends and expanding outside contacts and activities, leaving the Gauguin behind, at home with the children and the television set. In this situation, the Gauguin is often treated as a second-class citizen in the relationship, whose chief role is providing background support for the Caesar's brilliant career or exploits. For Gauguins, the balanced relationship requires assumption of equal responsibility, carving out a sphere of action for themselves in the relationship and not dodging out of hard decisions from a distaste for problem-solving.

XII

The Gauguin in Relationships

For the Gauguin-Emerson Relationship—Go to the Emerson-Gauguin Relationship.

For the Gauguin-Nightingale Relationship—Go to the Nightingale-Gauguin Relationship.

For the Gauguin-Beau Relationship—Go to the Beau-Gauguin Relationship.

For the Gauguin-Shelley Relationship—Go to the Shelley-Gauguin Relationship.

For the Gauguin-Einstein Relationship—go to the Einstein-Gauguin Relationship.

For the Gauguin-Austen Relationship—Go to the Austen-Gauguin Relationship.

For the Gauguin-Mozart Relationship—Go to the Mozart-Gauguin Relationship.

For the Gauguin-Caesar Relationship—Go to the Caesar-Gauguin Relationship.

THE GAUGUIN-GAUGUIN RELATIONSHIP

Maureen and Gary are twelve and ten years old, the children of Mike and Linda. Both children are angry with their parents, and cling to each other for support much more than opposite sex siblings of this age would normally do. Clearly they are turning to each other for some of the parenting that is missing from their relationship with their mother and father.

Maureen has virtually taken charge of many aspects of family life, assuming the tasks that her mother refuses to take responsibility for. She cleans the living room and kitchen if she plans to invite her friends over. She does a major portion of the grocery shopping. She washes and irons her own clothes and some of Gary's things as well. She manages to do this while maintaining excellent grades in school. She is widely viewed as a model child.

Gary in contrast is a little waif. He looks bedraggled, hair uncombed, shoe laces untied, often with a stain or a rip on his shirt. Gary daydreams in school, gets barely passing grades, and seems to disappear into the background and pass unnoticed in most situations. He has no friends.

Both children are responding to a lack of involvement and concern from their parents. If Mike and Linda, were asked why they are failing to notice their children's blatant needs, they would be hurt and bewildered. They perceive themselves as good parents. They are kind and loving, they certainly are never abusive, in fact, they are extremely permissive. They often take the children to the movies or out to dinner. They keep meaning to plan a family vacation to some really great place. They haven't gotten around to doing that yet, but they will. They are good providers. Not only is there plenty of food in the house, but Mike often goes out after dinner to pick up ice cream for everyone. When the children ask for money for something, they get it, if it is at all within the bounds of reason. What more could they do?

Linda has genuinely forgotten about the day that Gary came home crying and complaining of having hurt his arm on the playground. It was only when Maureen came home from a friend's house and made a scene that they all went off to the doctor's and discovered it was broken. She has also forgotten about the time last year that Maureen had the starring role in the school play and she became preoccupied and forgot to show up for the performance.

Mike feels that he is a good father too. When Maureen complained to him that he wasn't there for her, he was genuinely puzzled and distressed, but he then dismissed it as the sort of momentary dissatisfaction that comes over adolescent girls and that is basically groundless. He did promise to help her with a school project last week and he hasn't been able to get to it yet, but he certainly plans to. It's just that she always seems to pick an inconvenient time to approach him on it.

Gauguins are kind and loving, but until they become healthy, they are not focused on the world around them. They always mean well, but they often seem to lack the energy to put this goodwill into any form that might make it available to anyone else. Being asked to do things or to resolve situations tends to make them angry, and they are acutely uncomfortable with that feeling. One way to avoid the anger, is to blur the focus of the request so that they don't see it too clearly which makes it considerably easier not to comply with it.

Gauguins want peace and quiet and there is no one more likely to give it to them than another Gauguin. In examining the mutual attraction that could exist in this relationship, it is surprising that it does not occur more frequently. Probably the explanation for its rarity lies in another of their basic personality traits. When both parties are Gauguins, no one takes the initiative to initiate a relationship.

The problems in this partnership are more likely to be experienced by their children than by the couple themselves. It is hard to conceive of an argument more serious than what to have for dinner occurring between these two. Both hold to the philosophy that problems are in the mind of the beholder and that a problem unacknowledged is a problem solved. Both will be deeply committed to the other and to the marriage. Conflict will arise only should one partner experience enough emotional growth to begin to insist on addressing some of the issues that they have both been letting slide.

This couple are unlikely to have serious problems between each other, but eventually the outside environment will present problems that will intrude on this marital bliss. They are likely to forget to file income taxes on time or balance the checkbook. Both will tend to neglect minor home repairs until something is seriously wrong. No responsible person will be available to remember they need to clean up the garden before winter, or to put in the storm windows. Their lives are likely to be dotted with a series of near catastrophes as unmet responsibilities repeatedly catch up with them.

Addictions are a potential problem for Gauguins, who are prone to addictive behavior. If they find they have started to drink too much, it is unlikely that either of them will raise the issue with the other or work on finding strategies for turning the situation around. Overindulgence in food is also a common problem for Gauguins, and the lack of control and failure to acknowledge the problem will predispose them to fail to take meaningful steps to correct the situation.

The couple may have money problems, for the same reason that they have addiction problems. As long as the charge card still extracts money from the machine and goods from the stores, what difference does the monthly total make? This can go on until all of the charge cards are at the maximum and there is a serious amount of accumulated debt.

Obviously all of these issues stem from the same basic traits. Becoming aware and acknowledging that they tend to space out on their surroundings and neglect tasks and people, is the first step to creating change in this marriage. Making lists will be a major help to them, since they are badly in need of more structure. With adequate lists of tasks that must be accomplished and a time frame for accomplishing them, they can provide that structure for themselves. They will need two lists. There are the yearly tasks: Clean up the garden, start working on the income tax, etc. This list should be supplemented by weekly lists of things that must be attended to: Call the plumber, take clothes to the cleaners, go to the bank. This will not only bring order into their lives, but also begin to eliminate many recurrent problems that eventually must be faced.

Making the list is the first step, following through is the hard part. Gauguins must be particularly careful about procrastination. It comes so naturally to them that it's hard for them to stay aware of what they are doing. If the lists don't help and things are still falling apart, or if the children are still complaining or visibly demonstrating their unhappiness with the status quo, it's probably time to seek professional help, which is a real difficulty for this personality type. The statement, *"I have a problem."* goes against their innermost convictions. They tend to believe that time is the great healer and that everything will come out all right in the end. It is important both for the couple and for the children that the Gauguin couple steel themselves to the realities of the situation long enough to find a therapist and start facing the need for change.

GREATEST DANGER SIGNAL: The main danger in this relationship is that the partners will both fail to take adequate responsibility for the irritating daily requirements of modern life: bill paying, home repairs, etc. Because failure to attend to these details eventually catches up with people in very unpleasant ways, it can create a major degree of damage to the relationship. It is important for this couple to divide up the unpleasant and easily postponed tasks and to both assume responsibility for doing their share.

PRIMARY FOCUS: The primary focus for this couple should be on remembering to get out and do things. There is nothing wrong with staying at home and reading or watching television, but it can be carried to an extreme. Stimulation is important for all of us and it would not be a bad idea for them to find some way to insure that they have regular contact with the outside world. They could join a discussion group, a civic association or church group; or they could arrange to meet friends for dinner or entertain on a bi-weekly or monthly basis. Without taking this precaution, there is a danger that the marriage will become so dull and routine that the monotony of their lives will dam-age the quality of the relationship.

XIII

Finding the Right One

There are better ways to choose a partner than gazing across a crowded room and experiencing immediate infatuation, or marrying the person you've been dating because the time has come and they're there. Granted, there is no possible method of guaranteeing that you will find the one right person, this does not rule out considering the odds before making important choices. Examining the dynamics of hundreds of good and bad marriages to understand what makes some work and torpedoes others some pertinent insights emerge. It seems that there are some optimal combinations, a great many that will probably work out fine, and a few that should be left in the category of fun dates at best

This is advice for the non-committed, a theory obtained from the observation of varied relationships and from working with couples who want to improve their marriages. Life often evades or negates the best theoretical constructs, so that it is perfectly possible to have found the right relationship and to be happy in it whatever the personality dynamics involved. Any relationship can succeed if the two people involved are willing to work hard and have enough patience. Still, for those who have not yet found the perfect relationship, the chemistry in some matches is more effective and less explosive than in others and marital happiness is more likely between couples who are naturally compatible. For those still searching for the right person, these observations may provide a focus for the search.

Basically, the nine personality types can be broken down into three configurations of three for maximum compatibility. In each case, all of the combinations within these groups seem to function well together, and to have relationships that provide them with a reasonable degree of stability and pleasure. Emersons, Shelleys, and Mozarts compose a triad. Nightingales, Einsteins, and Caesars are another grouping, as are Beaus, Austens and Gauguins.

There is a theoretical explanation for the success of these configurations, and repeated observation appears to bear out the theory. Any two of the three in each group are more likely than most couples to find happiness and fulfillment in their relationships.

EMERSONS, SHELLEYS AND MOZARTS

The underlying principle that makes these three personalities fit together well is their essential honesty or authenticity. Emersons are scrupulously honest out of their own need to do the right thing and to be fair. They are people who genuinely cannot tell a lie. This trait extends past merely verbal correctness into all of their dealings. They may be mistaken, but they will not knowingly be or act in a dishonest manner. While this can become maddening when it is reduced to a type of Boy Scout naiveté in emotionally unhealthy or rigid people, it is an attractive trait in the healthy Emerson.

Shelley honesty is of a different cast; it is a more gut level quality. It is the aspect of their personality that makes it so difficult for them to express their feelings casually or on the spur of the moment. Shelleys simply cannot say that they feel something they don't feel and sometimes have a great deal of trouble saying anything, lest it not express exactly what they mean. They have a serious problem relating to people who express conventional opinions out of habit without seriously considering what they are saying, or those they believe to be talking superficially, or in platitudes. This search for emotional authenticity powers much of Shelley angst and is irritating to many people, but is generally understood and respected by the Emerson and Mozart.

Mozarts need to be happy and this need is the power behind their genuineness. It can be an almost physical kind of authenticity. The strength of their drive to fulfill their own desires as fully as possible creates an authenticity in action that parallels that of the Emerson and Shelley. Since Mozarts find it extremely difficult to subvert or deny their own needs, they are forced to acknowledge them, and in doing so, to reveal themselves as they truly are.

The basic core honesty and authenticity of these three personalities provides a strong unifying factor, which makes relationships between them work. The Emerson may rage or be bitingly sarcastic, but the emotion is genuinely felt and expressed. This authenticity is perceived intuitively by Shelleys and Mozarts, who can understand and relate to the feeling to some extent and be less upset or hurt by it than are other personality types.

In the same way, the difficulty Shelleys experience when expected to be emotionally facile, and their revulsion from any suggestion of easy sentimentality, is so palpably caused by the fear of distorting emotions or experiences, that Emersons and Mozarts can respect it, rather than being annoyed or censorious.

The Mozart's need to do whatever gives them pleasure may appear self-centered or selfish to others, but Emersons and Shelleys have a gut level understanding of what is driving the Mozart. So even when they set limits on some specific or too extreme manifestation of this pleasure drive, they continue to comprehend and appreciate its authenticity.

NIGHTINGALES, EINSTEINS AND CAESARS

The driving desire to acquire what will meet a basic need is the underlying tie between these three personalities. There is a total dissimilarity in the type and style of acquisition, but all three are collectors and possess the collector's focus. Nightingales are collectors of relationships. There is a strong need to meet new people and bring them into their orbit. They experience a genuine satisfaction in acquiring a new friend or a new group of friends. Their desire for more people in their lives may be partially powered by a sense of inner emptiness, which causes Nightingales to feel that they are not adequately loved. There is often a hope behind their search that the next person they add to their circle will be the special one who will be able to be there for them in a way that will meet this unfulfilled need.

Einsteins are collectors of information, knowledge, and theories. They often have difficulty completing projects, since there is always another book or paper, which they should read before they are able to consider themselves adequately knowledgeable on a subject. Their quiet and persistent acquisition of new information parallels the Nightingales' collection of new people.

Caesars are naturally expansive. They want to increase their influence, their wealth, their authority, and seek wider and wider fields in which to do this. Their collector's bent can be roughly categorized as the collection of more power and influence.

The focus on acquisition drives these personalities and creates a broad commonality among them. They must all expend time and energy to reach beyond the immediate intimate relationship in their lives in order to find fulfillment of their other need. Since in their separate spheres, each of these personalities has a similar requirement, they can understand and respect the time and attention demanded by each others' quests.

BEAUS, AUSTENS AND GAUGUINS

Beaus, Austens and Gauguins have in common the need to be comfortable within the conventional world. They are natural insiders. Good manners and appearances count for a great deal. For each of these personalities, social acceptability and group approval are highly important.

For the Beau, there is a very strong need to be admired and to have the respect of those whom they consider important. The correct clothing for an occasion, the appearance of poise and knowing the right thing to do are primary concerns. And with the exception of overtly competitive situations, they are accommodating and agreeable to most of the people they meet.

The Austen has a deep concern with being liked. Austens seem to be more worried than others about what the neighbors think, a trait which can make them great team players and cause them to be viewed as generally agreeable people, but can also lead to ingratiating behavior. The easy-going, obliging Gauguin can go along with just about anything that the partner suggests and certainly never rocks the boat in any gathering but they can be made deeply uncomfortable by behavior they consider to be unacceptable or unconventional.

This sense of community mores and its corollary desire to please, make the relationships between these numbers secure. The anger of Caesars and Emersons and the quirks in the behavior of Shelleys, Einsteins, and Mozarts can appear jarringly unconventional and unnecessarily abrasive to these personalities. They feel safe with partners within their triad, knowing that few boats will be rocked, few toes stepped on. Socially acceptable behavior and good manners will prevail.

Austen's are more likely than others to find happiness outside the bounds of this construct. While, like every other personality pattern, Austens function out of the same basic configuration of needs and drives, the patterns of interaction they display are quite widely divergent. This allows some of them to fit in well with someone outside the primary configuration. Emerson and Austens do have common bonds in their desire to do the appropriate thing, although their motivations for doing so, and their definitions of appropriate are very different. Nightingales and Austens have a strong desire to be helpful and caring in common, which can provide a bond and a commonality of approach for them. Shelleys and Austens have sensitivity and empathy in common, which in some cases allows them to bridge their differences.

The most practical way to apply this theory is to read the more detailed chapter on the interaction of your type with the two other personalities in your configuration and then to read the chapter in relation to the specific person you are considering or are already involved with. This allows you to understand the traits that may create conflict over time and to compare these traits to those of your optimal choices in order to make a reasoned decision.

XIV

A Final Note

The material in this book is based on a system of human development called the Enneagram, which describes nine personality types and their complex interrelationships. The traits and behaviors detailed here are merely an introduction to this incredibly rich and powerful method of understanding ourselves and the others in our lives. If you are interested in knowing yourself better and increasing your understanding of human behavior, I urge you to explore this system further.

You will not find the names by which I designated the personalities in books on the Enneagram. The literature uses a number, not a person's name. Thus, the Emerson is a One, the Nightingale a Two, etc.

Prominent authors in this field include David Daniels, Kathy Hurley & Theodorre Donson, Claudio Naranjo, Helen Palmer, Don Richard Riso & Russ Hudson, Elizabeth Wagele, and Jerome Wagner. Information about the Enneagram can be found at *www.intl-enneagram-assn.org*, the web site for the International Enneagram Association. There is also find an extensive bibliography on the subject there.

www.ingramcontent.com/pod-product-compliance
Lightning Source LLC
Chambersburg PA
CBHW032058280526
45784CB00012B/27